ROGER STEVENSON
DECEMBER, 1995

THE END OF
ECONOMIC MAN

THE END OF ECONOMIC MAN

Principles of Any Future Economics

GEORGE P. BROCKWAY

 Cornelia & Michael Bessie Books
An Imprint of HarperCollins*Publishers*

Grateful acknowledgment is made to Yale University Press for permission to reproduce two graphs from Hyman P. Minsky, *Stabilizing an Unstable Economy*, © 1986 by Yale University.

FIRST EDITION

Designed by Helene Berinsky

Library of Congress Cataloging-in-Publication Data
Brockway, George P.
  The end of economic man: principles of any future economics/George P. Brockway.—1st ed.
    p. cm.
  "A Cornelia and Michael Bessie book."
  Includes bibliographical references.
  ISBN 0-06-039114-6
  1. Economics. 2. United States—Economic conditions. 3. Economic man. I. Title.
HB171.B6499 1991
330—dc20   89-46076

91 92 93 94 95 CC/RRD 10 9 8 7 6 5 4 3 2 1

To the Absent Members

CONTENTS

Preface   ix

1. INTRODUCTION: *Why We Have Economics*   1

2. PSYCHOLOGY: *The Three Antinomies of Greed*   8

3. MATHEMATICS: *Why Physics Is Value Free
   and Economics Isn't*   20

4. PEOPLE: *Where Economics Is Grounded*   31

5. MONEY: *The Distinguishing Idea of Economics*   39

6. PRICE: *Reformulating the Law of Supply and Demand*   61

7. LABOR: *Where It All Begins*   73

8. GOODS: *Which Keep It Going*   87

9. CAPITAL: *Saving and Investing*   97

10. SPECULATION: *Why a Bull Market Is a Disaster*   106

11. PROPERTY: *The Labor Theory of Right*   119

12. PRODUCTIVITY: *Why Micro and Macro Don't Always Mix*   140

13. INTEREST: *And the Parable of the Talents*   153

14. INFLATION I: *The Myth of the Full-Employment Trade-off*   170

15. INFLATION II: *The Bankers' Classic COLA*   182
16. INTERNATIONAL TRADE: *How the Multinationals
    Are Different*   196
17. CONCLUSION: *The Prospect of Slow Deterioration*   221

Appendix A: On Perfect Competition   231
Appendix B: On Games   234
Appendix C: On Utility   237
Appendix D: On the Margin   243
Appendix E: On General Equilibrium   246
Appendix F: On Economies of Scale   256
Appendix G: On the Money Supply   259
Appendix H: On the Reform of Corporations   261
Appendix I: On Comparative Advantage   265

Notes   273
Index   291

PREFACE

economic man. *Econ.* A hypothetical man supposed to be free
from altruistic sentiments and motives interfering with a purely
selfish pursuit of wealth and its enjoyment.
        —*Webster's New International Dictionary, Second Edition*

To be fully human in the early Renaissance one had to
participate in the rebirth of the ancient world. To be fully human today
one must be not only doctor, lawyer, or Indian chief, but also a free,
responsible, and recognized actor in the economic world. This demand
is a theme in contemporary movements for racial, ethnic, and gender
liberation. As an ironic consequence, no one who is liberated can be
an ideal economic agent, for economic man (the ideal economic agent)
is a fanatic. He is a madman. He is possessed. He is not free and
responsible.

What, then, becomes of economics? As the discipline has developed,
it has depended upon economic man as an organizing principle, as mass
and energy are organizing principles of physics. Economists have deduced their laws from the supposedly rational behavior of this
monomaniacal monster of selfishness incarnate.

Monomaniacs wind up reifying their manias. Thus economics has come to concern itself with things—resources, the gross national product, the bottom line—rather than with people. In any future economics this concern will be reversed. Human beings will be more important than things, and what Carlyle quite properly called the dismal science will take on a new and friendlier aspect.

Accordingly, in the pages that follow, price explains (it is not explained); the law of supply and demand is reformulated; saving and investment are redefined; production and speculation are seen in conflict, as are wages and interest rates (but not profits); normal profit and actual profit are distinguished; the labor theory of value is supplanted by the labor theory of right; "productivity" is revealed as a question-begging question; high interest rates (the "Bankers' COLA") are exposed as a prime *cause* of inflation; international trade is understood to be different from intranational trade; and mores, morals, and morale become central economic concerns. On the last point it may be remarked that contemporary calls for reformed business ethics must go unanswered so long as economics—which analyzes business enterprise—systematically denies the relevance of ethics.

Although far broader and more systematic, this book necessarily covers some of the same ground as my earlier book (*Economics: What Went Wrong and Why and Some Things To Do about It*) and, in order to stand alone, repeats some of that material. A few especially technical or polemical questions are relegated to the appendixes. While most of the notes (which are in the back of the book) are bibliographical references, a few are discursive and carry the discussion further (or farther afield). The ones I particularly recommend are signaled by a small star (☆) following their superscript in the text.

Economics deals with ordinary, everyday affairs of ordinary, everyday people and should be written about, in so far as possible, in ordinary, everyday language. A few terms are nevertheless of such importance that I call particular attention to them. *Speculation* and *normal profit* are specially defined where they first appear. *Opportunity cost* ("perhaps the most fundamental concept in economics," according to the *MIT Dictionary of Modern Economics*) is, I trust, generally clear from its context.

As I have said on many other occasions, there is no idea presented here that is not directly or indirectly due to the teaching of the late Professor

John William Miller of Williams College. Even turns of phrase and sentence rhythms are often his, as readers of the five volumes of his published essays will recognize. In addition, much of the material covered was discussed with him in person or by correspondence. I make no claim that he would have supported what I have written, but my indebtedness to him is impossible to overstate.

I am also greatly indebted to Myron Kolatch, executive editor of *The New Leader*, who has, for almost ten years now, given me access to an alert and responsive audience. Other editors who have kindly given me permission to use material I originally published in their pages are those of the *Journal of Post Keynesian Economics, Challenge,* the *New York Times,* and *Washington Monthly.* Much of the material in Chapter 3 and Appendix C was included in a paper presented before a conference at Notre Dame University and published in Oliver F. Williams, Frank K. Reilly, and John W. Houck, eds., *Ethics and the Investment Industry* (Savage, Md.: Rowan and Littlefield, 1989). Much of Chapter 6 and Appendix I was presented before a conference at Brigham Young University. And much of Chapters 15 and 17 was presented before a colloquium at the University of Tennessee. I am grateful to the universities for the invitations to participate in the conferences and for permission to reuse some of my material here.

In the best tradition of scholarship, many professionals in several fields have been generous with information, advice, caution, and encouragement, even on points with which they disagreed. In particular, Professors Robert Averitt and Raymond Richman each read and commented on a complete draft of the manuscript. I have tried to have the wit to benefit from their criticisms and of course absolve them of all responsibility for the result.

Having served a term as a publisher myself, and having thus experienced at first hand the unreasonableness of authors, I am especially appreciative of the patient understanding and support of my old friend Simon Michael Bessie and his assistants Amy Gash and Miranda Book, and thanks are due Wendy Almeleh, my long-suffering copyeditor.

The penultimate draft of the manuscript was typed (word processed?) by Karen Lee Carey, who, as it happens, is a direct descendant of Sir William Petty, the founder of economic statistics referred to in Chapter 3.

Mary Platt, research librarian of the Chappaqua Public Library, performed expeditious miracles in getting books and journal articles for me.

Unless otherwise noted, all the statistics herein either come from or are based on *Economic Report of the President, Statistical Abstracts of the United States,* or National Income and Product Accounts in *Survey of Current Business.*

The index was prepared by Joan Haladay and S. W. Cohen.

THE END OF
ECONOMIC MAN

INTRODUCTION

Why We Have Economics

I

Economics is the study of the principles whereby people exchange money for goods and services.

Like all definitions, the foregoing is only a starting point. It also implies limits; economics is not all of life. Several of the few words in the definition—even "people"—will require separate chapters. Some may object that the definition excludes many topics that recognized economists often discuss. Barter is an example. Adam Smith, in fact, placed a propensity to barter at the very *fons et origo* of the discipline. Yet there is no proposition in any system of economics—classical, neoclassical, or whatever—that is clarified by a consideration of barter, while there are many that are confused thereby. This is not to deny that almost everyone occasionally engages in barter, or that in some parts of the world or on some levels of society or at some times, barter is or has been the dominant system; and it emphatically is not to imply that the lives lived in those places and times were or are unworthy of being lived or being studied. The point is merely that the modern world does not and could not run on barter, and no future economics will run on barter.

Of the words in the definition, "people" is obviously the most important. But Adam Smith took the wealth of nations for his subject, and modern schools concentrate on the gross national product or on a putative equilibrium or on the techniques of allocating resources to satisfy personal preferences.

At this point I can offer only a bare suggestion of why I propose such a sharp break with the recent past. In the early 1980s, when upwards of 14 million men and women in the United States were unemployed, and there was much debate about whether we were in a recession or a depression and how to end whatever it was, public attention was lavished on statistics supposed to indicate when recovery was finally under way. Among the "indicators," the rate of unemployment was understandably included. But this rate was, curiously, a "lagging" indicator. That is to say, contemporary economics held that something entitled to be called a recovery could be achieved leaving 6 or 8 or even 10 percent of our fellow citizens unemployed. Furthermore, it was widely insisted that 4 or 6 percent of us must always be unemployed if inflation was to be controlled.

An economics that regards several million people as of less importance than some level of prices will clearly differ in substantial ways from an economics that holds that full and just employment of men and women is a central economic problem.

II

Economics is a comparatively new discipline. Adam Smith is usually credited with being its father, and it was only in 1776 that he published *The Wealth of Nations,* the seminal book. Before that time, we find a few lines in Plato, a few paragraphs in Aristotle, a few admonitions in the Bible, some advice on farm management in Hesiod and later in Cato and Virgil, medieval sermons on usury and the just price, a flood of Renaissance pamphlets—several of them of considerable sophistication—together with some paragraphs in treatises on government. Until very late, the subject was what the Greeks said it was—*oikonomia,* household management. In the Renaissance, the nation was the king's household, and even by Adam Smith the nation is occasionally treated as an analogue of the private household. Indeed, we continue to find the same approach today.

When today's introductory textbooks tell students that they will learn about the efficient allocation of scarce resources, they are casting their subject as an aspect of man's struggle with nature. This was the problem for the Greek householder, for whom physical well-being, not to mention comfort, was inescapably precarious. This remained the problem for two millennia, but by Adam Smith's time its solution had become possible. It is a mark of Smith's genius that he recognized what had changed.

The steam-powered and water-powered machines of the Industrial Revolution concentrated production and brought forth the factory system, and the factory system made possible rapid progress in the division of labor. Plato had seen that the polis would be stronger if some men specialized in farming and some in soldiering, and it was common in quite primitive societies for the men to do the hunting and the women to do the gathering. These are instances of a division of labor of sorts, but they have nothing like the possibilities of the eighteen operations in the manufacture of pins that Smith described and immortalized in the opening pages of his book. Even a "small manufactory," employing only ten men poorly provided with machinery, "could make among them upwards of forty-eight thousand pins in a day. . . . But if they had all wrought separately and independently, and without any of them having been educated to this peculiar business, they certainly could not each of them have made twenty, perhaps not one pin in a day."[1]

Such an explosive growth of production (aided, we may note, by a bit of machinery and a bit of education) immediately changed the terms of economic endeavor. Subsistence need no longer be an all-absorbing problem. From the Industrial Revolution on, it has been possible in principle to feed, clothe, shelter, and provide health care for all mankind. That this has not been accomplished in fact is due to a failure of will, not a lack of means. It is a political problem. The economic problem, whose independence Smith declared, concerns human beings' relations with each other, not their struggle with nature.

III

By the middle of the nineteenth century, the scientific method was carrying all before it. If every event has a cause and if the universe is uniform, miracles are no longer sought or feared. Scientific inquiry, once fairly begun, is interminable. If human illnesses are natural, the human body becomes a part of nature. And if the human body is natural, it would seem that the mind, if it is human, must be natural, too.

At this point, a curious reversal occurred. It appeared early in Karl Marx, in works written fifteen years before *The Origin of Species*, though published posthumously. Like Rousseau, Marx saw mankind in chains and searched for the means of liberation. He found it in history, which to him was comprehensible only as it was lawful, and lawful only as it was impersonal and inexorable. He considered himself a materialist, and understood history to be materialist in the same way that classical mechanics was materialist.

Developing his ideas, he wrote, "It is not a matter of what this or that proletarian or even the proletariat as a whole *pictures* at present as its goal. It is a matter of *what the proletariat is in actuality* and what, in accordance with this *being,* it will historically be compelled to do."[2] What was launched in search of freedom has paradoxically come aground on sociohistorical compulsion. Marx was not the last to sail these murky waters.

We find mankind liberated from spooks and spirits, from lords and priests, by becoming mechanized. Once the universe was running like a clock, there was nothing for it but to fit us to a wheel in the works— perhaps a greater thing than a cog, but mechanical nevertheless. For us to be fit for this function, psychology had to subject us to mechanical controls. Or, as J. W. Miller said, we had first to lose our souls; then our minds; and finally, with the behaviorists, consciousness. Economic man is a prime example of this remarkable servomechanism.

IV

Medieval ethical doctrine, which included medieval economics, concerned a static society in which the proper relations of individual to individual and of individuals to God were immutable. It was a world of six foreordained events, from the Creation to the Second Coming, to which St. Augustine had added a seventh, the Eternal Sabbath. Though these events followed one after the other, they described a sequence, not a history. The various events had been and would be reached and passed regardless of what anyone did or did not do; and what was virtuous or sinful had no relation to any period but was from everlasting to everlasting.

During the Renaissance, the medieval ban on usury spurred the first tentative steps in the direction of fractional-reserve banking, which, coupled with double-entry bookkeeping, introduced a dynamism into business that was as fateful for the static medieval world view as was the cosmology of Copernicus. After Adam Smith, economic theory, following economic practice, abandoned religious dogma. It did not, however, reform its ethical base, but ultimately denied it.

In the second chapter of *The Wealth of Nations*, Smith announces that the "division of labor, from which so many advantages are derived, is not originally the effect of any human wisdom. It is the necessary, though very slow and gradual, consequence of a certain propensity in human nature which has in view no such extensive utility; the propensity to truck, barter, and exchange one thing for another."[3] This is clearly the theme of impersonality, but the definitive metaphor does not yet appear.

We hear of the invisible hand halfway through the book: "By preferring the support of domestic products to that of foreign industry, [every individual] intends only his own security; and by directing that industry in such a manner as its produce may be of the greatest value, he intends only his own gain, and he is in this, as in many other cases, led by an invisible hand to promote an end which was no part of his intention. Nor is it always the worse for society that it was no part of it. By pursuing his own interest he frequently promotes that of society more effectually than he really intends to promote it. I have never known much good done by those who affected to trade for the public good.

It is an affectation, indeed, not very common among merchants [Smith adds drily], and very few words need be employed in dissuading them from it."[4]

Smith's less metaphorical, but perhaps as frequently cited, statement of the idea comes even further on, more than two-thirds through the book: "[t]he obvious and simple system of natural liberty establishes itself of its own accord. Every man, as long as he does not violate the laws of justice, is left perfectly free to pursue his own interest in his own way, and to bring both his industry and capital into competition with those of any other men or order of men." This passage comes at the end of an attack on the physiocrats. But now Smith goes on to state explicitly the factor of the idea that gave it its historical power: "The sovereign is completely discharged from a duty . . . for the proper performance of which no human wisdom or knowledge could ever be sufficient; the duty of superintending the industry of private people, and of directing it towards the employments most suitable to the interest of society."[5]

Here Adam Smith made the wealth of nations seem an impersonal science on the model of Newtonian physics. Thus he changed irrevocably the conditions of our thoughts and lives. His words were so simple, so elegant, so appropriate to the spirit of the times that they carried instant conviction to all who heard them. Where only a few years earlier Rousseau had declared, "Man is born free, and everywhere he is in chains," the striking off of those chains now seemed an imminent possibility. And it would be done automatically, effortlessly, by the invisible hand, now that the heavy hand of sovereign lords was seen to be unnecessary. No one any longer needed to feel guilty in challenging the inherited authority of kings or the revealed morality of priests. The pursuit of self-interest would work, regardless of intention, for the benefit of all; and self-serving labor, freed of its taint of miserliness and greed, could achieve miracles of production, making use of the technical miracles of the natural sciences. The wealth of nations, which had previously been determined by military or dynastic maneuvering, could become the daily concern of commoners.

The free market, the free state, and free thought were thus intertwined in Smith's message. They did, in fact, grow up together—three robust children of the Enlightenment. As far as we know, all three depend on each other. Where one does not exist, the others have existed only in stunted form. In the ancient world, only personal wealth

or patronage of the wealthy could liberate thinkers from the deadening requirements of subsistence grubbing. In the medieval world, the Church sponsored scholarship, but on its own terms; even the great St. Thomas spoke harshly of intellectual speculation. Only in the modern world of the West do we find the ideal of a free state formed of all adult citizens, all of whom are free and responsible as thinkers of their own thoughts, as providers of their own sustenance, and as definers of their own relations with their fellows.

Just as thought could not be free if liable to persecution by secular or ecclesiastical authority, so government could not be free as a function of feudal rights and duties.

More than control of the purse was involved. That struggle had gone on for more than half a millennium, starting at least as early as Magna Carta in 1215. As long as the issue was between the king and his barons, no economic question was implied. The English barons, like the First and Second Estates on the Continent, fought for the right to raise revenue in their own way, and that way did not differ, so far as the ultimate taxpayers were concerned, from the way followed by the king. In both cases it was a question of household management. The lord, like the king above him and the paterfamilias below him, did with his dependents and his property as he thought best. At every level, exchange between domains was minimal; and within each domain the problems concerned much agriculture, some engineering, and, too often, the tactics of small-unit engagements.

What matters for modern government and modern economy is that there is a purse, that is to say, that there is an undifferentiated fund to support unspecified and unanticipated needs of government. Such a fund makes actual the idea of the general welfare; without it, government has only ad hoc functions specifically authorized. If democratic, specific authorization is constitutionally narrow in scope and small in scale. The New England town meeting, much admired by Tocqueville, went about as far as one can go in this direction. Modern government would be impossible as an amalgam of the Social Security Trust Fund, the Highway Trust Fund, and so on. The ambitious projects of the ancient world, like the Athenian acropolis or the wars against Persia, called for some sort of dictatorship, benevolent and limited if possible. A strong and continuing government needs a strong and continuing economy.[6]

We have economics because it frees us to govern ourselves.

2

PSYCHOLOGY
The Three Antinomies of Greed

I

All the great economists have turned to what they call psychology. Adam Smith opened his first book, *The Theory of Moral Sentiments,* with this sentence: "How selfish soever man may be supposed, there are evidently some principles in his nature, which interest him in the fortunes of others, and render their happiness necessary to him, though he derives nothing from it except the pleasure of seeing it."[1] Although he used the word "evidently," he produced no evidence; yet he went on to base the theory of his book on the principles in man's "nature" that he no doubt sincerely believed he had discovered.

John Maynard Keynes followed in his train. At a crucial point in *The General Theory of Employment, Interest and Money,* he wrote, "The fundamental psychological law, upon which we are entitled to depend with great confidence both *a priori* from our knowledge of human nature and from the detailed facts of experience, is that men are disposed, as a rule and on the average, to increase their consumption as their income increases, but not by as much as the increase in their income."[2] Of a lesser man than Keynes one might be tempted to say that he wrote so emphatically because his evidence was so slight. In any case, whatever evidence he might have had, he adduced none; and one may scour all the psychology textbooks in the land without coming across the faintest adumbration of this allegedly dependable psychological law.

The psychology invoked by economists has, it must be acknowledged, borne little relation to that studied by psychologists. This anomaly was noted as long ago as 1925 by Wesley Clair Mitchell, founder of the National Bureau of Economic Research, who made what must be judged a preliminary and superficial attempt to tie his economics to the then-fashionable behaviorist psychology of John B. Watson.[3]

Economics has to come to ground somewhere. Almost universally, the ground chosen or assumed has been self-interest, an apparently simple, straightforward, and obvious concept. It is, nevertheless, easier to understand what is meant by the idea of self-interest or the pleasure-pain principle than to use the idea to further understanding. Every time Galileo released a brass ball at the top of an inclined plane, it rolled in the same way, accelerating in the same way. But regardless of Adam Smith's notion of a propensity to barter, sometimes a deal goes through, and sometimes it doesn't. One person will see self-interest in a swap and the next won't. This seems, so to say, perfectly natural. They're different people. Everyone is different. People are differently endowed and come from different backgrounds and have different needs, wants, hopes, expectations, fears, understandings, interests. Everyone is strange but me and thee.

In all honesty, human beings behave very strangely indeed. With the reports of thousands of cultural anthropologists before us, we know that there is scarcely a practice commonly seen in one part of the world that is not shunned in another. Even in Smith's day enough was known of the customs of the Chinese and the American Indians and, nearer at hand, some sadly disreputable Frenchmen, to understand that their behavior differed from that of a Scottish scholar who lived much of his life with his mother.

What, then, becomes of human nature? If people act differently because they *are* different, what is gained by claiming they are of the same nature because they act out of self-interest? Self-interest would appear to be as various as humanity. Is there such a thing as self-interest, after all?

The usual answer to this question says that it's *enlightened* self-interest that is really uniform. The form of the answer appears again and again in the history of Western thought and again and again as a proposed solution to economic problems.

The distinction between self-interest and enlightened self-interest seems the same as the familiar distinction between appearance and reality. We are used to mistrusting the appearance of things; it is prudent to look for the underlying or hidden reality. "Things are seldom what they seem," sings Little Buttercup in *Pinafore*, "Skim milk masquerades as cream." Nor is this search merely a question of prudence; it is also a mark of wisdom. It is a major theme of most, if not all, religions, which celebrate the superior reality of some world other than this, or the superior force of some supernatural power. It is a recurring concern of poets, who probe with Wordsworth "something far more deeply interfused," with Eliot "the world of perpetual solitude."

The notion of the underlying reality of enlightened self-interest (however defined) is the very model of an a priori judgment. It assumes what it pretends to prove. It claims that we should behave in a certain way if we knew what's good for us. If we don't behave in the prescribed way, it's because we don't know what's good for us. There is no way of attacking or even defending this form of argument. Enlightened self-interest is a dogma no more successful in subduing the riot of human behavior than is self-interest without the enlightenment.

II

In the conventional story, economic suppliers (or producers) are profit (or income) maximizers; and economic demanders (or consumers) are utility (or satisfaction) maximizers. Economic man maximizes both profit and utility. Not surprisingly, there is a considerable literature questioning the realism of these propositions. Given the enormous range and variety of what people do, not to mention the comparative effectiveness of their doings, it is argued that these multitudinous doings cannot all be examples of profit maximization. In the same way, it is said that the different ways we spend our money—certainly idiosyncratic, frequently wasteful, occasionally counterproductive—suggest that utility maximization is also a protean idea without real definition.

There is much merit in these objections; yet there is also force in the rejoinder that it would be strange not to try to maximize profit or utility, as the case may be. If you can get more of either, why shouldn't you? Indeed, since maximum profit arguably comes from the most efficient use of scarce resources, can it not be said that you have a duty to seek it? After all, this is the way Adam Smith's invisible hand seduces selfish behavior into producing public good.

Let us say that I am a profit-maximizing man. Not only am I clever, bold, and ruthless; not only do I stretch the law as far as it will go in my favor (but prudently no farther); not only do I push my employees to the limit and deal as sharply as I can with my suppliers and my customers; not only am I admired and feared as a keen and tough competitor—beyond these delightful qualities I am necessarily a workaholic. As long as there's another dollar—another penny—to be made, I am after it, not like a hawk (I have no time for soaring), perhaps like a badger. If there's no way to squeeze more out of my regular employment, I'll go moonlighting; and when I finally fall into bed, if I lie awake, I am scheming ways to increase my profit tomorrow.

Unfortunately, I never get to enjoy my winnings. I'm too busy to. If I were to relax a moment, a main chance might pass me by. Literature is full of monsters like me. Dickens would have had to shut up shop if he hadn't had such people to write about.

Literature is also full of utility maximizers—charming wastrels who live a life of endless pleasure. Women were supposed to be enchanted by them. Until very recently, women were themselves supposed to live such lives. As Veblen saw it, it was only when women were successful in this utility-maximizing way that their profit-maximizing husbands enjoyed any utility—albeit a derived utility—from the profits they piled up.

So we have a conflict. A profit maximizer has to forgo utilities for lack of time. And unless a utility maximizer can manage to be supported by someone else, he (or she) will not have resources to pay for possible pleasures.

No producer is only a producer, and very few besides children, the senile, and the infirm are only consumers. Since producers are also consumers, they must be both profit maximizers and utility maximizers, and that is impossible.

Can we narrow the situation down and say that economic man is a profit maximizer when he is producing and a utility maximizer when he is consuming? If so, we must then ask why he is producing at this moment instead of consuming. Why is he moonlighting instead of gazing at the moon? If he has a job, he has accepted the responsibility of maximizing profits at certain hours of the day, but why did he take the job? Why not emulate Henry Thoreau? (Of course, Thoreau was also an exemplary producer; goods he created still yield profits and utilities, all over the world, a century and a quarter after his death.)

An obvious modification of the scheme calls for utility maximizers to do their best, subject to the constraint of their wealth, while profit maximizers are clearly subject to the constraints of their abilities and their luck. But even an incompetent man may be a workaholic and so unable to enjoy even the few utilities available to one of his accomplishments, while a remittance man may steal enough time from his pleasures to make a little profit for himself, just for fun. Thus the proposed constraints are, if precise enough to support a calculation, limited to a single case; if they are vague enough to be general in application, they are also so general in implication that no useful inference may be drawn.

This conclusion is not merely a rhetorical flourish. If you translate your thoughts into mathematics, you will reach the same conclusion very quickly. Taking the problems of maximization literally (and how else should we take them?), we find that the decisive constraint in every case is that of time. There are only so many hours in the day. Hours devoted to profit maximization are not available for utility maximization, and vice versa. We can solemnly write this proposition in the form of an equation: $P + U + W = 24$ (profit-maximizing hours plus utility-maximizing hours plus wasted hours equals twenty-four hours in a day). Valid though this equation may be, it does not tell me what values I should give to P or U or, for that matter, W.

The proper allocation of our time is a question each of us must decide. Our lives depend on our decisions. They are acts of will. They are mathematically indeterminate and without mathematical solution, as we have seen them to be illogical and without reasonable solution. These are no mere quibbles but go directly to the heart of conventional

economic theory. Nor is appeal here being made to the realism or
unrealism of the assumptions. Such empirical appeal is not without
validity, but it is not being made here. Our appeal is to logic. Any
theory that is illogical at the start will be illogical forever after. GIGO,
as the computer people say.

III

In talking about self-interest and profit maximization and
utility maximization, I have refrained from calling them by their common everyday name, which is greed. Economic man is greedy. Since
everyone is some kind of economic man—a producer or a consumer or
both—it would appear that everyone is greedy, which is manifestly
untrue.

There are four possible resolutions of the difficulty. The first is to
claim that whether people really are greedy or not, they act as if they
were. But this claim gets us nowhere because it raises again a question
of fact. Granted that Mother Teresa is not greedy, does she really act
as if she were?[4]

A second way out is described by Professor Amartya Sen: "The real
issue is whether there is a plurality of motivations, or whether self-
interest *alone* drives human beings."[5] Putting aside the question of
whether it can be meaningful to speak of human beings as driven, and
granting a plurality of motives (some of them doubtless contradictory),
we see that one motive must be selected as ultimately efficient or the
models economists construct will run only by unexpected fits and starts,
like a Model T operated by Laurel and Hardy. Whether greed is the
single motivation or the efficient motivation is a distinction without a
difference.

The third way is little more than a quibble over terminology. Shying
away from brutal "greed" and even from the relatively genteel "self-
interest," some say that an economic system exists to provide people
with all possible freedom to choose whatever they want whenever they
want it. The popular press has characterized a whole generation as so
motivated—the "me generation." But these formulations are essen-

tially identical; "greed" and "self-interest" and "me first" all come very close to the same thing.

The fourth way is what is known as partial analysis, which is signaled by the Latin ablative absolute *ceteris paribus*—other things being equal. This phrase is invoked so frequently by economists that they often drop in its abbreviation ritualistically, as a Tibetan monk spins a prayer wheel. *"Cet. par.,"* they will say, and go about their business. What they are doing is holding unchanged all except one of the factors of a situation or equation and then varying that one to see how it affects the outcome or solution.

To nonprofessionals it often looks as though economists were merely spinning wheels, because other things generally are not equal; but partial analysis is a perfectly legitimate procedure and in perhaps the majority of economic problems the only procedure. It is used all the time in business, in assigning costs to different parts of an operation, in deciding which advertising pitch pulls best, and so on.

What partial analysis does with the greed question is merely to say that, other things being equal, people want more of whatever it is they want. Moreover, *cet. par.*, people want more money, because, *cet. par.*, money is the best means of getting whatever people want. Thus Mother Teresa, who may be perfectly altruistic and scornful of anything for herself, may, other things being equal, be eager for more money to support her charitable causes. She won't compromise her beliefs to get that money but, *cet. par.*—that is, when those beliefs are not affected—she'll go for it. And I, holier than thou though I may be, am the same. With a stroke of the pen, we're all made alike again; willy-nilly, we're all transmogrified into the classical economic man.

None of this is to say that Mother Teresa is greedy or that I am or that you are. We may sometimes act out of self-interest, just as the most depraved miser may sometimes act altruistically. Other things being equal—all contrary considerations aside—the miser would be willing to be a benefactor of his fellowmen, or some of them.

The same sort of reasoning applies to every honorable or dishonorable activity you can name. Aside from things I will not or cannot do, I'd rather be rich than poor (I hear that rich is better). I'd also like to be an internationally respected philosopher and a better bird watcher, have a better second serve, and be well and truly beloved. All of these motives are true under the partial-analysis rule, and they are just as true as my greediness.

We seem, however, to have proved too much. If greed can be established under the partial-analysis rule, every sort of motive or trait or predilection or interest whatever—together with its contrary—can be equally established. Greed is on no surer footing than altruism. Amusingly enough, conventional economics reaches the same conclusion. Competition between perfectly greedy producers is supposed to drive prices down to cost—but perfectly altruistic producers would set prices at cost out of the goodness of their hearts.

We have proved nothing at all. Partial analysis is valid in treating specific and limited problems; it is powerless before a universal problem, such as *all* economic action. Partial analysis can yield only partial results; it cannot yield general results. Whether antiseptically presented as self-interest or as profit maximization and utility maximization, or brazenly acknowledged as greed, the presumed psychological foundations of economics are fallacious.

IV

Without the *ceteris paribus* disclaimer, the universality of economic man cannot be claimed; but with the rule, every sort of man or woman is universal. Nor would it make sense to claim a statistical universality. One can't be a little pregnant, and one can't be sort of universal. Why should economists have singled out what nonprofessionals call greed as the basis of their study?

On the face of it, it is an astonishing choice, for greed or covetousness is one of the seven deadly sins. Not venial but mortal. This is no casual opinion, but the settled judgment of mankind. A fat anthology could be compiled of notable statements to this effect, and a bulky portfolio collected of artistic embodiments of the idea. From King Midas to Silas Marner, it has been well understood that greed shrivels the soul. St. Augustine wrote, "Every disorder of the soul is its own punishment,"[6] and secular humanists would join the religious in this formulation.

In persisting in talk about greed, economists are like the drunk in the old burlesque skit who searched at the street corner for a wallet he had lost in the middle of the block because the light was better at the corner. Thus Sir James Steuart, nine years before *The Wealth of Nations*, wrote, "Were every one to act for the public, and neglect himself, the statesman would be bewildered."[7] Steuart's statesman prefers self-centered constituents because he thinks he knows how they'll behave in any situation. In the same way, economists assume they know what greedy economic man will do.

It is not enough, however, for economic man to be greedy; a greedy fool is as unpredictable as a sentimental altruist. Professor Frank Hahn put the apparent solution in a convenient form of words: "I am rather convinced that the rational greedy economic agent will continue in a central role."[8] Economic man must be both rational and greedy. But it is not so easy to be both.

Rationality is the mark of humanity. It is the foundation of responsibility, as responsibility is the foundation of freedom. Rationality is not a tool usable toward some indifferent end; it is itself the end. It is achieved with struggle and is forever at risk. It is the method and the objective of all the arts and sciences. The alternative is nonsense—not an error or a mistake, but nonsense.

How, then, can it be possible to be both rational and greedy? It is not possible. The rational greedy economic man is a contradiction in terms. It is not rational to demean oneself. Our greedy economic man is a fool, after all.

These are what I shall call the Three Antinomies of Greed: (1) Profit maximization and utility maximization cannot simultaneously rule us. (2) Other things being equal, greed and its contrary are equally universal. (3) Foolish greed is unpredictable, and rational greed is absurd.

Any one of these is conclusive. Together they overwhelm.

V

Neither self-interest nor utility maximization nor greed will do, and other psychological groundings are no better. Karl Marx hoped to release the creative and productive instincts of mankind by devising an economy in which it would be "possible for me to do one thing today and another tomorrow, to hunt in the morning, fish in the afternoon, rear cattle in the evening, criticize after dinner, just as I have a mind, without ever becoming hunter, fisherman, cowboy, or critic."[9] Herbert Marcuse thought that this notorious passage from *The German Ideology*, written in 1846, was a joke, and others have thought it a young man's aberration. But the same notion appears thirty years later in *Critique of the Gotha Program*, where Marx announces that in the communist future, production will not be a problem because it will have "increased with the all-around development of the individual."[10] Mao's China, during the Great Proletarian Cultural Revolution, made an attempt to reduce Marx's vision to practice. The result was chaos, satisfactory only to rampaging "youth."

While it might consequently occur to a commonsensical person to question the premises of self-interest or greed or creativity on which these various programs are based, the point here is that motivation is the wrong idea, anyhow. It suggests what people do automatically, what they are programmed to do. In so far as psychology inquires into such doings, it is no longer a suitable foundation for political economy. It played a historical role in helping to free us from absolute kings. But the issue now is not freedom from, but freedom, that is, autonomy.

VI

A consequence of economists' preoccupation with their special pseudo-psychology has been distraction from proper economic concerns. Keynes spent many pages of his great book analyzing the various motives for what he called liquidity preference, and his successors have spent many pages discussing his analysis. Yet in the end it does not matter whether money is withheld for the transactions motive or the precautionary motive or the speculative motive.[11] The economic consequence is the same either way; it is the withholding that matters. When the economic consequence is considered, it is seen (as we shall see in Chapter 10) that liquidity preference is effectively the same as speculation, although the motives may be quite different.

Economics and the law are both divisions of ethics. An important distinction between them is that motive or intention is central in the law but is insignificant in economics. A man is discovered with a smoking gun in his hand, standing over a bleeding corpse. It may be quickly proved that homicide has been committed by the man with the gun. But what did the man intend? If the killing was done with malice aforethought, it was murder. If it was done in a sudden rage, it was manslaughter. If the gun happened to go off when the man tripped, it was accidental death. If the killer shot to defend himself, the homicide is justifiable. And if the killer is unable to distinguish right from wrong, he is not a criminal, but may be, as they say, institutionalized. That a man has been killed is the beginning, not the end, of the law's concern.

With economics, it is the other way entirely. The intentions of economic agents matter only to them or to those entitled to pass judgment on them, but not to the economy—and not at all, as far as economic consequences are concerned, even to the agents themselves. Entrepreneurs may, with the best intention in the world, set the price for their products too high (or too low) and thus ruin their companies, their investors, their employees, and themselves. Their good intentions do not mitigate their companies' losses or the consequent diminishing of the GNP. Or, monetary authorities may raise the interest rate with the intention of keeping prices down; if the actual consequence is that prices are raised, that is what matters, not the intention. Or, three centuries ago mercantilists held that money was gold or some such commodity, which they therefore accumulated; they prospered, not because they had gold, but because, having lots of what for them was money, they kept the interest rate down.

Intentions of course matter in ethics and the law. They do not matter in economics proper. Thus all talk of profit *motive* or liquidity *preference* or *propensity* to consume is beside the point. Motive, preference, and propensity are psychological concepts. The economic questions are profit, liquidity, and consumption *tout court.*

Nothing in the foregoing denies (or affirms) the validity of any proposition in psychology or the virtue of the study of psychology. Every human action can be studied from the points of view of all the natural sciences and most of the social sciences. Nothing I do is without physical aspect; there is never a time when I do not obey the laws of motion, when I can step off a moving train without experiencing a rude, but equal and opposite, reaction. Nothing I ever do is without physiological aspect. If you prick me, I will bleed, and the blood will fall to the ground at the rate of 32 feet per second per second. Nothing I do is without emotional content, and your assault will make me angry or sad. Nor is there much I do that is in principle noneconomic; if I stay home to nurse my wound, I'll also suffer a loss of income. But the speed of the fall of my blood is irrelevant to my loss of income.

Just as it would be a confusion of terms to say that the attraction of positive and negative charges for each other is an expression of love, or that the stars in their courses reveal the greatness of Beethoven, so it is a confusion of terms to search for psychological explanations of economic events.

There is, however, one discipline that seems a special case: mathematics, if only because economics seems always to involve numbers. In the modern world, the authority of mathematics has rivaled the authority of psychology. That authority must now be examined.

3

MATHEMATICS

*Why Physics Is Value Free and
Economics Isn't*

I

Galileo, on the basis of a few almost-casual observations, proposed a mathematical formula for the velocity of any falling body, excluding all sorts of irrelevant data, and then devised measurable experiments that confirmed the formula. In the same way, Newton combined the astronomical findings and theories of Copernicus and Kepler with Galileo's formula to produce universal laws of motion. He then sought observations that would confirm these laws. At first he failed, and put his study aside. The story goes that a few years later, working with new figures, he became so excited as he saw confirmation looming that he had to call in a friend to finish the calculations.

In the social sciences an early, if not the first, work along these lines was done by John Graunt, a haberdasher and captain of militia, who studied the mortality records of the City of London and prepared what he called a "Table showing one hundred quick conceptions, how many die within six years, how many the next decade, and so for every decade till 76." His work appeared in 1661, twenty-six years before Newton's *Principia.* Graunt apparently prepared his table for fun, but it was quickly taken up by the nascent insurance business, and a general statement of the principles behind such work was made by Sir William Petty, a friend of Graunt's.

Because of this statement, Petty is credited as one of the founders of modern statistics, which he called political arithmetic, and which he defined as "the art of reasoning by figures upon things relating to the government." Petty was a minor sort of Renaissance man, a professor of anatomy at Oxford, the organizer of the survey of Cromwell's grants of land in Ireland, a landlord himself of some fifty thousand acres in County Kerry, and an occasional essayist on economic subjects. A longish essay or short book, published posthumously because it contained references to France offensive to Petty's patron Charles II, was *Five Discourses on Political Arithmetick.* "The method I use," Petty wrote, "is not yet very usual; for, instead of using only comparative and superlative words, and intellectual arguments, I have taken the course . . . to express myself in terms of number, weight, and measure; to use only arguments of sense, and to consider only such causes as have visible foundations in nature."[1]

One would think that with Graunt and Petty and several others on the Continent, economics was well under way on a course parallel to that of astronomy and physics. It is therefore with something of a shock that we listen to Adam Smith pronouncing a full hundred years later, "I have no great faith in political arithmetic."[2]

What had gone wrong?

The biographical reason for Smith's rejection of political arithmetic no doubt turned in part on his vehement rejection of mercantilism, one of the principal themes of his book. Petty, like others of his time, was a mercantilist. Though it is most unlikely that Smith had not read Petty's work and it is certain that he was aware of the discipline Petty had named, yet Petty himself is not named in *The Wealth of Nations.* This omission is surprising because, as Professor Heilbroner notes, over a hundred authors are referred to by name in Smith's treatise.[3]

Personality aside, the episode would seem to suggest some reason to be wary of statistics in economics. Smith had what seemed to him, and still seem to us two centuries later, sound reasons for opposing the Corn Laws. These reasons owed nothing to the figures that had been collected, even though they were in Smith's favor. "I mention them," he said, "only to show of how much less consequence in the opinion of most judicious and experienced persons, the foreign trade of corn is than the home trade."[4] He refused to bother himself about the accuracy of the figures and thought they proved nothing except the size of the problem. By the same token, the figures that persuaded others, including Petty, of the merits of mercantilism carried no conviction to Smith.

This sort of thing still goes on. In the past hundred years we have collected unbelievable quantities of statistics on everything one can imagine, especially on all aspects of economic life. The annual *Economic Report of the President* is thought to need 125 pages of statistics to support 285 pages of text. Yet that report is subject to debate within the establishment and to scorn from outside. It is commonplace—even expected—that economists will agree on figures and will dispute irreconcilably about their meaning.

A situation like this does not occur in the natural sciences. Once Simon Stevin showed that the velocities of falling bodies are not proportionate to their density, no student continued to hold Aristotle's side of the question. Newton was no doubt dismayed when his first calculations failed to demonstrate the inverse-square law. He may even have suspected that the number he had been given for the radius of the earth was wrong. But he did not pretend that the number didn't matter, that the law held regardless of the number.

Why should economists behave differently? The record suggests a fundamental difference between natural and social science. General acceptance of some difference is indicated by the usual division of the sciences into the two broad classifications, with physics always in one group and economics always in the other.

"Number, weight, and measure" will not actually take one very far in economics. One may no doubt count the bushels of wheat each farmer grows and then add the output of all the wheat farmers in the land to get the national output. And one can do the same for tons of coal and for almost anything produced by farming or mining. One can even classify and total the types and grades of steel produced by steel mills. Thereafter things get much more complicated. Some steel goes into stovepipes and some into cannons, some into bridge girders and some into snuff boxes. A pine forest may yield ships' spars, residential clapboarding, and paper products. Tables of the numbers, weights, and measures of these products may be of interest to individual producers, but they are too diverse for inferences of any generality. You cannot, as the saying goes, add apples and oranges.

It should, moreover, be noted that to divide fruit into apples and oranges, even to separate fruit from steel girders, is illicit on the premises of political arithmetic. An apple and a needle both have number, weight, and measure and therefore, on the premises, should be added together. Carry it a step further: It is illicit on the premises to distinguish a good apple from a rotten one or a potato from the dirt that is turned up when it is harvested. Newtonian mechanics works as well with a rotten apple as with a good one, but it would appear that economics may be somehow different.

II

A strong statement in favor of mathematical thinking was made by William Stanley Jevons, who argued in 1871 that *"our science must be mathematical, simply because it deals with quantities.* Wherever the things treated are capable of being *greater or less,* there the laws and relations must be mathematical in nature."[5] His point, Jevons insists, is not merely that mathematical notation is used, because "If we had no regard to trouble and prolixity, the most complicated mathematical problems might be stated in ordinary language." Rather, he holds that "There can be but two classes of sciences—those which are *simply logical,* and *those which, besides being logical, are also mathematical."* A logical science "determines whether a thing be or not be . . . but if the thing may be greater or less, or the event may happen sooner or later, nearer or farther, then quantitative notions enter."[6]

As so often happens in the history of thought, Jevons claims both too little and too much. The sort of question he assigns exclusively to logic—to be or not to be—is not merely characteristic of Hamlet but is also the basis of computer circuitry and so is the mathematics par excellence of our day. On the other hand, very little of logic is as restricted as Jevons suggests. The universal affirmative proposition of the form "All apples are fruits" certainly seems to meet his standard. But this proposition may be converted by immediate inference to the particular affirmative "Some fruits are apples," which is something else.

In any case, it by no means follows that all "sciences" that deal in quantities are merely mathematical. The obvious exceptions to Jevons's rule are legion, from penology to pharmacology. Criminals are sentenced to prison for a number of days or years or are required to pay a fine of a number of dollars; but no one supposes that judges do or should turn to mathematicians for advice in imposing sentence. Likewise, it is usual to prescribe 6.5 grains of aspirin for a headache, but the prescription does not appear in any mathematics text.

A task of algebra is to explore the relationship between dependent and independent variables. A decision as to which are dependent and which independent must be made to get the equation into usable form. One may debate whether the interest rate depends on the rate of inflation, or vice versa; and not only the shape of the equation but the deduced policy recommendations will be at stake. And there is still a prior question: Do the given variables have a dependent-independent relationship at all? Or, if they sometimes have such a relationship, is it regular?

The answer to these questions is by no means obvious or automatic. We may, for example, brush aside as frivolous Jevons' proposed connections between sunspots and the stock market, but an astronomer as distinguished as Harlan Stetson took the matter seriously enough to write a book about it. The illustration is more sharply focused by the fact that shortly after he wrote his book Stetson joined in the furious attack on Immanuel Velikovsky's best-selling quasi-literal interpretation of biblical cosmology.

The point is that neither the sunspot question nor the biblical question is definitively answered by mathematics. One can of course make errors in any mathematical calculation, and such errors certainly vitiate the conclusion; but mathematical correctness is no guarantee of a meaningful answer. Stetson rejected Velikovsky, not because of faulty mathematics, but because if Velikovsky were right, the entire structure of modern science would crumble. More than astronomy was at risk, because astronomy is consistent with physics, and physics with chemistry, and chemistry with biology. In the same way, economics must be consistent with ethics in the broad sense and with all humanistic concerns, nor may humanism be inconsistent with natural science if our life is to be intelligible.

Contemporary economics leans heavily on analytic geometry. A curious fact about the rank jungle of multicolored curves choking the pages of the textbooks is that numbers rarely attach to them; and when numerical values are represented, they often turn out to be estimated or wholly imaginary—a schedule showing the supposed (or denied) price elasticity of wheat, the kinked oligopoly demand curve, and so on. In almost all cases no one knows what the actual figures may be; the given figures are assumed in order to illustrate a theory.

The problem lies not in the fact that the actual numbers are truly difficult to come by or even, in some instances, impossible to come by. No one has been to the interior of the sun; yet astrophysicists talk confidently of what goes on there. This is possible because natural science is a unified structure. What the astrophysicist can observe about the sun can occur only if what he theorizes about the interior is true. Hence it *is* true. Revisions occur every day, but the system stands. The textbooks talk as though a similar system works in economics, but actually it does not. Every business—especially every one selling by mail—has experimented with price changes and found instances where a price increase has increased sales. Nothing like this happens in natural science, where there never are exceptions supposed to prove the rule.

III

In the article in which Wesley Clair Mitchell called for an alliance between economics and behaviorist psychology, he also urged a shift from qualitative to quantitative work. "Our qualitative theory," he wrote, "has followed the logic of Newtonian mechanics. . . . In the hedonistic calculus which Jevons followed, man is placed under the governance of two sovereign masters, pain and pleasure, which play the same role in controlling human behavior that Newton's laws of motion play in controlling the behavior of the heavenly bodies. . . . The mechanical view involves the notions of sameness, of certainty, of invariant laws; the statistical view [introduced by Maxwell] involves the notions of variety, of probability, of approximations."[7]

This odd analogy invites a couple of comments. First, there is no qualitative-quantitative split between Newton and Maxwell; they are both quantitative through and through. And, as we have seen, Jevons was as enthusiastic a supporter of quantitative methods in economics as anyone since; nor was he unaware of the fact that the numbers he worked with were imprecise. "Many persons," he observed, "entertain a prejudice against mathematical language, arising out of a confusion between the ideas of a mathematical science and an exact science . . . but in reality, there is no such thing as an exact science, except in a comparative sense. Astronomy is more exact than other sciences, because the position of a planet or star admits of close measurement; but, if we examine the methods of physical astronomy, we find that they are all approximate. . . . Had physicists waited until their data were perfectly precise before they brought in the aid of mathematics, we should have still been in the age of science which terminated in the time of Galileo."[8] This debater's point could serve Mitchell as well.

A second and more important comment on Mitchell is that the world of Maxwell, Einstein, and Heisenberg is not less subject to invariant laws than is the world of Newton. In physics, to be sure, the detailed precision of optics is confined to relatively gross phenomena, such as the refraction of a beam of light upon hitting a body of water. In a given experiment, the intensity of the beam and the angle of refraction never vary, regardless of the date of the experiment or the name of the experimenter. But whether a particular photon will be refracted or reflected cannot be said; the beam is the statistical result of a lot of photons. Yet nothing that can be said about a particular photon is in conflict with what can be said about gross phenomena. On the contrary, explanation of gross phenomena allows for, and must allow for, the diverse paths of determinate and regular proportions of photons. It does not happen that today 10 percent of the photons are reflected, although yesterday, under identical conditions, 20 percent were reflected, while the day before, the figure was 12. One would scarcely know how to grind and coat lenses in such an unreliable world, which would always be more or less out of focus.

A key phrase, of course, is "under identical conditions." We have, however, already seen that conditions for self-interested economic man are never identical. The behavior that economists try to describe statistically is in fact in constant flux. Indeed, it is exactly this shifting of demand and supply from here to here, from high to low, from this to that, that is supposed to be measured by the market. The "market" of a beam of light is constant; the economic market is forever unstable.

As Sir Thomas Browne said of the song the Sirens sang, the explanation of the market's rise and fall is not beyond all conjecture. But such explanation will not be of the same order as the explanations of optics.

IV

The attraction of mathematics for economists is no doubt enhanced (as Jevons suggests) by the hope that somewhere, somehow, they will discover something similar to Newton's inverse-square law. At first glance, Newton's problem and the econometricians' problem do seem similar. Both are confronted by a universe of infinite detail and variety, and both are sustained by the hope that, somewhere in that booming, buzzing confusion, orderly and reliable laws may be discovered. In fact, Newton experienced the order and reliability every moment of his life and could not—literally—have taken a step otherwise. The notorious apple neither flew away erratically nor disintegrated in midair, but fell solidly, as anyone would expect.

The orderly reliability of nature not only is free of the invocations of priests but also is free of the hopes and fears of ordinary men, including the scientists who study it. Experiments will come out however they come out, naturally, regardless of the intentions of the experimenters. In fact, if experimenters are found to have influenced the results, the experiments are discredited and the experimenters disgraced.

It is not, however, the impartiality of experimenters or observers that distinguishes natural science from social science. If social scientists report what they wish they'd found rather than what they did find, they are as surely discredited as are natural scientists who falsify their data. It is in their different subject matters that the difference between natural science and social science lies. Physics is value free because electrons know no value. The events reported by social scientists are not value free because the human beings who act in these events have values. By acting this way rather than that, they declare that they judge this way to be better—that is, more valuable. Both natural scientists and social scientists may incidentally reveal their personal values in their writings, but a report of human action will always concern the values of the human actors.

The universe of physics is a universe discovered by human beings, but it does not depend on human beings for its operation. Distance and clock time are not values; it makes no sense to approve or disapprove of them; Margaret Fuller could not refuse to accept the universe. It is a fact that the chemical bond works in the way Linus Pauling discovered, and neither Linus Pauling nor anyone else can change it.

"The values of an objective science like physics," Max Planck said, "are wholly independent of the objects to which they relate."9 No value appears in the physical description of an object. A physical description defines an object that obeys physical laws, not an economic object obeying economic laws, whatever they may be. A physical description of the piece of green-backed paper in my pocket does not reveal what makes it money or what money does. Any good that I buy with my money will obey physical law, but that fact is not what will make it a good. Every service that is performed must rely on physical law, but that fact does not explain what is economic about it. Every object is a physical object, and any object may come to be an economic object; but only some objects are actually economic objects. Whether or not a particular object becomes an economic object depends upon what human beings do with it.

Money, goods, and services are human values. Economic production and consumption are human activities. The consumption of food is essential to life, but that fact is in biology and says nothing about the price of apples. You may be convinced that apples are physiologically better for you than acorns, and your conviction may affect the price you are willing to pay; but it is only the price that is an economic concern.

As distance and clock time are fundamental physical concepts, money, goods, and services are fundamental economic concepts. Both lists can be extended, but one distinction will always separate them; the former are value free, while the latter are value bound. If it made a difference to the laws of physics what Linus Pauling (or anyone) felt about electrons, physics would collapse. If it didn't make a difference how much money Linus Pauling (or someone) would pay for an electron microscope, either the microscope would not be economic good, or economics would collapse.

The vocabulary of physics is amoral—not antimoral, but amoral.

Mass, force, and velocity have no moral implications because the laws describing them have no alternatives. The vocabulary of economics, in contrast, abounds in ethical terms. It is impossible to define "good," "service," or even "utility" without making ethical judgments. Every object has mass, but not every object has utility. Moreover, some people may consider a certain object a good while others do not, but there can be no disagreement about the equivalence and direction of action and reaction. There is no other or better way for a body to fall in a vacuum than $S = 1/2gt^2$; this is not because physicists don't happen to be interested in making this a better world. There is no unchanging price for a bushel of wheat; and this is not because economists don't happen to be interested in a stable universe. The price of wheat depends upon what people do, but bodies fall as they do regardless of what people do or think.

Economics is not value free, and no amount of abstraction can make it value free. The econometricians' search for equations that will explain the economy is forever doomed to frustration. It is often said that their models don't work because, on the one hand, the variables are too many and, on the other, the statistical data are too sparse. But the physical universe is as various as the economic universe (they are, to repeat, both infinite), and Newton had fewer data and less powerful means of calculation than are at the disposal of Jan Tinbergen and his econometrician followers. The difference is fundamental, and the failure to understand it reduces much of modern economics to a game that unfortunately has serious consequences.

V

After a couple of pages of moderately abstruse mathematics, Keynes remarks, "I do not myself attach much value to manipulations of this kind; . . . they involve just as much tacit assumption as to what values are taken as independent . . . as ordinary discourse does, whilst I doubt if they carry us further than ordinary discourse can."[10] Alfred Marshall, Keynes's early mentor, wrote in the introduction to his influential textbook that "it seems doubtful whether any one spends his time well in reading lengthy translations of economic doctrines into mathematics."[11]

To these sentiments may be added the observation that mathematics derives power not only from the conciseness of its notation but also from its stability. Mathematics knows only the present tense and does not deal in particulars. Two plus three *equals* five. It is mathematically meaningless to say, "Two plus three used to equal five," or "will equal five next year," or "sometimes equals five." It is also mathematically meaningless to say, "Some two plus three equals five," or "Two plus three equals five when you're counting sheep," or "when certain people do certain things."

A mathematical relationship is reciprocal; it can go either way, and it can retrace its steps. If $2x - y = 4$, then $y = 2x - 4$, and $x = (y + 4)/2$, from either of which can be derived $2x - y = 4$, which is where we started. In economics, if you buy a shirt, you cannot sell it back for the same price, nor would there be any reason to do so unless something was wrong with it (in which case you didn't buy it but refused delivery). More important, economics operates in calendar or historical time, which is not reversible. Last spring I paid two men for two weeks' work painting my house. If I could somehow get the paint off the house, that wouldn't give the men back their labor or get the paint back in the cans, not to mention the money back in my pocket.

4

PEOPLE

Where Economics Is Grounded

I

The people of our definition of economics now take center stage, and they do so as autonomous and responsible persons, not as specialized organisms whose nature is to behave according to certain rules, nor yet as entities obedient in some essential way to mathematical or physical formulae.

Autonomy is not atomicism, nor is it possible in a state of nature. All attempts to define mankind in jungle terms are more or less elaborate exercises in anachronism, taking more or less educated contemporary people and setting them down in a jungle to see what they will do. Such people are not naked apes but the product and beneficiary of a long history. Robinson Crusoe was an Englishman far from home, not a savage with a gun and an old nanny goat. There was no way he could not be an Englishman except by laboriously becoming something else, and that something else would not be a child of nature. Not even Friday was a child of nature.

If not children of nature, what were they? Children of some sort of society, of course: a family, a band, a tribe, perhaps a nation. A society is extended in two dimensions—spatially and temporally. The extent of the dimensions sets limits—or provides opportunities, which is the same thing—for the society's members. The temporal dimension is history, including its subdivision, biography.

The case for history is the same as the case against it. The case against history argues that since the past controls the present, since the antecedents of the present can be discovered, since the present is continuous with the past, the present was really complete in the womb of time. The future, too, was likewise complete. This is a theme well known to poets and ruminatively inclined scientists, and readily developed. "Given the distribution of the masses and velocities of all the material particles of the universe at any one instant of time," wrote Laplace, "it is theoretically possible to foretell their precise arrangement at any future time."[1]

This view seems at least to grant significance to the past. It would appear that the more I can learn about the past—even though my knowledge will hardly approach that required by Laplace—the better I can understand the present and foretell the future. It is, however, all a sham; for though I foretell the future, I can do nothing about it. The future was foreordained, as was my knowledge of the past and my understanding of the present. Knowledge of this sort is not mine at all but was in effect dictated to me by the same process that arranged the other particles, and it cannot be used for good or ill because nothing can be changed. It is hard to say what it is, but it obviously is not an aspect of autonomy.

Does autonomy then require denial of the significance of the past? Many say so. Men of action like Henry Ford call history bunk; it was fashionable in the 1960s to call it irrelevant; professional educators scorn attention to dates; and inspirational writers urge us to consider each day the first of the rest of our lives, advising us to put the past behind us, to forget it. Denial of the past reduces life to an alleged series of instants, each of which is the first in the rest of our lives. But the alleged series never appears as a series. The past is denied, and tomorrow never comes; so there is only the instantaneous and unrelated present. The situation is like that of the arrow in Zeno's paradox, which didn't move because at each instant it was where it was and not somewhere else. Nevertheless arrows do move, as St. Sebastian is our witness. If arrows move in spite of Zeno, perhaps there is an opening for us and our autonomy.

Such an opening is sometimes sought in the interstices of the warp of compulsion and the woof of chaos, where for the past half century

Heisenberg's uncertainty principle has seemed to offer a space for lawlessness within the frame of order.

Lawlessness, however, is chaos, no matter how framed. Wherever chaos might be, nothing of any effect could be found or done. The uncertainty principle points in a different direction. It states that of any particular electron, "We can either measure the position very accurately . . . or we can make accurate measurements of the velocity and forgo knowledge of the position."[2] Science is concerned with electrons as a class, not with particular electrons nor, *a fortiori*, with particular or unique objects or events.[3] This is no new discovery. The glory of science has been its success in discovering natural laws, and a law describes what an event has in common with other events. But whatever an event has in common with others is precisely what is not unique or individual about it.

II

The way I define myself will dictate the outcome of my search for autonomy. If I start searching in a state of nature, whether nasty or benign, I shall, at every crucial point, find my norm to be an irresponsible existence. If I start in the Garden of Eden, I shall forever yearn for a similarly carefree Heaven.

But if, instead of starting elsewhere, in some erewhon-nowhere of the imagination, I start where I am, what then? If, instead of looking for impersonal laws, I start with myself, who am I? If, instead of directing my attention to others' self-interest, I consider my own self-assertion, what do I find? What does it mean to be a person?

The first requirement of being a person is being—existence. *Cogito ergo sum; dubito ergo sum*—there are many ways of saying it. But I do not think unless I have something to think about, nor can I doubt unless I have been credulous. There is, in short, no way of making a standing start; I am always in the midst of life.

Existence requires continuity. Continuity requires identity. I cannot continue in any meaningful sense except as I remain in some way the same. Continuity requires time, and time is not definable unless the present is in some way different from the past.

Self-assertion requires self-maintenance. I must maintain my identity through the time of my existence. I must; I am required to do so; I am compelled to do so. This is a special and curious compulsion. It does not come from outside, like a slave driver's whip. Nor does it come from inside, like a neurosis. This compulsion is the same as my existence. The alternative is nonexistence, nonentity, nothingness.

The self that I maintain—the life that I live—is always threatened with dissolution. Only I can forestall that dissolution. If my dissolution is forestalled, I am the one who does it; it is my doing. I can always let myself go—in indolence, drugs, or death: myriads of ways. If I do not let myself go, I hold myself to my life, to the situation in which I have my being—a situation that is extended in space and in time, in society and in history.

Yet of course I am continually letting go because I cannot hold on. The present is inexorably taken away from me. What makes the past past is change in my life. I am plainly in an impossible situation: I must hold on, I must let go, in the end I shall be defeated. This impossible situation is, nevertheless, the only one possible, the alternative being nothingness—an extinction so complete that it is not even *my* extinction. That same alternative, moreover, forces on me responsibility for my impossible situation. I am the one who must hold on here and let go there, for I do not exist except in this, my holding on and letting go. I do not exist except in my doing, in my willing and acting, and in my accepting the consequences of my acts.

There is no gainsaying the fact that this program is uncongenial to the prevailing temper. People today see themselves in the grip of forces beyond their control. Although C. P. Snow's two cultures fail to understand each other, they tend to agree on their basic irresponsibility. The one is a stranger and afraid, the other a sophisticated servomechanism. Both are in a world they never made. These are the fruits of analysis that starts outside of myself. If I am not I at the start of my search for myself, then there is no one searching, and no search and no discovery.

This much may be granted by the modernist outlook; but almost immediately a move is made to shift off the point, and I am asked to listen to stories about how my search is controlled by my id, or how my perceptions are limited by my genes, or how my judgment is affected by the appearance or nonappearance of certain trace elements in my brain cells. All of these stories may well be true, but they are not the point. The point is that these stories do not tell themselves; someone tells them. They do not sound in a silence. If they are meaningful, they are consistent; and if they are consistent, their consistency will include the teller, for without a teller—you, me, or someone—they cannot be told.

Many are tempted to say that consistency is a false or unnecessary or impossible demand. If so, they cannot tell you or me about it, for their telling depends on the physiological regularity of their voice production and our hearing, on the physical regularity of acoustics, on the historical and social usages of their words. Communication demands at least these consistencies; and as Tom Lehrer says, if you can't communicate, the very least you can do is to shut up.

You may tell stories about my id, genes, and trace elements and thus try to deny my autonomy—and even succeed in doing it. But *your* autonomy as a storyteller still remains and must remain. You may be able to prove that I am out of my mind, crazy, irresponsible; but you cannot at the same time prove your own irresponsibility, for if you are irresponsible, your proof is not worth attending to. At this point some have claimed that they may (willy-nilly) be telling the truth because they have been programmed to do so. Such alleged meaning can only be an external accident, as a watch with a dead battery or a broken mainspring is correct twice a day. The trouble is that there is no way of knowing when the correct accident occurs and so no way of identifying its correctness.

The possibility of asserting truth requires the possibility of error. The possibility of depending on the reliability of nature requires human fallibility. Galileo was a human being; Newton was a human being; Einstein was a human being. A remarkable thing about these human beings is that we have selected them for our attention, brushing aside other human beings who contended that the earth was flat or that old ladies could fly on broomsticks or what you will. These other human beings were, we say, wrong, and we can give reasons. The human beings we attend to were right, and again we can give reasons. The important thing about their rightness is that it didn't come naturally. It was laboriously and rationally won and confirmed. They might have made mistakes, and certainly did so on other occasions. In short, the certainty of physics depends upon the possibility of error. Human beings can make mistakes and so can assert truths, including those of physics. Being fallible, human beings cannot be like Galileo's brass balls rolling down an inclined plane. As Ortega said, "Man has no nature, what he has is history."[4]

The foregoing may seem simple and commonsensical and too obvious to bother with. To emphasize its importance, let me boldly say that it is the comprehensive theory of which Einstein's theories, both the general and the special, are instances. Einstein's initial problem was that of synchronizing two clocks. It turned out that the task of synchronization could not be performed except by identifying the specific coordinate system of a specific observer, who said that in his system, from his point of view, the clocks were synchronous. In the Newtonian world of absolute space and time—a coordinate system zeroed by Copernicus on the sun—the point of view of the observer was not considered. In effect, he did not exist. But in actuality he (you and I) does exist, and it was Einstein's great achievement to make his existence and his motion consistent with the existence of a physical world in motion.

In the same way, I am insisting that the consistency of every universe of discourse depends on the integral inclusion of the observer, the experimenter, the storyteller. His or her autonomy must be part of the system. If there is no autonomous observer—if you and I don't exist— there is no way of saying that the system exists. There is no saying at all.

The thrust of what must be postmodernist thought is that consistency demands autonomy. Put it the other way around: No system—no universe of discourse—that denies autonomy is consistent with its own existence. This is true of physics and psychology, the systems that many have tried to substitute for economics, and it is true of economics itself.

III

We must not forget how we got here. The fathers of economics told us they were studying the implications of our self-interest. For our part, we concluded that our subject was rather our self-maintenance or self-assertion, and we have found that, even for the most abstract and recondite sciences, such assertion is an indispensable point of departure. This assertive self, therefore, is no insignificant thing. It is always with us.

The assertive self is what is generally called the will. There are three aspects of the will that are especially important for our study of economics: it is embodied, it has a past, and it has limits.

To say that the will is embodied is merely to say that I am part of my world. Whatever the world is—matter or energy or spirit or what you will—that I am also. If it were not so, the consistency we have spoken of would be empty and our accounts of the world meaningless. On the most ordinary level, if I were not part of the world—and the world not part of me—I could simply let it go, forget about it, pay it no mind. Of course, my body would then melt, thaw, and resolve itself into a dew, but this disintegration of my body would not, on the premises, affect me. All who believe this are welcome to act upon it. Those of us who remain will conclude that the natural world is not a matter of indifference to us, because our body makes us a part of it and it a part of us. That we are embodied is constitutional, not accidental.

The limitation of my will follows from its existence. Whatever exists can be defined. Whatever is defined is this, not that. I am *not-you*. Because you are thus essential to my definition, you are, in the most fundamental sense, essential to me. If I destroy you, I destroy part of myself. My existence may require your destruction, as in war; but whenever and however I wrong you, I diminish myself. This is the ethical sanction; there is no other.

My autonomy requires this sanction. It is not imposed on me but is flesh of my flesh and bone of my bone. In detail, it may be concerned with my superego, with encapsulated love for or fear of my parents, or with what I learned before (or after) the age of seven. But in principle, and regardless of the details, it is an aspect of the compulsion that I maintain my existence.

As a consequence of the compulsion to maintain my existence, I must maintain yours; and on this requirement economics is grounded. Economics is not a question of an alleged propensity to barter or to seek profit, nor is it a question of the properties of numbers. Nor since the Commercial and Industrial Revolutions has anyone's comfort or physical existence been an insoluble concern. Household management is not now the problem—not even of the national household.

Economics is a question of the relations of human beings with one another. These relations are free; therefore they can be judged and controlled. Whatever is determined is beyond control.

Economic relations are special relations in that they are all concerned with money. Money is the distinguishing idea of economics. Without money, all the other economic ideas either do not appear (price) or fall back into general ethics (rights) or general psychology (demand) or general physiology (consumption) or agriculture and engineering (production).

To money, therefore, we now direct our attention.

5

MONEY

The Distinguishing Idea of Economics

I

According to tradition, money was invented in Lydia, a small kingdom in western Asia Minor, in the seventh century B.C. Before that time and place many of the functions of money were served in various ways, but money as something special did not exist. It was unknown to the heroes of whom Homer sang. There is little mention of it in the Old Testament. Yet without money our present civilization could not exist, could not have come into existence. As we cannot escape history, we cannot escape money.

David Hume and many others have written that money is a convenience: " 'Tis the oil, which renders the motion of the wheels more smooth and easy." But it is more than that, and different from that. It is not a convenience or a tool. A hammer is a tool; it is useful—arguably necessary—in building a building, but the finished structure—even the partially finished structure—can be, and is, described and defined without reference to hammers used in construction. A yardstick, however, is different. Measuring is essential not only in the construction of the building but in the specification of the size of the whole and of the parts, and of the relation of part to part. Without measuring, the structure is formless, and a description of it is merely a list of building materials and their sense qualities. Measuring is similarly necessary and creative in economic affairs, and economic measuring is done with money.

In general, measuring is a comparing of something with some standard. By laying a ruler across this book, you determine that the page is about six inches wide. But how long is an inch? Well, an inch is 1/36 of a yard, and since 1893 a yard has been 3600/3973 of a meter. Originally, as one of the reforms of the French Revolution, a meter was defined as 1/1000 of a kilometer, which in turn was 1/10000 of the surface distance from the equator to either pole. Of course that distance could not be measured directly, especially not by laying a meter stick along the route ten million times (that would be a literally circular fallacy). Instead, reliance was put on geometry, which gave the circumference of the earth as $2\pi r$, and the distance from the pole to the equator as $2\pi r/4$. The radius of the earth is stated in terms of some unit of measurement. When it was first calculated with reasonable accuracy, by Eratosthenes in the third century B.C., the unit was the stadium, which may have been equal to 600 of some king's feet. In Newton's time, and in the time of the French Revolution, the unit was the yard, which may have been the circumference of some king's belly or the length of some king's stride. So we have come full circle after all: A yard is defined in terms of a meter, and a meter is defined in terms of a yard.

In the meantime, frequent refinements in measuring the radius of the earth led to unsettling changes in the length of a meter. Consequently it was agreed that a meter was the distance between two scratches on a certain platinum-iridium bar. This bar, which was deposited in Sèvres, outside Paris, was obviously more precise than the meter stick incised on a slab of marble that in 1848 was built into the wall of the Chancellery (now the Ministry of Justice) in the Place Vendôme in Paris, where it can still be seen. But both meter sticks—the marble one and the platinum-iridium one—were arbitrary. The present standard, in use since 1960, which is equal to 1,650,763.73 wavelengths of the red-orange light given off by krypton-86, is more convenient since it can be used by scientists everywhere (provided they have the right instruments), but it is no less arbitrary. In the end, as it was in the beginning, we stand up and declare that *this* is a meter, and no fooling.

There are two further points to be made about measuring. First, the relationship between the measuring standard and the thing measured is not reciprocal. This book is about six inches wide; but an inch is not defined as 1/6 of the width of this book. The standard defines the thing, not vice versa; the alternative is circular reasoning of the sort that threatened at the start of the metric system.

Second, the meter standard, although perfectly arbitrary and, moreover, consciously agreed upon, is not a convention in the sense that a red light means danger or stop or the port side of a ship, or that a tennis set, which used to have to be won by two games, can now be settled by a tie breaker. The nautical rules of the road, which are conventional, require ships meeting head on to pass red to red, that is, left side to left side; and everyone, with the exception of the British, the Japanese, and some others, has adopted the same system for highways. It is convenient to have an agreed-on system; but it would not be impossible for drivers of cars meeting each other to get out and debate the right of way, as I have seen happen on a narrow road in Greece. Without the rules of the road, no one has the right of way, but the right of way implies nothing beyond itself. Using a yardstick, on the other hand, defines spatial relations, and hence space. Space is an inevitability, not a convenience. A game, of course, is not even a convenience. The introduction of the tie breaker changed the strategy of tennis, but this matters only to tennis players, and no one has to be a tennis player. One can't help being spatially oriented, and the orientation had better be measurable. If not, the physical universe is beyond comprehension, and ordinary life chancy.

II

The ancients were casual about weights and measures. The cubit was the distance from one's elbow to the tip of one's middle finger. Obviously this changed from person to person, and in the same person from time to time. Limited attempts at standardization were made then (or have since been made by scholars), so that it is said that the ancient Egyptian cubit was 52.5 cm, while the Greek was 46.29 cm; the Hebrew 44.65 cm, and the Roman 44.36 cm. Measurement of time was even more vagrant, since everywhere except in Egypt the time from sunrise to sunset was divided into twelve hours, and likewise the time from sunset to sunrise, the length of an hour thus varying from day to night, from season to season, and from latitude to latitude. The Western world consequently had no reliable clock until the fourteenth century, and even two hundred years later so much ingenuity was invested in making clocks that showed the phases of the moon and the like that fine measurement was disregarded and Galileo had trouble timing his first experiments.

In any event there was little need for universal systems of measurement until the rise of experimental science. As long as the world was a parade of miracles and portents, measurement played no role in understanding, and replication of awesome events was unthinkable. Precision was, to be sure, required in building, and it was readily attained: foundations were level, the proportion of part to part was meticulously observed, and stones were fitted one to another so closely that a knife blade could not be slipped between them. Such precision, however, did not need to be universal; it merely needed to be consistent within the bounds of each separate building. Whatever the cubit used in the construction of the Parthenon, it was strictly followed, but a different unit could have been used for the Odeon of Herodes Atticus, a stone's throw away. In the same way it was, within the memory of men now living, not unusual for New England farmers to erect barns using not a yardstick but a "story pole," various multiples of which yielded the desired proportions. I myself have used a story pole and found it handy in building a trued and squared playroom in a roughly finished cellar.

Local systems of measurement are satisfactory for local purposes. Among many examples, medieval Vienna required its bakers to measure their loaves against standard sizes carved on the wall to the left of the main portal of St. Stephen's; in Renaissance Ragusa (Dubrovnik), the standard cubit was that of a statue of Roland or Orlando that still stands in the town square. Specific large projects, such as those of Eratosthenes and Newton, could make do with some local system; and in any case, astronomy had long had one important universal system— the Babylonian invention of degrees, minutes, and seconds for measuring angles.

Although the scientific revolution had started in the sixteenth century, it was not until after the invention of the metric system that the remarkable burgeoning of physical science began. In the same way, trade requires reasonably stable measuring units, and the spread of such units calls trade into existence. The Lydian invention, which was quickly and widely embraced in the Mediterranean world, made possible the slow, halting, and still-continuing shift away from a world of plunder and rapine.

The facts that trade grew so slowly, that almost every jurisdiction boasted its own currency, that statistical information was almost nonexistent, and that for two and a half millennia the only money that men were conscious of was coined metal—these facts for a long time hid the further fact that although both a yardstick and a dollar are measuring units, they measure in fundamentally different ways.

III

When my wife and I were buying our present house I made some measurements, using a steel tape I've since lost, and determined that the room I'm now writing in was eleven feet two inches by sixteen feet seven inches. That was twenty-five years ago. This morning I measured the room again, using a wood (presumably birch) yardstick given me by the local hardware store. The answer this morning was the same as that a quarter century ago: eleven two by sixteen seven.

Now, when we bought the house all those years ago, we paid a certain number of dollars for it. Of course, we gave the seller a certified check, but we could have legally tendered him a stack of dollar bills. If I were to sell the house today, I'd receive from the buyer a certified check, but the number of dollars represented by the check would (I trust) be considerably greater than what we paid. If the buyer tendered me a stack of dollar bills, they'd look almost the same as those of twenty-five years ago, but it would take many more of them to accomplish the same purpose. The house would be substantially the same, but the price would be different. On the record it's hard to avoid concluding that the measuring unit has changed.

Nothing like this happens with physical measuring units. The steel tape I lost expanded or contracted a bit as the weather was warmer or cooler, but this change could, if necessary, be allowed for, or the temperature controlled. If a thermometer is calibrated so that the freezing point for distilled water at sea level is 32 degrees and the boiling point 212 degrees, then the normal temperature of the human body will be 98.6 degrees today, as it was yesterday or last century. If the boiling point is taken as 100 degrees and the freezing point 0 degrees, it is easy to make the appropriate conversions from Fahrenheit to Celsius. Without this uniformity, chemistry would be impossible or infinitely reduced in power. A talented cook can achieve brilliant results by seasoning to taste; but if you want to get water from hydrogen and oxygen, your proportions have to be precise, and precise proportions always give you the same result.

It is clear that a dollar does not measure physical properties of objects, nor does a yardstick measure economic properties. Nowhere is there a standard for the franc or the dollar similar to the platinum-iridium bar at Sèvres. Even when the dollar was said to be redeemable for 15 5/21 grains of gold 9/10 fine, there was no need for—indeed no possibility of—comparing a dollar bill with a lump (very small) of such gold. Furthermore, a mason can lay his meter stick against a stone he wants to measure and immediately have his answer, but there is no point to laying a dollar bill alongside something one wants to buy. A physical measurement is direct and absolute, but a monetary measurement is somehow different.

Unlike shoes and sealing wax, money is ambiguous in its meaning. The dollar bill I have in my pocket is an asset to me, but represents a debt of the nation. The balance in my checking account is also an asset to me, but it is a liability to the bank. On the other hand, the check I put in the mail to my creditor will be an asset to him but a debit to me. In contrast, goods are goods to whoever holds them and are nothing to anybody else, except as they enter into and so swell the national commerce.

Another ambiguity of money was revealed by Keynes's analysis of liquidity preference, which is partly a function of the convenience of keeping money at hand for the transaction of ordinary business, partly a preparation for speculation, and partly a function of holding money as a store of wealth because of uncertainty about the trend of the economy (and that, too, is a form of speculation). A strong preference for liquidity thus indicates grave doubts about future business, and at the same time great faith in the continuing strength of the money-issuing institution, which strength must in turn be based on the state of business.

IV

We should not be surprised to have discovered that economics and Newtonian physics, which are fundamentally different, should have fundamentally different ways of measuring. It is nevertheless disturbing to find money floating, as it were, between goods, instead of setting an unequivocal value to each one; and this idea has been resisted, and is resisted to this day.

Historians as well as economists feel a recurring need for some sort of constant that will permit comparisons of income and costs from year to year or century to century and from place to place. Hence the Bureau of Labor Statistics publishes the Consumer Price Index and the Producer Price Index, while the Federal Reserve Board publishes the Industrial Production Index. There are many other indexes, both official and unofficial, at this level of sophistication.

Lay citizens speak of the purchasing power of money and call attention to the declining value of the dollar. This way of speaking seems to assume that money has value, like any good or service, and that this value can be measured. Measuring the value of the dollar would mean comparing it with something else, either the "market basket" of the Consumer Price Index or something similar. Although the contents of the market basket can be changed by legislative or executive or merely bureaucratic fiat, the basket seems real, while money seems only nominal or, as Marx called it, a "purely ideal or mental"[1] form of value. But measurement, as we have seen, is not reciprocal; so if the "value" of money is stated in terms of a market basket, the basket becomes the standard of measurement, and money becomes a curious commodity with an elevated price.

There is no objection in principle to making this market basket, or any part of it, or anything else our monetary unit. As everyone who has had a little Latin or Anglo-Saxon knows, many ancient peoples counted their wealth in terms of cattle, as the Masai do today. This is clumsy and imprecise, but not impossible. But if we did something like this, we should not delude ourselves into thinking we had established a "constant dollar."

No market basket is the same to different people at any given time. My wife and I set up housekeeping many years ago; so we became relatively unconcerned with the price of furniture. Nor is that basket the same in different historical situations. Of all the things in the basket, the price of bread is sometimes urged as basic, and it was indeed a central issue in the French Revolution. But today food is so small a part of the family budget, and bread so indifferent a part of the diet, that all the bakeries in the land could shut down tomorrow without causing much inconvenience, let alone starvation. It is the same with indexes of industrial prices; the price of steel is of less importance to a book publisher than it is to a builder of office buildings, and it is more to a builder today than it was before the inventions of the elevator and the electric light made skyscrapers possible.

The constructors of indexes are of course not unaware of such shifts of demand, and they try to keep up with them by shifting and refining the contents of their market baskets. Such shifting obviously compromises the constancy of the index, which thus becomes a historical standard, like any other form of money.

Among other things, indexing is an attempt to escape history and to reduce economics to natural or automatic happenings. It is also in direct conflict with the system it pretends to serve. Conventional economics says that a market economy, through constant shifts in the relative prices of goods and services, is the most efficient way of allocating limited resources. But to measure with "constant dollars" is to nullify market price shifts.

Although the attempt to devise a constant dollar is often launched in the hope that the economic world can thereby be placed beyond the reach of human judgment and the errors and vices to which it is prone, it is not so easy to escape the necessity for judgment. Indexing, in fact, depends on judgment from the very beginning, for someone (or a committee of someones) must decide which items are to be included and how the various items are to be weighted. And someone must decide how the weighting is to be changed from time to time. In 1982 a considerable shift in the Consumer Price Index was caused by a shift in the weighting of the mortgage rate as a factor in the cost of housing. A further change was made in 1986, and, of course, there will be more.

In the extreme case, indexing is far from harmless. The reason is appropriately given in a 1923 lament of Hans von Raumer, minister of economics in the Weimar Republic. "The root of the evil," von Raumer complained, "is the depreciation adjustment [that is, the index]. Inflation goes on unchecked because one must add enormous increments onto wages and prices alike, and these in their turn work in such a manner that the depreciation provided for actually occurs through the inflation thus caused."[2]

V

Starting, very likely, with the first coinage in Lydia, there has also been a search—or a longing—for some rare and durable commodity (usually gold or silver) to act in the same way as an unchanging yardstick. The trouble with this notion is that money has never been merely a rare and durable commodity. Even when such a commodity has been the money of account, the work of money has also been done in other ways. A society in which the only acknowledged money is gold, and in which fractional-reserve banking is unknown or prohibited, will still do much—perhaps most—of its business on credit. Small retail transactions may be carried out with cash on the barrel head, but any work done for hire—to take the simplest case—involves credit. Either the work is paid for in advance, in which case the hirer is extending credit to the hired, or, in the more usual case, the hired extends credit by doing the work first and being paid weekly or monthly or when the job is done. There is, in fact, no other way of doing such business; if the pay were measured out as the work proceeded, both the hired and the hirer would be too preoccupied to get any work done.

This credit relationship does not, of course, increase the number of gold coins circulating in the economy. If in my business the application of a hundred dollars' worth of labor to a hundred dollars' worth of raw materials will produce something I can sell for three hundred dollars, I need only a hundred dollars to get things rolling. I use my money—all hard coin carefully counted out—to buy the raw materials. When my employees have done their work, I take the finished product and sell it for the three hundred dollars, again hard coin, a hundred dollars of which I pay to my employees, leaving me with my original hundred dollars plus a hundred dollars' profit. Putting the profit aside for consideration in another chapter, we see that my implicit credit arrangement with my employees, together with my skill or luck in selling the product quickly (or in advance), made it possible for my hundred dollars to underwrite the work of several hundred dollars. Everything was paid for in hard coin. No substitute was offered or accepted. Credit made work for my employees, a profit for me, and goods for the purchaser.

There are three important lessons to be learned from this little scenario. The first is that money is not merely a method of measuring a static situation but is essential for planning and contracting ahead. The employees and I could agree on the work and the pay because money enabled us to compare the value to each of us of their present work and their future pay. As a yardstick measures and thus defines a static situation, money measures and thus defines a dynamic situation, one in which people reach present agreement for future action. Without money, the employment relationship is at best sharecropping and at worst slavery.

The second lesson is a corollary of the first. Money functions in planning ahead; it is commonly called a store of value but is more precisely called a store of buying power. My employees can agree to work today for money next week because money next week will be useful. Money next week can be useful because it is not consumed in trade. Goods and services are ultimately consumed, but money is not.[3] Money may be lost in speculation, as we shall see in Chapter 10, but it is not consumed. The work for which I pay my employees will be over and done with, but the money I pay them will perform its function again and again. Indeed, if it could not do so, it could not function at all. My employees would not accept my gold coins for their services if they could not subsequently use the coins to buy goods or services themselves.

The third lesson is that as the functioning of a yardstick defines space, so the functioning of money defines commerce. In its functioning, money creates commerce. It calls enterprise into existence.

VI

If you want to know how much money you have, how do you set about counting it? You can count your spoons and arrive at a precise number that will satisfy even an analytical philosopher. Bertrand Russell writes, "If a set of numbers can be used as names of a set of objects, each number occurring only once, the number of numbers used as names is the same as the number of objects."[4] This may seem like an odd procedure, but you can follow it with your spoons and will then know how many people (presumably counting them the same way) you can invite to dinner.

When you seem to do that with the cash in your pocket, it would appear that the folding money is a different sort of object from the coin. The number of greenbacks you have is less significant than the figures engraved on each one. Still more esoteric and insubstantial is the money you have in a checking account, which can nevertheless be added to and subtracted from and thus counted. But there's more to it than that. You may have some stocks and bonds, perhaps all of them listed on the New York Stock Exchange and so sufficiently liquid for you to sell them at a moment's notice; the money you can get for them nevertheless varies from moment to moment. Others of your holdings are probably less liquid. If you have a house for sale, it will almost certainly take you weeks, and may take you months, to find a buyer willing to pay you almost what you hope it's worth. What you might get for your books and furniture is even more dubious.

Your stocks and bonds and house and chattels are counted as part of your wealth but not part of your money. This seems a distinction without a difference, because your credit depends in part on your wealth. For most of us, with comparatively little net wealth, our credit depends on our income. In either case, we can spend our credit like ordinary money—and more easily than ordinary money, a credit card being more convenient to handle than a pocketful of change. The total credit we have is not fixed, and it depends upon our continuing sources of income, that is, upon us as going concerns.

Because I don't throw away all my junk mail, I now have three bank credit cards, not to mention a couple put out by department stores—

each stating a different line of credit. Almost every mail brings me another that I can have merely for answering a few not remarkably searching questions. In addition, my bank tells me I can overdraw my account for a trifling fee, and four other banks offer to refinance my mortgage at a bargain rate only three times what I paid when I bought the house.

All of this is credit. But it is not money. It is not even potential money (whatever that might be), for at least some of these eager purveyors of credit are likely to exchange information and begin to wonder whether I'm such a good risk after all.

To become money, my credit or pseudo-credit must become actual. I must draw it down—that is, borrow on it. It then becomes actual and determinate. Credit becomes money by becoming debt. Money looks both ways, like a contract. It is an acknowledgment of indebtedness. Federal Reserve notes, which are, as they say on their face, "legal tender for all debts, public and private," were issued by the government in payment for some good or service, and the government will take them back in payment for some fee or tax. Until the government does take the notes back, it is in debt to whoever holds them.

Money is a generalized claim on the economy. The claim can take many and various forms. The actuality of the claim is what matters. In a primitive society the claim comes into existence through saving. In a somewhat more advanced society (such as the one of our employment scenario of a few pages back), there is also the factor of income anticipation in the employees' lending of their labor power. In a capitalist economy, profit anticipation is the major driving force.

As conventional economics imagines the world, profits are immediately spent, preferably reinvested. There is then no need for borrowing or lending except to help someone in an emergency. (The absence of necessary borrowing partly explains the inability of equilibrium economics to find a place for money in its system.) Production then creates its own demand, and economic progress is serene and steady. There are no failures, there is no waste, and there are no unused resources or unemployed workers. Because the future is unforeseeable,[5] we do have failures and waste. Our profits are consequently too small to employ all the resources and workers. But they could be employed if we could anticipate the results. Entrepreneurs cannot guarantee results, but they can try to anticipate them. They borrow to achieve them, thus creating money.

VII

Different (and knottier) problems appear when attempts are made to determine the national money supply. One may regard with some bewilderment the lists of objects that make up the Federal Reserve Board's definitions of M1, M2, M3, and L. M1 consists of currency, traveler's checks, and checking deposits (M1A includes only checking deposits in commercial banks, while M1B also includes NOW accounts and deposits against which checks can be drawn in savings and loan associations and certain other institutions). M2 adds ordinary savings and time deposits, money-market funds, and overnight Eurodollar deposits, but it does not count time deposits of $100,000 or more. M3 has no $100,000 limitation and also counts repurchase agreements. Finally, L includes all the foregoing plus non-bank public holdings of U.S. savings bonds, short-term Treasury securities, commercial paper and bankers' acceptances, net of money-market mutual-fund holdings of these securities. In February 1990 the seasonally adjusted totals were M1, $801.2 billion; M2, $3,254.2 billion; M3, $4,064 billion; L, $4,881.8 billion.

The range of the estimates is extraordinary. L is some six times as large as M1 (which was the money supply the Reserve tried to control until very recently) and one and a half times M2 (the supply the Reserve now has its eye on), and of course M2 is four times M1. The very variety of the estimates indicates that there is no "realistic" way of counting our national money—at least no way that would satisfy a Bertrand Russell. The reason, of course, is that our money is not real in the sense that our spoons are real. Money is not a commodity, not even a commodity of a special sort. It is certainly physical; it may be metal or paper, stone or beads, an entry in a ledger or a byte in a computer bank; its physical specifications are not what make it money. It is money because it is used as money—because it functions as money.

The recognition that money is not a commodity is a historical turning that is still not complete. It marks the transition from mercantilism to capitalism. Mercantilism was not altogether unlike a barter system. Merchant adventurers traded commodities for gold and silver, and both they and their sovereign hoarded gold and silver, which they could do because gold and silver were commodities.

Business practice today has generally made the turn. Enterprise is ongoing. The actual market is open; it is not "cleared." But theory, especially monetary theory, is still quasi-mercantilist. As we scan the hodge-podge of items the Reserve lists under its Ms and L, we are struck by the fact that all of them, except for a few in L, are static. They are sitting in bank vaults or on computer disks. They may be ready for work, but they're mostly not working, and there's no assurance that they'll ever be called to work. They are in effect hoards, finite and physical, like the treasure heaped up by the mercantilists.

VIII

The difficulties encountered in measuring the national money supply loom especially large in a widely accepted theory of inflation (a subject to be more extensively discussed in Chapters 14 and 15). In brief, the theory holds that the greater the money supply, the higher the price level. More money will be chasing fewer—or the same—goods; so prices will rise. It seems obvious.

Let us assume that half the citizens of your village have a supply of some one good, and that the other half have a supply of some conveniently coined money. Say 100 goods and $100. If goods are exchanged for dollars, the price will be a dollar a piece. But suppose the president or the chairman of the Federal Reserve Board or the Sugar Plum Fairy decrees that when the sun rises over Passamaquoddy Bay tomorrow morning, everyone who went to bed with $100 will wake up with $200. When the exchange is made now, the price has jumped to two dollars a piece. Now generalize the situation. Introduce as many goods as you need or want, and you will be tempted to conclude that doubling—or merely increasing—the money supply is a sure prescription for inflation.

The silent—and illicit—assumption is that everything that is brought to market in your village is sold, that the villagers spend all their money in buying it, and that the market is cleared. It has been an exhausting day, and one not likely to be repeated.

David Hume, a progenitor of the quantity theory of money, was also one of the first to observe (but perhaps not appreciate) the error. "If the coin be lockt up in chests," he wrote, " 'tis the same thing with regard to prices as if it were annihilated: If the commodities be hoarded in granaries, a like effect follows. As the money and commodities, in these cases, never meet, they cannot affect each other."[6]

The only money that matters is functioning money. The money in the chests will stay there until someone lowers the price at the granaries, or, conversely, the commodities in the granaries will remain until someone offers a higher price for them. In both cases, it is an offered and accepted price that initiates the exchange, not the quantity of money or the quantity of goods. In both cases, a prudent price setter may well consider estimates of available quantities of goods and amounts of coin in setting the prices, but these aren't the only, or even the primary, considerations; cost (whether average or run-on) is almost certainly another. Furthermore, there is no law requiring price setters to be so prudent. Many a price is set whimsically or even foolishly—and it is no less set. It is the same way with the price taker.

Price setters and price takers are always and everywhere human beings, and human beings are always and everywhere autonomous. Prices are set by human beings, not by things, nor by quantities of things.

IX

It is not necessary to know exactly what the money supply is before acting to increase or decrease it. The curious fact, however, is that what is actually done by the Federal Reserve Board has no direct effect on any of the items listed under the various Ms and the L. The Federal Reserve doesn't issue traveler's checks, and it doesn't create commercial paper or bankers' acceptances. It doesn't even print more banknotes, at least not initially. What it does do is make it more or less expensive, or more or less difficult, for banks to lend money.

If it wants to contract the money supply, the Reserve generally does one or both of two things: (1) By raising the federal-funds rate and the discount rate (interest rates that banks pay for short-term loans from member banks or from the Reserve) the Reserve increases the banks' cost of funds and hence the rates the banks charge their customers. (2) By selling government bonds at attractive prices, it leads banks to commit their reserves to government bonds, rather than to business loans, and increases the interest that banks can earn in perfect safety, consequently inducing them to raise the rates they charge their commercial customers. Thus, the immediate effect of the Board's operations is to raise the general interest rate. The Reserve also has the power to increase banks' reserve requirements, thus reducing their capacity to lend, but has not used it since 1979.

Although the Reserve has, from its beginning, had control of the money supply among its objectives, and although it has, since October 6, 1979, taken monetary control as its primary duty, to the exclusion of concern for the interest rate,[7] the immediate effects are on the interest rate. The Reserve's theory says that the money supply is the independent variable, but the practice treats the money supply as a dependent variable (which it is).

Of course, the interest rate has an effect on the price level, for it is a cost of doing business. Books written only a few years ago tended to make light of this cost, for the rate was then low. At the present time, however, interest costs are more than 20 percent of GNP, and the interest expense of the typical corporation is in excess of 25 percent of gross income.

The cream of the jest is that a high interest rate, introduced to contract the money supply, usually with the intention of lowering prices, has actually increased costs and so has forced increases in prices. Moreover, should the Board use its currently disused power and increase banks' reserve requirements, the consequences would be similar, at least in the short run. For the demand for money is a demand that must be constantly met by every business. It is difficult or impossible to change plans rapidly on short notice, because business is an ongoing affair. Thus a sudden reduction in the supply of borrowable funds would force businesses to pay higher interest rates and charge higher prices (or absorb losses) at least until their plans could be modified (reduced, actually) to meet the new conditions.

Unlikely as it seems today, the Reserve might decide to increase the money supply. It in fact tried to do so from time to time during the Great Depression. It turns out that while a contraction of the supply is said to have an effect after a two-year lag,[8] an attempted expansion may have no effect at all. Economic agents will respond as seems reasonable to them. Some will no doubt be expansive but certainly not all. Making it easier to lend does not necessarily increase borrowing.

Except for the deficit-creating borrowing the government itself does and for the coins and notes in circulation, the government does not create money. The textbooks say that bankers create money by lending it,[9] but actually bankers produce nothing except some useful services. The active partners in the creation of money are borrowers. If no entrepreneur plans a better mousetrap, if no consumer longs for something beyond his or her means, if no speculator schemes for a big killing, the banker sits idle. The banker can refuse to support plans, longings, and schemes and can thus single-handedly *not* create money; but the first and essential step in creating money is taken by borrowers. If no one borrows, no money is created, regardless of the intentions of bureaucrats and the complaisance of bankers.

No one borrows money for the fun of it. It would be an expensive pastime, especially when interest rates are usurious. Borrowers want borrowed funds for one of four purposes: to spend on consumption, to invest in productive enterprise, to refinance existing indebtedness, or to speculate. Only the first two purposes contemplate the buying and selling of goods and services, and only the first is certain to have such an effect.

If you buy something for your own use, you have unequivocally been a factor in aggregate demand. But if you hire workers, build a factory, stock a warehouse, you do not necessarily add to aggregate supply. Enterprise is systematically uncertain. What's to come is still unsure. It is on this point that the "real bills" theory, touted by the Federal Reserve and others in the 1920s, foundered. Properly worried by the amount of money going into speculation, the Reserve tried to dam the flow and channel loans into productive enterprise. Short-term loans were especially favored, because real things were usually an immediate consequence. Loans resulting in real things were called "real bills." Since the output of real things increased at least as fast as real bills, there was not too much money chasing too few goods; therefore, it was argued, increasing the money supply by real bills could not cause inflation. (As will be seen in Chapters 14 and 15, I do not hold the foregoing theory of inflation.)

In spite of its best efforts, the Reserve found its statutory powers insufficient to restrict the flow of money into speculation. Greater powers, however, would not have substantially changed the outcome. It was the systematic uncertainty of enterprise that rendered the real bills doctrine irrelevant. Real output is not necessarily economic production. Things may be manufactured and services made available but there is no guarantee that anyone will buy all or any of them. The price may be too high, the quantity offered too great, the specifications unattractive, the timing wrong, the advertising misdirected. Or the entrepreneur may merely have bad luck. As demand must be effective, supply must be effective too. Wanting something you can't afford is no part of demand, and offering something nobody wants is no part of supply.

Because of the uncertainty of enterprise, an increase in the supply of money, caused by the borrowing of entrepreneurs, is not always followed by an increase in the effective supply of goods. We have already seen that a price increase does not necessarily follow an increase in the money supply, because markets are not cleared. Of course, prices may be affected in some way, because nothing in the economy—the world we live in—happens perfectly smoothly. Yet a forward surge in the money supply and hence probably in the economy is as likely to reduce the price of bread as to increase it. Expanded demand for bread may lead to economies of scale. Or newly affluent demand may be up-traded from sliced bread to croissants.

Money enters into all economic transactions. The activities of suppliers are therefore affected by the interest rate, as are the activities of demanders, a high rate being constrictive for obvious reasons, and a low rate expansive. If economic agents are even aware of the supply of money, it is because the monetary authorities have announced that that is what they are controlling. Economic agents must then try to estimate resulting movements of the interest rate, for it is the interest rate, the cost of using money, that concerns them. An indication of businesspeople's lack of interest in the money supply is the small space given to news of it in the business press. *Forbes* reports none of the supply measures but reports extensively on interest rates.

Frequent fluctuations of the interest rate introduce an inhibiting and costly uncertainty into business planning and are disruptive of financial markets. In twenty-four out of forty years (1950–89) the prime jumped up or down by 10 percent or more. In thirteen of those years the jump was more than 20 percent, and in one it exceeded 50 percent.

Both money and commodities are creations of economic activity. High activity calls both into being—that is what economic activity is and does—and high activity is at least made possible by low interest rates.

In short, all prices are expressed in terms of money, but the supply of money has no direct and unequivocal or even unidirectional effect on the price of anything.

Monetarists nevertheless contend that there are so many different interest rates that control of "the" interest rate is impossible,[10] while control of the money supply within a narrow range is entirely feasible.[11] The contention, however, is beside the point. Just because it may be easy to control the money supply is no reason for controlling it. It would be easy to control the mining of silver, but it would be idle to do so. The money supply would be the thing to control if it determined the price level either directly or through an effect on the interest rate. Since its actual effects are either negative or indeterminate, its control, which has been a central objective of the Federal Reserve since 1951, is either mischievous or meaningless.

The control of interest, which is an inescapable cost both of living and of doing business, is at the heart of the matter. It is certainly true that there is, at any given moment, a bewildering array of interest rates. But businesspeople are not bewildered; their bankers tell them quite clearly what the applicable rate is. Consumers are not bewildered, for the same reason. Bankers are not bewildered; the various rates are not independent of one another, and their interrelations are mysteries only in the medieval sense that their mastery is essential in the banking profession. Nor need the monetary authorities be bewildered. They, too, can master the interrelations of rates. They can, moreover, readily calculate what may legitimately be called "the" rate by dividing the total annualized interest charges paid by domestic nonfinancial sectors by the total indebtedness of those sectors.

X

Since money exists, it is necessarily limited. Ultimately, the limit is set by functioning, and the possible functioning is set by the state. Marx thought the state would wither away, and both monetarist and neoclassical economists tend to agree with him that all public questions are economic questions. But willy-nilly, for good or ill, directly or indirectly, the state is responsible for the uses to which money may be put and for the fees that may be charged for these uses. To take a simple example, money may not be used to buy stolen goods or to suborn perjury, and these prohibitions have at least some effect on the demand for money.

In the United States, the Federal Reserve Board controls the lending capability of the banking system, thus limiting the functions money can serve and who can use it. Not everyone who wants to borrow can do so. In effect a sort of triage is imposed. In the years when Regulation Q limited the interest banks could pay on deposits, and state usury laws limited the interest banks could charge on loans, the triage tended to be guided by bankers' judgments of the security of the loans; but in the years of deregulation, bankers have been forced by their higher cost of funds to favor aggressive borrowers willing to pay high interest rates.

Overnight every sort of company was put into play, taken over, bought out, merged, broken up. Wall Street apologists pretend that the result is the triumph of efficiency and vision over stodginess and lethargy, and it is true that considerable fortunes are made for many lucky stockholders and investment bankers. Yet industrial efficiency should increase production of goods and services, while the general result of all the speculative activity has been stagnating production, falling wages, and rising prices.

The rising prices have alarmed the financial community, especially the Federal Reserve Board, which has adopted policies that have narrowed the triage and ensured that speculation, rather than efficiency and vision, would rule the American economy. Any general control the Board now attempts hurts the producing economy more than it does the speculating economy. Until the government is again willing to take responsibility for the uses to which our money is put and to regulate and tax accordingly, no other outcome is to be looked for.

XI

As a practical matter, it has always been understood that money depends on credit or faith, that it passes from hand to hand because people have faith that it is what it purports to be. When the king of Lydia put his stamp on a lump of electrum, traders all over the Mediterranean had faith that the lump weighed what the stamp said. It was no longer necessary for traders to carry scales and weights with them at all times—as was done until recently on the Gold Coast—and make an elaborate ritual of the simplest transaction. Buying and selling could be accomplished in the few minutes it took to count out and examine the necessary coins.

Clipping and counterfeiting, to be sure, became worrisome, and various ways of combating them were developed. One of the most remarkable was devised by thirteenth-century Florence, where it became customary to circulate brand-new florins in small leather bags sealed by the mint. It is noticeable that acceptance of these purses was still an act of faith; it was assumed that they contained genuine and sound florins because one had faith in the inviolability of the purse and the legitimacy of the seal.[12]

Faith in money neither starts nor ends with the currency itself. Obviously something more than appreciation of the design or printing is at work in the acceptance of inconvertible paper money. It is made legal tender by law or acceptable by custom. It, too, can be counterfeited and so circulates only on faith in its genuineness; to this extent it is like coin. In the same way, checks can be forged or kited, balances can be overdrawn, and banks can fail.

The more fundamental and fruitful faith is in the society as a going concern. What is at stake is not the purity or genuineness of the money per se, but confidence in the continuity of a society in which money can be spent. The South will not rise again; so Confederate money is of value only to collectors, and Confederate war debts (and thus war credits) were wiped out by the Fourteenth Amendment.

An unstated reason for the persisting interest in gold—in "hard money" generally—is an aloofness from the present polity. This is often more than liquidity preference; it expresses a willingness to opt out of the present society and an expectation of maintaining one's position in a successor commonwealth. This, too, is an act of faith, and one not infrequently belied by the event. Hoards invite plunder or confiscation. The Inca's treasure did him no good.

Nor does faith in money stop with faith in a society in which money may be spent. What matters at least as much is that the society will be such that what is bought with money may be peaceably used and enjoyed. Society is a going concern. Thus the acceptance and circulation of money are possible when we have faith in our fellows and in the society created with them.

6

PRICE

Reformulating the Law of Supply and Demand

I

Now that we have money, we can have economics, and in economics a primary question is price. How is it arrived at? At least since Adam Smith the answer has been that price is the resolution of a tension between supply and demand. If the supply is small and the demand is great, the price will be high, while a large supply and a weak demand will result in a low price. We seem to have known this always, to have learned it at our mother's knee, and never to have had occasion to doubt it. It is one of the Enlightenment's self-evident truths.

Yet the law of supply and demand was not revealed to the Greeks, the Jews, the Romans, the Ostrogoths, or the schoolmen of medieval Europe. In the ancient world justice was a reciprocal relationship between individuals, and so was trade. Aristotle cites the Pythagoreans as recommending literal reciprocity, a theory that with the Jews was the Mosaic talion law—an eye for an eye and a tooth for a tooth. After giving reasons for prefering proportionate reciprocity, Aristotle writes, "It is by exchange that men hold together. That is why they give a prominent place to the temple of the Graces—to promote the requital of services; for this is characteristic of grace—we should serve in return one who has shown grace to us, and should another time take the initiative in showing it."[1]

Aristotle evidently understood grace to be more than prudence or calculation. In *The Republic* Plato had shown, as Adam Smith was to show two millennia later, that the division of labor increases output and that as a practical matter it makes a just society necessary.[2] But Aristotle had his eye out for what holds the polis together, and what he glimpsed was a system of mutual obligations freely entered into and objectified in exchanges of goods and services.

The Church Fathers, whose precepts were based on the equality of all men before the Lord's throne, developed the idea of the just price. "Therefore," St. Thomas argued, "if either the price exceed the quantity of the thing's worth, or, conversely, the thing exceed the price, there is no longer the equality of justice; and consequently to sell a thing for more than its worth, or to buy it for less than its worth, is in itself unjust and unlawful." He saw, however, as his mentor Aristotle had seen before him on the question of justice in general, that this admirable rule was not altogether easy to apply. Among exceptions, he cited "for instance, when a man has great need of a certain thing, while another will suffer if he be without it. In such a case the just price will depend not only on the thing sold, but on the loss which the sale brings on the seller. And thus it will be lawful to sell a thing for more than it is worth in itself, though the price paid be not more than it is worth to the owners." Putting aside the question of what a thing is "worth in itself," we are still left with the implication that trade will be typically conducted in parochial face-to-face exchanges, for only thus will buyer and seller approach the ability to judge each other's needs and potential sufferings. Even then, Aquinas adds, it "depends on a kind of estimate."[3]

The Church's rules, exceptions and all, became meaningless when Venetian merchants traded glassware in Beirut for spices to sell at home. The Venetians certainly got much more for their Murano goblets than they could have done at home, while the Levantines are likely to have held up their end.

Society has an interest in price that may be different from that of either of the traders. In primitive environments a successful hunter may demand such returns for his spoils that he puts the band or tribe in thrall. Modern examples are perhaps less dramatic but still ubiquitous: Are the services of any corporation executive worth $5 million a year? Did high wages paid to steelworkers ruin the industry and damage the economy? On the other hand, are the wages paid to teachers so low that educational standards suffer?

Thus the idea of the just price has persisted. Advocates of any form of price fixing have acted in the name of justice. This was true of the medieval and Renaissance guilds; it is true today of marginal utility analysts, of labor unions and proponents of agricultural price supports, metropolitan rent controls, and prohibition of international "dumping." Utility regulation seeks prices that will be fair to both those who have invested in the utilities and the public.

II

The idea of justice was not foreign to the free market. The invisible hand was supposed to achieve a result compatible with moral sentiments and so to attain a natural as opposed to a theological justice, a natural price as opposed to a just price. Adam Smith wrote, "When the price of any commodity is neither more nor less than what is sufficient to pay the rent of the land, the wages of the labour, and the profits of the stock employed in raising, preparing, and bringing it to market, according to their natural rates, the commodity is then sold for what may be called its natural price."

Smith is careless here. There are no "natural" rates in economics. $S = 1/2gt^2$ expresses a natural rate, but there is no natural rate of wages or profits in bringing a commodity to market. There are often customary rates and legal rates, but such rates can be changed, as $S = 1/2gt^2$ cannot.

We may, however, forgive this slip because Smith recognized that once goods were brought to market, the "natural" price had nothing to do with the price actually paid. What then controlled was what he called effectual demand, "which is different from the absolute demand. A very poor man may be said in some sense to have a demand for a coach and six; he might like to have it; but his demand is not an effectual demand, as the commodity can never be brought to market in order to satisfy it."[4]

The effectual demand may be so great that "a competition will immediately begin" among those who want and can afford a certain commodity, and this will push the market price above the natural price. And if the effectual demand is weak, competition among sellers will force the market price below the natural price. A high market price will attract new producers to the field; the resulting increased availability of the product will deflate the competition among the buyers; and the price will fall. A low market price will have the opposite effect. So the market is supposed to tend toward the natural price, at which point price will be in equilibrium.

III

The ideal market is served by many competitors producing many interchangeable goods. There are usually substitutes available for any scarce commodity; while a stone won't serve the purposes of bread, cake may. To forestall cartels, producers must be able to enter or leave the market easily. There must be many consumers, too, for a monopsonist can control a market as readily as a monopolist; a manufacturer who has only one buyer for his product is at the mercy of that buyer—unless he is able to co-opt him, as our arms merchants are said to co-opt the Department of Defense.

When many producers can supply easily substitutable goods, all have to take the price the market will bear. Even the giant oligopolies of the *Fortune* 500 are too small in relation to the total market to set their prices as they please. They are price takers. On the other hand, if I want to buy a certain kind of car, I haven't much choice in what I have to pay. The president of General Motors doesn't care whether I buy one of his cars or not. There are too many like me. I am a price taker.

In a freely competitive world, every buyer and every seller—that is, everyone—is a price taker. Prices come from the reconciliation of supply and demand or the tension between them. The market sets the prices. But if the market sets the prices, all economic agents—both buyers and sellers—are price takers. They are passive agents—a contradiction in terms. The market is presented as an impersonal process, an automatic process, one that no person controls and hence all persons can enjoy. It seems a Cartesian paradise.

But it is a pathetic fallacy. A market can't do anything. It is a place, a condition—not an agent, a doer. Of course, it is a figure of speech. No one pretends that the market literally sets prices. How could it? It can't speak or read or write or make gestures. Yet prices are somehow set. What actual event is hinted at by this figure of speech?

The textbooks reduce the competitions to two curves, a supply curve rising gracefully upward to the right, showing that more goods are supplied as the price is raised, and a demand curve, falling gracefully downward to the right, showing that more goods are demanded as the price is lowered. Where the two curves cross is the price that the market is supposed to set. It is said, moreover, that at this price the market is cleared; all that is brought to market is sold, and there is no incentive to bring more.

Everyone in business knows that this is not the way the world turns. Something like this may be imagined by market research, but the curves that predicted the success of the Edsel were scarcely objective in the sense that a graph of Boyle's law, relating pressure and heat, is objective.

In the market, what is objective is the price. Supply and demand are determined by price, not the other way around. Demand is not what I'd like to have, or what I desperately need, or what I might buy. All that is formless and indeterminate. Demand is what I actually buy at the price quoted. Supply, too is indeterminate. A novel nobody wants to read is not, as a book, a factor in supply (it may, however, be a supply of scrap paper and be sought after as such). In short, supply and demand are dependent variables; the independent variable is price.

Supply and demand are always equal, at any price; their equality follows from their definitions. Supply is what is sold, which necessarily equals what is bought, which is demand. Neither supply nor demand is satisfied all at once. The market is not a one-time thing, like the auctioning off of a bankrupt farm. Not only does it take time for supplies to be produced; it also takes time for demand to develop. Fifty years ago the demand for a dishwasher or a TV set or an automobile with automatic shift was weak. Of course, these products were not so efficient then as they are now; but also people didn't know they wanted them, and initially they didn't know such things existed—because they didn't.

Whether or not demand is or can be manipulated, both demand and supply take time; so the market must stay open. And if it is correct to consider a free market in some way necessary to a free society, it is a mistake to think of a market being cleared in a succession of essentially unconnected and irresponsible happenings.

The whole idea of market clearing is foreign to the idea of business enterprise. I want the market to be cleared if I am auctioning off my goods and chattels; but if I am in business, I want to stay in business. If I am a book publisher, I do not close up shop when I sell an edition of a textbook. I order a new printing and look around for another book to publish; I must publish or perish, and I set my prices accordingly. In the same way, even a fishmonger, whose wares must be sold today, sets his prices with an eye to tomorrow's business.

At this point cost becomes a factor, as it was in determining Smith's "natural" price. In setting prices for a continuing business, I must consider what it will cost me to reproduce or replenish my supply. Yesterday's costs are sunk, but tomorrow's must be met. Everyone's business has the same problem; hence it seems reasonable to say that price is determined by cost.

But my costs are not "natural"; they are my suppliers' prices, and my suppliers' costs are their suppliers' prices, and so on ad infinitum. No cost is original. No supplier is without costs, which are somebody else's prices.

Ricardo thought that the regress was stopped by the fact that the ultimate cost is labor, and that laborers have certain bare necessities— the simplest food, the cheapest clothing, the minimum housing. The cost of labor cannot fall below the cost of these necessities, and so their cost seemed to him to be the irreducible cost upon which the price system is based.[5] Yet these so-called wage goods, too, are produced, and produced in the same ways as other goods. A firm producing such goods can reduce its prices by controlling its costs in the same ways other firms do. There is thus no final or natural price for wage goods; hence no natural price for labor; hence no mathematically determinate system of original costs or prices or values. The regress is infinite.

The only way to stop an infinite regress is not to let it get started, and of course this one does not get started in the real world. What actually happens is that some person—some willful human being or corporation of human beings—for some reason that is personally satisfactory (regardless of how it may appear to anyone else) names a price for some commodity, and some other willful human being accepts it. "Willful" is perhaps too strong; yet "willing" is too weak: What I am naming are free, responsible, and decisive acts.

IV

Trade starts with a price, whether quoted by producer, middleman, or consumer, but the quotation is not made in a vacuum. It does not appear de novo, a complete surprise to all concerned. It is not the first offer made on earth. The person quoting the price is not the first ever to have bought or sold.

In short, prices have histories. Wheat was sold at a certain price yesterday. If today I make a bid much lower than that, I shall buy no wheat. If my price is much higher, I shall place myself at a disadvantage with my competitors, who will have bought at yesterday's lower price and so can undersell me in the bread market. Or they may make an effortless profit by selling me what they bought. As the price I offer was not the beginning, so it is not the end of the history of wheat prices. It will have an effect on subsequent offers and acceptances.

A pricing decision may come out of a computer, or it may be a gut feeling or the result of tossing a coin, but it is a decision. Even the computer's answer depends on someone's decisions about the relevant data and the proper program.

A pricing decision is an act of will. It is a free act. It is determining, not determined. Like all acts, it is limited. It is an event in an ongoing world, not an imaginary world. Furthermore, I am limited to the prices I actually set. I set these prices, not some others. I do this, not that. A something is limited; the alternative to limitation is nothingness.

Price determination is not the only willful act in business. The decision to be a haberdasher rather than a bookseller is similarly willful. Determining the prices of shirts and ties is secondary and subordinate to deciding to be a haberdasher and also to deciding what clientele one intends to attract, what kind of haberdasher one intends to be. All these acts are rational in the sense that one can give reasons for them. None is rational in the mathematical sense that it is the determinate answer to an unequivocal problem.

With the willful act we arrest the infinite regress that has plagued us hitherto. When we say, "This is what I'll sell at that price," "This is what I'll buy at that price," we launch ourselves into the future; we progress, not regress. Accepting—seeking, rather—the consequences of our action, we declare our membership in, and responsibility to, an ongoing world.

Léon Walras, who was no amoralist, distinguished at considerable length between economics as an ethical science (which most of his followers today would not recognize); as an art, which taught how to achieve moral ends; and as pure science, which taught how it worked. Toward the close of the nineteenth century, John Neville Keynes, the father of John Maynard, made a similar tripartite analysis. In our day, Milton Friedman, perhaps indulging a puckish humor, has quoted favorably from the senior Keynes's work.[6]

But there is no such thing as pure economics. Physics can be studied—must be studied—without regard to the willful act of any individual or any group of individuals. (This is not to deny that it takes a willful man or woman to be a physicist.) But there are no sterile events in economics. Walras, whose work was hailed by Joseph A. Schumpeter as "the only work of an economist that will stand comparison with the achievements of theoretical physics,"[7] opened his analysis, after a long introduction, with the observation, "Value in exchange, when left to itself, arises spontaneously in the market as the result of competition." But this pure parthenogenesis is immediately corrupted by willful humanity: "As buyers, traders make their *demands* by *outbidding* each other. As sellers, traders make their *offers* by *underbidding* each other."[8] Walras's emphases underline acts of will.

Without those traders making their demands and offers, there is no economics, pure or applied. With those traders, economics becomes inextricably immersed in questions of morals. I do not mean merely that trade is impossible unless traders abjure fraud (at least up to a point), although certainly this is true. What I mean is that demands and offers—the fundamental elements of "pure" economics—are not acts of God or events of nature but acts of human beings who necessarily define themselves by what they do, including especially what they do in the marketplace. Perhaps more to the point: Demands and offers can be described and understood only as acts of will. If they are not free and responsible acts, economic discourse collapses into theology or physics.

Economics is therefore an ethical discipline, a normative discipline, a humanist discipline, a historical discipline. It is ethical, normative, humanist, and historical through and through—not just on holidays, nor just for show, nor because of the good-will value of an appearance of honesty. Ethics is there at the beginning, or it is not there at all. If ethics is excluded from economics, which studies the principles of business enterprise, it is also excluded from business.

All exchanges involve ethical questions. In everyday life we cannot live at a constant fever pitch of deliberation. In a famous chapter in his textbook on psychology, William James laid out the importance of habit in allowing us to get on with the business of living without worrying over "which sock, shoe, or trouser-leg [to] put on first."9 In the same way, social customs and trade practices—what Arthur Okun called the invisible handshake—allow us to go about our work without constantly weighing and agonizing over the ethical implications of our actions. Nevertheless, all exchanges *ipso facto* involve other people and so by their very nature present ethical questions. A virtuous act enlarges the person and a vicious act cancels or constricts some possible enlargement. "I could not love thee, dear, so much, loved I not honour more" expresses conflict but not contradiction. A rational exchange looks to the maintenance of both trading partners, but nineteenth-century Social Darwinism and twentieth-century theory of games (among many examples) contemplate the destruction of one partner by the other and hence the destruction of the exchange and the repudiation of its genesis. This is irrational.

Exchanging goods and services is only one of the principal ways of meeting other minds, of being recognized by others, of recognizing oneself, of becoming conscious of one's limits and so of one's powers. We meet one another as buyers and sellers, as teachers and pupils, as patrons and clients, as friends, as lovers, and also as competitors and enemies. Society depends on these relationships. Individuality as we know it depends on them. Their development is a work of history. They have not always been as they are now. Only a hundred years ago loving was much different from what it is today, as can be seen by comparing Anthony Trollope's *Phineas Redux* with John Updike's *Rabbit Redux*. The differences in ways of economic exchanging are, if anything, greater.

Without noneconomic interests, economic interests cannot be defined or named. A home dishwasher is sold and bought because it is appropriate to a certain way of life; it is not everywhere and always an economic good. Even a mathematical economist like Professor Gerard Debreu was constrained to say, "The fact that the price of a commodity is positive, null, or negative is *not* an intrinsic property of that commodity; it depends on the technology, the tastes, the resources, . . . of the economy."[10]

Different sorts of exchange—and also different possible exchanges of the same sort—are in conflict with each other. The meaning of a commitment is understood only as it conflicts with another. The conflict results not in the obliteration of one by the other, nor in a trade-off that diminishes both, but in a comprehension that modifies and may intensify both. An unconflicted commitment, like that of economic man, is obsession or madness. A resolved conflict is personality; one resolves to be the person one becomes. The controls of economic activity are those that maintain not only the economic modes but the other modes as well—that maintain and rationalize the conflicts among them.

V

The traditional law of supply and demand has been the indispensable cornerstone of all economics since Adam Smith. The theory of the self-regulating market depends on it, and self-regulating markets are supposed to determine all prices—not merely the prices of ordinary commodities, but also wages and interest rates.

In Chapter 2 we confronted the traditional theory with the Three Antinomies of Greed. In Chapter 5 we noted the turning from mercantilism to capitalism—from money as a special sort of commodity to money as debt. In the present chapter we have marked another turning point to any future economics. Price becomes a primary economic fact, not a fact to be explained. By restating the law of supply and demand, making price the independent variable on which supply and demand depend, we have opened up consequences both powerful and liberating.

First, the infinite regress in which economics has been entangled is stopped before it gets started. Previously, when price was a variable determined by the intersection of supply and demand curves, the regress on both sides was infinite. The quantity of anything supplied varies with its cost or price, likewise the quantity demanded. If price must be explained, these prices must be explained; so each factor cost was said to be determined at the intersection of its own supply and demand curves, both of which had price as one of the variables, and so on, ad infinitum.

On the demand side, the regression has tended to take leave of economics altogether. Demand was said to be determined not in terms of price or money but in terms of psychological satisfaction, which could in turn be explained in terms of physiology, physiology in terms of chemistry, chemistry in terms of physics, atoms in terms of electrons, electrons in terms of quarks—and still there is no end, as the newest more powerful atom smasher will demonstrate.

Second, while the classical regress has led steadily away from human beings, the restated law of supply and demand, by defining price as determining rather than determined, places price setting and price taking at the start of economic activity, thereby recognizing that economic goods are human goods, and establishing price setters and price takers—human beings—in positions of responsibility and freedom. It will no longer be necessary to make heroic—which is to say, contrary to fact—assumptions about the "nature" of humanity. Greed need no longer be the engine driving economics but can again be recognized as mortal sin.

The cynic of Oscar Wilde's witticism—he who knows the price of everything and the value of nothing—is today balanced by the dogmatist who knows the value of everything and the price of nothing. A task of any future economics will be to bring price and value together, to establish their economic identity; and this will be done in part by proscribing certain economic acts—particularly certain low (or high) wage rates and interest rates—just as certain acts are proscribed in love and even in war. Economic activity—like all human activity, from love to war—will be understood as a mode of self-definition, and so will no longer be beyond ethical judgment.

Finally, economics will have a clearer and more obvious relevance to our daily lives in our mundane world. Selling and buying will be seen for what they are—ordinary activities in which ordinary people ordinarily engage. They will not be the less significant for that.

7

LABOR
Where It All Begins

I

The great economists have all been essentially decent men. The meaning of the myth of Midas has not been lost on them, nor have they been able to stomach the proposition that a miser fingering his hoard is the pinnacle toward which civilization has been building. On the other side, they are all children of the Reformation, they are all celebrants of the work ethic, and they all earned the acclaim accorded to achievers.

With this background, it is not surprising that they have almost all been at least half persuaded that the true, the real, the fundamental, the everlasting standard of value is labor. The theme is announced by Adam Smith: "Labour alone, therefore, never varying in its own value, is alone the ultimate and real standard by which the value of all commodities can at all times and places be estimated and compared. It is their real price; money is their nominal price only."[1] (The words "real" and "nominal" aren't the same as those of medieval philosophy, but they do give rise to similar difficulties.)

Smith's successors made the point in terms somewhat different from his. Ricardo argued that the issue was the commodities "necessary to enable the labourers, one with another, to subsist and to perpetuate their race." Keynes held that "the unit of labour" was "the sole physical unit which we require in our economic system." Marx was in general agreement: "How, then, is the magnitude of [use-value] to be measured? Plainly by the quantity of the value-creating substance, the labour, contained in the article."[2]

Yet, it is a matter of common observation that the amount of labor required to produce a commodity has almost nothing to do with either its use-value or its exchange-value. Useless artifacts, shoddy artifacts, defective artifacts, illegal artifacts, unhealthful artifacts, dangerous artifacts, all require labor, some of them much more labor than articles of good repute. It is not the amount of labor embodied in them that makes them useless, shoddy, defective, illegal, unhealthful, or dangerous, nor would more labor necessarily correct their failings. Again: a house in the Houston suburbs, which was worth a quarter of a million dollars a few years ago, can be had for half that price today. It is the same house, and the amount of labor it embodies is the same, if not actually more. Again: It took much labor to install asbestos ceilings in classrooms; but the asbestos was worse than valueless; it was harmful and had to be removed—with the expenditure of more labor.

Marx sought to get around such difficulties by insisting on "socially necessary" labor.[3] Socially necessary labor is labor that produces a socially useful product. Marx said, "[N]othing can have value without being an object of utility. If the thing is useless, so is the labour contained in it; the labour does not count as labour, and therefore creates no value."[4] Thus it is not labor that is the test of value, it is value that is the test of labor. A corrupt tree bringeth forth evil fruit, but the evil fruit proves the tree to be corrupt, not the other way around.

It is not always easy to say exactly what labor is. The army sometimes taught rambunctious soldiers to mind their manners by having them dig a hole six feet wide, six feet long, and six feet deep and then fill it up again. There was plenty of labor involved in the exercise, but not much economic consequence. Yet the labor was, at least in theory and perhaps even in intention, socially useful, because the result was supposed to be a better disciplined soldier. Similar problems arise in trying to find a common measure of skilled labor and unskilled labor, efficient labor and inefficient labor, mental labor and menial labor, labor paid and unpaid, earnest labor and timeserving.

Consider the CEO of a *Fortune*-500 company, who has six or eight division presidents "reporting" to him, but really running the company, as much as anybody does. From sheer boredom he may throw himself into politicking somewhere, or he may throw the company into a frenzy of mergers and takeovers and spin-offs. Either way, the net consequence is not much greater than the soldier's six-by-six-by-six hole in the ground. In what sense is the soldier or the CEO laboring? How can their disparate laboring be a universal standard of value?

There are two ways of reducing what they do to a common denominator. The first is to accept their pay as the yardstick, or perhaps some ingenious accounting of the value they add in production; but such a solution equates money values with real values, and it was precisely to avoid this equation that the notion of a labor standard was introduced. The other possible measuring unit is time; the unit of labor is an hour of laboring. This is the solution Marx adopts in his theory of surplus value, where he argues that the distinction between skilled and unskilled labor is confused, that skilled labor is relatively insignificant, and that the capitalist appropriates the same proportion of the output of skilled and unskilled labor, anyhow. "We therefore," he concludes, "save ourselves a superfluous operation, and simplify our analysis, by the assumption that the labour of the workman employed by the capitalist is unskilled average labour."[5]

Even this simplification has to be underwritten by concern to define "average labour." On a spread of two pages of *Capital*, we find peppered the following adjectives: "useful," "normal," "suitable," "socially necessary," "normal" again, "average," "normal" yet again, "average" again, and "usual." This of course is an array of synonyms rather than a definition. Marx does, indeed, give a definition, and it is a surprise: The capitalist, he says, "has bought the use of the labour-power for a definite period, and he insists on his rights. He has no intention of being robbed."[6] And so on. Thus "average labour" is what the capitalist, backed by his penal code, says it is; it is not a "scientific" standard at all.

II

The Clayton Antitrust Act declares that "the labor of a human being is not a commodity or article of commerce." Marx, however, thought it was, at least in the capitalist mode of production. Capital, he wrote, "can spring into life, only when the owner of the means of production and subsistence meets in the market with the free labourer selling his labour-power."[7] For labor power to be a salable commodity, Marx held that it had to be "free" (by which he meant unrestricted), and that the laborer had to be "free" (that is, unconnected and without resources).

If we accept these conditions, we may doubt whether Marx's scenario was ever staged in its pure form. Since his time, in any event, the capitalist nations have all enacted not only minimum-wage laws but also laws governing child labor and hours and conditions of work and vacation and unemployment compensation and old-age security and freedom to join labor unions and much else.

Labor is certainly not an ordinary commodity. It cannot be alienated more than once. An ordinary commodity can be sold and resold until it wears out, but free laborers sell their time only once. They work from sun to sun, and tomorrow is another day. Speaking more strictly, employers do not buy laborers' time or labor power; rather, they pay a fee (wages) for the temporary use of it, as a borrower pays a fee (interest) for the temporary use of money. The employer who "buys" today's labor power cannot sell it to someone else, who might in turn resell it. There are of course exceptions: slavery and peonage (which are different modes and so don't count), possibly certain sports and entertainment contracts, and some hiring practices, especially of farmhands and longshoremen. All of these are limited in their incidence.

If labor is not a commodity, and if it is not a standard either, what is it? It is, what no one will ordinarily question, essential. It is fundamental, primary, irreducible, original, basic, ontological. It is, moreover, human. We do with it what we will; we will what we do with it. How we labor is one of the principal ways in which we assert ourselves. We define ourselves by what we do and how we do it and how we treat the doings of others.

III

Labor may not be a commodity; yet we expect to be paid for our work. The program of "From each according to his abilities, to each according to his needs," first enunciated by Louis Blanc, then publicized by Marx in his *Critique of the Gotha Program*, and enshrined in the Soviet constitution, has not had broad appeal, at least among those with the abilities to make themselves heard. Even the towering prestige of Mao Zedong could not advance the idea much beyond sloganeering. We must assert ourselves in the world and must likewise look there for recognition.

The laborer who makes the most insistent—and usually richly rewarded—claim to recognition is the entrepreneur. Historically, the entrepreneur was both capitalist and executive. Adam Smith and Karl Marx and John Stuart Mill, if they made the distinction at all, thought of the executive as a sort of overseer or foreman or clerk of the works or supercargo. He represented the owners, was an extension of their will, followed their orders. Occasionally he was able to accumulate funds of his own, whereupon he became a capitalist in his own right and abandoned his subservient position.

This structure, which was comfortably suited to individual proprietorships, partnerships, and even joint stock companies, was carried over, in the latter half of the nineteenth century, to the new limited-liability company. Arguing from one analogy or another, legislatures and courts developed a theory of the corporation whereby each share of stock, like each citizen of a democracy, had a vote in the election of the directors, who acted as a sort of legislature, established company policy, and hired the managers to execute that policy.

Even as this theory was being developed, it was recognized as a legal fiction. Subsequent critics, like R. H. Tawney, emphasized the corporate divorce between ownership and work. A. A. Berle and Gardiner C. Means documented the passing of control of the typical corporation from stockholders and directors to management. The shift of control to management tended, as John Kenneth Galbraith argued, to change corporate objectives from profit maximization to the protection of what he called the planning system and its technicians.[8] Today all public corporations are at risk of seizure and dismemberment by raiders interested neither in control nor in work.

Joseph A. Schumpeter was probably mistaken in seeing these changes as the result of "technological progress." Business may indeed, as he said, be increasingly conducted by "teams of trained specialists who turn out what is required and make it work in predictable ways." There is also much evidence that "Bureau and committee work tends to replace individual action." But it is not true that "the leading man . . . is becoming just another office worker—and one who is not always difficult to replace."9

The leading man has not in fact sunk into gray anonymity, as he would have done if his role had actually been reduced by technological progress. He is as colorful and as active as ever. His activities have been redirected, as Keynes understood, not by technology, but by the development of the stock and futures exchanges, the voracious appetite of "institutions" for securities, and the consequent opportunities for arbitrageurs and raiders to make enormous fortunes out of takeovers and spin-offs. Keynes observed that "there is no sense in building up a new enterprise at a cost greater than that at which a similar enterprise can be purchased; whilst there is inducement to spend on a new project what may seem an extravagant sum, if it can be floated off on the Stock Exchange at an immediate profit. Thus certain classes of investment [a footnote explained that these classes include practically all investment] are governed by the average expectation of those who deal on the Stock Exchange as revealed in the price of shares rather than by the genuine expectations of the professional entrepreneur."10

The triumph of speculation over enterprise does not, of course, eliminate the human element. The leading man (in Schumpeter's phrase), no matter what kind of activity he leads, still needs animal spirits (in Keynes's). Someone must undertake to do whatever is done. It is convenient to continue to call him (or, it may be, her) the entrepreneur, though some of his or her activities would not be recognized by Marx or Mill or by Schumpeter or Keynes.

The entrepreneurial function, Schumpeter wrote, "does not necessarily consist in either inventing anything or otherwise creating the conditions which the enterprise exploits. It consists in getting things done."11 The person with the special and comparatively rare talent that satisfies this function was earlier characterized by Frank H. Knight as an economic surd—that is, irrational. No perfectly prudent person is an entrepreneur; the risks of failure are too obvious and too great. As Keynes said, "If human nature felt no temptation to take a chance, no satisfaction (profit apart) in constructing a railway, a mine or a farm, there might not be much investment merely as a result of cold calculation."[12]

All of this is true; yet it is not impossible that the case for the entrepreneur has been overstated. There may be no industry without him, but industry depends also on those who toil in the vineyard, and it has occurred to many to wonder whether all that toil is necessary or desirable. Hesiod's *Works and Days,* which might be said to be the first economics text, as well as one of the oldest of literary works to come down to us, announces a theme that still teases mankind. After an invocation to Zeus, Hesiod laments:

> From men the source of life has been hidden well.
> Else you would lightly do enough work in a day
> To keep you the rest of the year while you lounged at play.

More recently, the same idea inspired Thoreau to retreat to Walden Pond, and more recently still, so-called alternate lifestyles have been celebrated.

Against these seductive notions, it has been argued that Thoreau's experiment depended not only on Emerson's support but also on the industries that originally produced the shanty boards and used windows and one thousand old bricks that he bought secondhand. Somebody worked at those industries, even though Thoreau didn't. Even Marx advanced a similar argument, contending that the historical role of capitalism was the rationalization of production necessary to make decent work and leisure generally available in the communist future. It is unquestionable that grinding poverty was the common lot in the Western world until very recently.

It is, however, equally unquestionable that hunters and gatherers, where they still exist, live comparatively toil-free lives, and that an appropriate ordering of priorities would enable even a New Yorker to work a stress-free thirty-five hours a week and have twice that time free for libraries and museums and botanical gardens and such. It would therefore seem necessary to recognize that the common laborer is as much an economic surd as is the entrepreneur. They are both essential for the work of the world; but there is no reason why either should work so hard at it—no reason, that is, except that work is one of the ways in which we define ourselves.

IV

In the meantime, entrepreneurs and managers are paid very richly, and common laborers are paid very poorly. Several executives were paid more than $5 million in 1988. These sums were compensation for one year's labor and are said to have been earned. (It may be assumed that they were also snugly sheltered, but that is another question.) There were more than 36,000 people who reported *taxable* incomes in excess of a million dollars in 1987.

When justification is sought for such astronomical sums, attention is usually called to the responsibilities accepted by the corporation CEO. If a workman on the assembly line makes a mistake, it is likely to be caught by someone else; and if it isn't, the possible damage is limited. But if the CEO makes a wrong decision, he may bankrupt the company. Furthermore, the workman cannot make a *correct* decision that is more than routine, while the CEO may, with a clever move, multiply the company's earnings many times.

The importance and difficulty of all this decision making is certainly overrated. As Galbraith somewhere points out, difficult decisions usually are difficult because they are close, and close decisions tend to be close because there is not much to choose among the alternative possibilities. In such situations, it doesn't make much difference which way the ball bounces. Really important decisions, on the other hand, decisions that do make a difference, are often blindingly obvious.

That this analysis is in general correct is indicated by customary corporate practice. Apologists for big business—especially those inimical to government—are fond of contrasting the risky career of the business executive with the life tenure of the civil servant (in such discussions, the volatile life of the elected official is not mentioned). As a matter of fact, however, it is rare for a CEO to be dismissed for malfeasance, let alone for misfeasance or nonfeasance. In most companies it would be lèse-majesté to suggest that the old man had made a mistake. The life of a CEO is so stable that it caused some fluttering when Robert Townsend suggested in *Up the Organization* that the term of a corporation president ought to be no more than five years. If decision making were all that difficult, a CEO's life would not be such a happy one.

Although the difficulty of decision making may be exaggerated, it is true that most people are willing to let someone else do it. Successful business executives do display a willingness to make decisions, however easy or difficult, and are rewarded for that. In addition, they are said to have valuable experience to call on. Again there is something to the argument, but again perhaps less than is claimed for it. For it is reasonable to inquire how they came by all that experience. They were, as the saying goes, lucky enough to be in the right place at the right time, and not uncommonly they inherited the right place.

In any case, as people climb the corporate ladder, several important things are being tested beyond their ability to do sums in their heads and their cheerful willingness to anticipate what their boss wants. Perhaps most important of all, they are exhibiting their ability to learn, and especially their ability to understand at a glance how things work. If they're going to get ahead, they've got to have a quick ear and a sharp eye.

It must be acknowledged that the quick ear and the sharp eye are far from common. At the same time, it is possible that we may have here another of those nature versus nurture problems, like the debate over whether women are naturally slow at mathematics or merely are brought up that way. One's genetic composition (whatever that may mean), home environment, and formal education may be of the most promising, but a few years in the lower reaches of a large organization that happens to be riddled with office politics can be devastating. The winners in such contests prove themselves adept at politics; and if they're good at their jobs too, that's a plus. The losers' talents never have a chance to develop.

The winners, in fair contests as well as in foul, gain something more than pay raises. They gain experience. They have increased opportunities to practice the use of their eyes and ears. They learn by doing. Perhaps more important, they join C. Wright Mills's "power elite" and gradually expand their business connections so that they are eventually on familiar terms with the most "useful" people among their firm's customers, suppliers, and competitors, not to mention lawyers, bankers, and regulators. All of this makes them—or seems to make them—many times more valuable to their firms than the inexperienced, dispirited, though almost equally talented, losers. And this is said to justify the enormous difference in their salaries.

There is also, in the minds of the directors who formally set the high CEO salaries, another justification. They believe that they must pay their CEO well, or he (it's almost always "he") will decamp for some competitor that does pay well (after all, he knows them all), thus subtracting his skills from their company and adding them to the competition. It is not impossible that this reasoning is sound, especially since paying him an extra million, say, to hold him, is just a drop in a *Fortune*-500 bucket. Moreover, if he really and truly can increase his firm's profit by a million and one dollars (and who's to say he can't?), he will have proved, as standard economists say, the marginal utility of his raise.

This reasoning may remind us of the free-agent auction in baseball. And indeed the same principles operate, with the same results: astronomical salaries for a few stars, who are expected to attract the crowds, whopping raises to keep the most important and most powerful of the rest in line, and higher prices for the paying customers. This is a curious situation in which one individual, or a very small group, can have what Galbraith calls countervailing power[13] against a large corporation or even against the economy as a whole.

V

At this point it may repay us to look a little more closely at the compensation of one of these fortunate few. Let us suppose a bright and well-educated young man of twenty-one, who does not inherit his position but is thought to be of "management potential." In the present state of the business world, it would not be quite realistic to suppose a young woman in the same situation. So a young man. He starts work for a *Fortune*-500 company, not as an apprentice sweeping the factory floor, nor even as a clerk running errands in accounts receivable, but as a management trainee. He is by no means at the bottom of the ladder, but it's still a long way to the top, and at every rung he's in head-to-head competition with others like himself, many from outside his company (and he may shift companies himself). If he gets to be CEO at age fifty-one, he will have prevailed in perhaps ten such contests—a competition rather like a tennis-club ladder, in which one periodically challenges the player above or is challenged by the player below.

At any rate, our man finally makes it to the top. The question is, How much better was he than his competitors? The difference may be thinner than a double-edge razor blade. Jimmy Connors was undisputed 1982 Wimbledon champion, but he and John McEnroe won the same number of games in the final match and even scored the same number of points. Beyond that, it is, as the announcers say, a game of inches.

Let's give our man all the credit we can. Let's suppose that, at each rung of the ladder, he shows himself 10 percent better than his competition. That is, one must admit, a pretty big margin if he runs into any competition at all. So if we give our hero a 10 percent superiority at every stage, we're not understating his attainments.

On this assumption it is reasonable to claim that when he finally pulls himself to the top, he has proved himself ten powers of 1.1 (1.1^{10}), or 2.59 times, better than the losers in the first contest. Thus it would seem reasonable for his pay to be 2.59 times theirs. If the permanent losers, with modest seniority raises, got themselves up to $35,000 at age fifty-one, the winning CEO should be earning 2.59 times that, or $90,650. Giving him the breakage, it would be $91,571.

This is of course ridiculous. There is no *Fortune*-500 CEO who doesn't make many times $91,571, without even thinking of fringe benefits, options, and other perquisites. A $5-million-a-year man gets fifty times the amount we've calculated for a more-run-of-the-mill CEO. And consider: $5 million is 150 times the pay of the losers in the race, who were no fools to begin with, or about 500 times the poverty level for a family of four.

It is doubtful that anyone really believes that these fantastic differentials can be justified on any basis of amount of work or difficulty of work or contribution to the general welfare. It is sometimes contended, not without a show of reasonableness, that if a foreman (or forewoman) supervising six or eight workers receives a paycheck one or two thousand dollars higher than the workers', the CEO supervising sixty or eighty thousand workers is entitled to a proportionately higher reward. Or if the CEO of a firm with annual profits of a million dollars takes home fifty thousand a year (and probably much more), the CEO of a company earning a billion dollars would be entitled to take home fifty million. Of course, no *Fortune-*500 CEO does (the really large salaries are paid by financial companies). One reason why no *Fortune-*500 CEO does is that he is actually supervising not sixty or eighty thousand people, but six or eight subsidiary presidents, who in turn supervise six or eight vice presidents, who in turn supervise six or eight division heads, and so on down the line. This is, moreover, the chain of command; the CEO has an extensive staff to assist him and so do all his subordinates, except those at the end of the chain.

In the end, the argument is that in a free country with a free market, one is entitled to get whatever the market will bear. If the demand is great, it is right to reap the benefit of that demand. If there is strong demand for computer programmers and if few are available, competition will push their salaries up. The same is true of common laborers, though they tend to get pushed in the other direction. It is all a question of supply and demand.

So it is said. One would have to be a fool not to be aware that given the way a modern corporation is set up, the CEO and those at the top can pretty much write their own tickets or, to change the figure, design their own golden parachutes. It is difficult to contemplate some recent performances of this sort without disgust. But this is not the present point. For the moment it is enough to observe that when you rely on the market to justify your salary, you are reducing your labor—and yourself—to a commodity, a mere thing.

VI

The aims of a human life are, as Freud said, loving and working. These are two of the ways in which we declare our membership in society and acknowledge our obligations. These declarations and acknowledgments are not passive; they must be actively pursued, and in this some are more fortunate than others.

On the other side, one has no obligation that is not confirmed by rights. Society can do little about loving—except to refrain from admitting impediments—but working is at the very heart of it. A political economy that fails to allow its citizens to contribute to the common weal fails fundamentally.

This is not a matter of prudence or of benefit-cost analysis. The citizen's right to make a contribution is equal to society's right to hold him or her to obedience to the laws. No one has a right to a particular job with a particular firm, but everyone has a right to make a contribution. As a consequence, the state must be, as used to be said, the employer of last resort. The last resort is not the citizen's but the state's. It is the state's obligation to enable its citizens to advance the state's purposes. In this, as in so much else, the New Deal was creative and prophetic, and the postwar years have seen a steady erosion of morale.

The problem is not, as the nineteenth century conceived it, one of forcing people to work by threatening starvation. Nor is it one of enticing people to work by promising rewards. As Galbraith showed in *The Affluent Society,* the economy can proceed very prosperously with large numbers of potential workers on the dole, but the citizens cannot proceed in that way.

VII

Self-justification—not market justification—is crucial if self-definition is the ground of labor. It would be absurd to find one's meaning in one's work and at the same time to declare the work unworthy. Such absurdity does, however, abound, whence the banal apology of businesspeople caught in sharp or mean practice, that they're not in it for their health.

Searching for the legitimation of private property, John Locke wrote, "As much land as a man tills, plants, improves, cultivates, and can use the product of, so much is his property."[14] He felt that a man's legitimate possessions were limited to what he could produce and use before it spoiled, but he granted that money as a store of value allowed one to pile up as much as one had a mind to. This piling up, it may be noted, was to be strictly in money, not in producers' goods. As early as Aristotle, however, it had been seen that the "so-called art of money-making" had no limit. This of course was a fatal defect to the Greek mind. Those who practiced this art were, Aristotle said, "intent on living only, and not upon living well; and as their desires are unlimited, they also desire that the means of gratifying them should be without limit."[15] Such people are still with us. The other day the son of a Texas oil multimillionaire dropped out of college, went to work for his father, and in short order had made some millions of his own. The father was asked why the son needed to do this. "What else is there to do?" was the rejoinder.

In all candor, it must be admitted that this sort of thinking is perfectly congruent with the introductory paragraphs of many (if not most) of today's economics-principles textbooks. In terms of desires or wants or material gain, there is no limit to money making or the bottom line or, for that matter, to the GNP. No invisible hand guides them. The compensation of labor—executive labor as well as common labor—has no "natural" standard; it is not a "scientific" question. It is an expression of the standards, the ideals, the will of society and its members. It is an ethical question. It goes to our mores, our morals, our morale.

Wage scales are, from top to bottom, a social creation, and they are an indicator of the sort of people we are. We demand to see expert tennis and so pay the top players in excess of a million dollars a year. We don't demand to see expert croquet and so pay croquet masters little or nothing. I myself share the preference for tennis; nevertheless I recognize that there is nothing in the relative difficulty of the sports or the relative rarity of the requisite skills to justify the million-to-zero differential. The same is true of the relative contributions of the CEO and the unskilled laborer whose job he has just eliminated. The CEO and his company would be valueless in the Amazon rain forest or on the Antarctic icecap; their value is a social value. There are certainly differences in the social contributions of the CEO and the laborer, and even of the tennis star and the croquet shark. But the ranking of these differences and the prices that are put on them are not natural phenomena; they embody social judgments in which we all share.

That we Americans allot the richest rewards of our economy to speculators is a question of mores; that we still allow one-sixth of our fellow citizens to be ill housed, ill clad, and ill nourished is a question of morals; that we shrink from our problems instead of attacking them with eagerness, generosity, and hope is a question of morale. The questions are obviously interrelated.

8

GOODS
Which Keep It Going

I

Natural objects become economic goods by being acted on by economic agents. All work is limited, and so is what is produced. Every activity (not merely economic activity) has a base in nature; as Troilus told Cressida, the act is a slave to limit.

Natural resources are valuable because of their importance in a particular economy, at a particular time and place. For us today, petroleum seems essential, and it is for our economy. But it was insignificant in Adam Smith's time (when coal was only coming into its own), and the world will not come to an end when the Arabian sands run dry. The world will be different, but it will not end. No resource is absolute.[1]

For this reason, the familiar definition of economics as determining the optimal allocation of resources begs the question. It assumes that resources are absolute, whereas a resource is recognized as a resource precisely and only because of the way it is allocated in the present economy. An optimum is such only in relation to a given standard or given constraints. One can speak of the best economics textbook or the best red wine, but not of the best thing or the best good. Whatever allocations a given price system achieves are optimal only in relation to that price system. The allocation argument is circular. It is, moreover, notorious that, left to himself, economic man will destroy the ecosystem, wasting topsoil, polluting air and water, and spreading poisons with profit-maximizing abandon.

When we talk of economic goods, we have more than subsistence in mind. Subsistence, as we have remarked, is a physiological problem. Even for Ricardo, the subsisting laborers were producing something more than their own and their employers' sustenance. What made that something a good?

Let us begin by inquiring how a service becomes an economic good. That nothing intrinsic to the service makes it an economic good a few examples will show. Home cooking of the highest quality is not an economic good, but hash slinging of junk food is an economic good. Home handiwork is not an economic good, but hired plumbing is. Whether you pray standing on the corner of the street or in your closet with the door closed, what you do is not an economic good, but when a priest or parson prays for you, that is. It is even possible to argue that our hapless soldier digging that hole in the ground is performing an economic service, since he does it in the line of duty, for which he is paid.

Economics is a necessary part of modern life, but it is not all of life. An economic service is work done for pay, regardless of what else may be said about it. The service may be good, bad, or indifferent—performed shoddily or with grace. It may be one of general usefulness, as maintaining telephone communications. It may be one of special usefulness, as praying for the faithful. It may be one of nil or negative usefulness, as offering a teetotaler a drink in a restaurant. All that matters is that it be done for pay. Since it certainly is not uncommon for people to be so delighted with their work that they do it for pleasure, it is more precise to say that an economic service is paid service.

This insistence on pay is not arbitrary. The alternative is to consider everything anyone does—at least everything that involves two or more people—as economic. Such analyses quickly reduce to such absurdities as Marx's theory that slavery is latent in the family[2] or the variation of this theory that sees marriage as an exchange of sexual favors for security. That some marriages may seem like that, even to the partners, says nothing about most marriages, and certainly nothing about any humanistic view of marriage. Furthermore, if such an exchange were truly economic, one would have to look for the resulting income, which could be stated only in money. Without an actual monetary exchange, the statement would be arbitrary, and the taxing authorities would be dragged into foolish calculations. If the husband leapt from the marriage bed to prepare breakfast, would his wife's income be greater than if he turned over and went back to sleep? If so, by how much?

Insistence on a monetary transaction makes an economic service an ephemeral good. The service doesn't exist unless it is done and paid for, and once it is done, that is the end of it. They also serve who only stand and wait—provided they are paid for it. An unemployed waiter produces no economic value. Nor can services be stockpiled. In slack times, or in anticipation of a strike, I cannot take extra rides up and down in the office elevator and so be prepared for crowded or nonexistent service to come. We have already noted that labor power—the power to perform a service—cannot be resold.

In all this, services seem different from material goods. But all material goods are also more or less ephemeral. Not only do moths and rust corrupt and thieves break in and steal, but material things may lose their marketability, which, in fact, many material things never had.

Prompted by personal enthusiasm, by the acclaim of respected critics—by any number of things—a book publisher may produce more copies of a novel than he can sell at any price. There may be several thousand left after the regular sale at the full price and even after the remainder sale at the lowest price that repays the cost of handling. In the end, to make room in the warehouse, the rest are shredded if there is a sufficient need for waste paper or dumped in a "sanitary" landfill otherwise.

This is not an esoteric scenario in the book business, and it has myriad parallels in other lines, even under communism. In the heyday of the Gang of Four that followed Mao, several streets of Shanghai were lined with hundreds or thousands of good-size steel boilers quietly rusting under the plane trees. Somebody had no doubt been praised for exceeding a quota, but what was turned out (if not still there) has had to be reduced to scrap. These things happen, whether as a result of American know-how or in accordance with Mao Zedong Thought, because no one can foretell the future.

The novel was an economic good (we are not commenting on its literary merit), not because of the labor (that did the writing and tended the machines that made the paper and printed the books), the land (whose trees were made into paper), the capital (that provided the paper mill, the printing press, and the warehouse for the publisher's inventory), or whatever other factors of production you care to name. All these were necessary, but they were not sufficient to create a good. The factors of production resulted in an artifact, not an economic good.

The artifact became an economic good as it passed from hand to hand through the economic system. The passing did not have to be constant, but it did have to have a constant potential. Once the possibility of movement was foreclosed or abandoned or ended, the economic value of the artifact vanished.

At every stage, the product depends on the system, and the system is prior. While today's product may modify tomorrow's system, it could have been produced only because today's system was already a going concern. The system includes the market but is not confined to that; there is scarcely an aspect of the society and its government that does not bear on it. Putting it in its most obvious terms, an automobile is worthless without roads and gasoline and people who know how to drive. The Inca's hoard, as we have remarked, was worth nothing to him in the face of the destruction of his society; with distribution facilities destroyed, a stock of corn would have done him no better. Goods and services have no economic value unless they are available to an effective demand. The author of our landfilled novel has friends and relatives unable to find the book in a convenient bookstore. The sales are lost; rather, they never existed, and so more books go to the shredder or dump. Many things for which there is a brisk demand in one society are unsalable at any price in another. Few refrigerators are sold to Eskimos living on ice floes, or so we are given to understand.

The wealth of a nation consists not in its mass of material things but in its system. The natural resources of South America are not greatly inferior to those of the United States, but the wealth of the two regions is vastly different. The distinction was not understood by bankers who made large loans on the basis of the resources. The land of India is far richer than that of Japan, but the comparative wealth of the two nations is reversed.

Nor is accumulated capital crucial. As John Stuart Mill pointed out, capital is constantly being consumed and reproduced, and this fact explains "what has so often excited wonder, the great rapidity with which countries recover from a state of devastation; the disappearance, in a short time, of all traces of the mischiefs done by earthquakes, floods, hurricanes, and the ravages of war."[3] In 1871 the fledgling German Empire imposed a 5-billion-franc war indemnity on France, intending to impoverish her for a generation, but in spite of the loss of Alsace and Lorraine, and in spite of the disorders following the Paris Commune, the entire debt was paid off in two years. At the end of World War II, Germany was in ruins, but in short order it became again one of the most prosperous nations of the world—and this without the eastern provinces.

What is true of national wealth is true of goods. What counts is system, a going concern.

II

"Consumption is the sole end and purpose of all production," wrote Adam Smith, "and the interest of the producer ought to be attended to only so far as may be necessary for promoting that of the consumer. The maxim," he added, "is so perfectly self-evident that it would be absurd to attempt to prove it." The maxim certainly does seem self-evident. Why bother to produce something that's not going to be used? Yet in the history of economics, the maxim has been remarkably little attended to. Smith himself noted that "in the mercantile system, the interest of the consumer is almost constantly sacrificed to that of the producer."[4] The same was true of medieval guilds; it was true of Karl Marx, who insisted that distribution was not the issue;[5] it was true of Andrew Carnegie, who amassed wealth in order to give it away, and of Thorstein Veblen, who satirized the conspicuous consumption of Carnegie's contemporaries; it is true today of Marx's followers, who inveigh against consumerism, and also of the supply-siders, who think of themselves as exemplary anti-Marxists.

These views, as R. H. Tawney suggested, were no doubt focused by the Church's doctrines of the sins of avarice and gluttony.[6] The rival teachings of Calvinism had a similar effect. Salvation was solely a question of divine election, and mundane triumph was a possible forecast of election; therefore it was only prudent to work hard to give the forecast a chance to show itself. At the same time, it was imprudent to enjoy the fruits of the triumphant labor, because anyone who did so obviously valued this world more than the next and so could scarcely be one of the elect. Thus predestination led to vigorous emphasis on production and to studied indifference to consumption. As is the case with success in every line of endeavor, the example of Calvinist businessmen had a widening influence on others of other faiths or of no faith. We have already met the Texas oil multimillionaire whose son left college to make his own millions. "What else is there to do?"

In spite of the self-evident priority of consumption, Adam Smith placed his emphasis, like the others, on production. The title of his book was *An Inquiry into the Nature and Causes of the Wealth of Nations*; he did not promise a discussion of the uses of wealth, nor did he supply any. Given the state of the world then—given the state of the world now—the overwhelming problem has been to produce enough to feed, clothe, and shelter the huddled masses of the earth. Until that political problem is solved, it seems frivolous to fuss about the purposes of wealth. But the fact remains that most economic activity is neither directly nor indirectly concerned with the subsistence problem. Economic theory likewise has its mind on higher things; and when it thinks of consumption at all, as Ricardo and Malthus did, it concludes that the mass of mankind is forever condemned to abject poverty, like it or not, while the work of producing the pleasures of the rich and well-born provides employment for the poor. There is no suggestion that these pleasures, whether dainty or coarse, serve otherwise than as a goad to envy, ambition, and emulation.

III

The most enthusiastic advocate of production *à outrance* will hesitate over agricultural practices that maximize this year's crop but deplete the topsoil. He understands that overcutting the forests of the Himalayas will result in crop failures in India and floods in Bangladesh. The amount of production, in short, cannot be stated except with a time frame, and there is nothing sacrosanct about the calendar. Indeed, it is now fashionable to argue that American industry has faltered because executives have been maximizing short-term gains. On the other hand, who is eager for pie in the sky by and by?

Even if the time question were satisfactorily solved there would still remain the problem of counting. How do we know that production is being increased? The problem looks simple enough for a book publisher or a boilermaker; just compare the number of books or boilers manufactured this year with the number manufactured last year. But we have seen some of the books shredded and some of the boilers scrapped. Very well, one can count what's left. Counting will work well enough provided what is counted is homogeneous, as would be the case with a small foundry making only one style and size of boiler. But even a very small publisher will publish many different sizes and kinds of books, and it appears that they are not thought of in terms of size or weight or number of pages or number of words or number of anything. A think piece on economics will cost more, word for word, than a popular novel, regardless of intrinsic merit.

We have drifted from adding up numbers of things to adding up prices of things; there is no other way to solve our problem. But is this a rational solution? If prices are what matter, it is no trick to increase them. Anyone could do it in a trice, simply by debasing the currency. This has been done more than once in the history of the world. It has even been done in reverse; when in the 1950s France exchanged one new franc for ten old francs, did that cut French production by 90 percent?

Now, this is all obvious enough, and economists have long since solved the problem to their satisfaction by the construction of indexes. But we have noted that such constructions all depend on judgment. There is no shirking the responsibility of judging. Even when responsibility is refused at the start of analysis, it presents itself again and again. The persistence of the problem is a reliable indication that the initial refusal to accept responsibility was illicit, and that wants are not absolute but are liable to judgment.

I cannot be judged—nor can I judge myself—except by what I do. Consumption, to the extent that it is not merely physiological, is an activity. It is as much an activity as is production. The consumer is, like the entrepreneur or laborer, an economic surd, a human being. No one is driven by necessity to work as hard as producers do. No one is driven by necessity to consume as much as consumers do. Production and consumption are acts of will, not of necessity.

What, then, is it that consumers do? How can these doings be judged?

IV

Thorstein Veblen judged the behavior of consumers, especially those with a great deal to consume, very severely. His position was that the economic "struggle is substantially a race for reputability on the basis of an invidious comparison." What he called "the habit of pecuniary emulation" was not the only motive for economic activity, but all other motives were "greatly affected" by it. In order to demonstrate one's reputability, one supported conspicuous consumption, which was as lavish as one could make it, but not formless. In fact, the prescribed pecuniary canons of taste and dress, which required the conservation of archaic rituals and observances, were so difficult to master that they were specially assigned to the leisure class, which was mostly made up of women. Under a veneer of quasi-scientific objectivity, Veblen plainly despised what he analyzed, and contrasted pecuniary emulation with the instinct of workmanship. "[T]he end of vicarious consumption," he wrote, "is to enhance, not the fulness of life of the consumer, but the pecuniary repute of the master for whose behoof the consumption takes place."[7]

That much of the world runs as Veblen described—though perhaps less now than a century ago—and that what he described was deserving of his scorn there is no doubt. Nevertheless, his analysis left consumption essentially outside the economic process. It was the end—in the sense of terminus—of economic activity, but it was an unworthy end of unworthy activity. The contrasting instinct of workmanship perhaps led, in some not fully explained way, to fullness of life, but the enjoyment of this presumed fullness was a private affair.

Consequently, it remains that "the very idea of consumption itself has to be set back into the social process," as Mary Douglas and Baron Isherwood say in their book *The World of Goods.*[8] These writers are concerned with "an anthropology of consumption," but their analysis opens the way for economic theory. They point out that in the history of anthropology "enlightenment has followed a decision to ignore the physiological levels of existence which sustain the behavior in question." Accordingly they see consumption not as sustaining life but as "the joint production, with fellow consumers, of a universe of values. Consumption uses goods to make firm and visible a particular set of judgments in the fluid process of classifying persons and events."[9] Darwin made a similar observation regarding taxonomy. "With plants," he exclaims in *The Origin of Species,* "how remarkable it is that the organs of vegetation, on which their nutrition and life depend, are of little significance!"[10]

The universe of values does not exist except in the process of becoming firm and visible. By what I spend my money on—the clothes I wear, the food I eat, the furniture, books, music, and pictures with which I surround myself—I discover and refine the standards to which I repair and thereby demonstrate to others the sort of person I am, the sort of people with whom I associate and whose good opinion and good fellowship I value.

The problem of judging consumption is not different from the problem of judging production. In neither case does one face the problem as a newborn babe or from behind a veil or blindfolded. One is in the midst of one's life, of one's society, of one's times, of one's history, and one does not exist otherwise. No solution will be valid that disregards the situation in which one finds oneself or forgets what the past has left unsolved.

I am the judge of my purposes, but I am not the only judge. If my actions are unworthy, it is my soul that is shriveled. I pay the price and have my reward. But society also has an interest in what I do and is my judge because I am literally nothing if not social. All of this works both ways. Individual and society are symbiotic, reciprocal, mutually necessary, ontological. Society is literally nothing except as a membership of individuals, and this fact lays upon me the right and requirement to judge society. If a society's actions are unworthy, all the citizens suffer. All Americans were diminished by the Vietnam War; all are diminished by economic policies that condemn fellow citizens to lives of desperate poverty; all are diminished by the persistence of unjust laws.

The point is simply this: I define myself, even to myself, by what I do. There is no other way. What I do includes what I, as an economic agent, consume—what I do with my money. I must confess that I am not strong enough or wise enough or good enough to be proud of everything I do. Yet I insist on my responsibility because only the responsible are free. In classical economics, consumers are said to be sovereign. What does this mean, except that consumers are responsible for the values of the economic world? Whatever consumers do—what they actually do—defines and enlarges or diminishes their humanity, and the humanity of all of us.

Consumption is no less a human activity than is production.

Consumption has consequences, not only for the consumer, but for the economy. What is consumed today must in some way be replaced so that we can live to consume another day. Economic consumption and production do not end, any more than the market is cleared. Failure to consume the quantity of goods produced will of course discourage further production. A drop in production will cause roughly proportionate drops in employment and investment, and these will affect subsequent consumption. And so on.

The relation of production to consumption is historical. It is linear, not cyclical. The drop in production that follows a drop in consumption is not a correction that restores a previous equilibrium; it is a determinant of a new situation, which will have consequences yet to be discovered.

9

CAPITAL

Saving and Investing

I

The goods we have been discussing are consumers' goods—
things and services to be used and enjoyed. Their role in the economy
is systematically different from that of producers' goods—things and
services to make consumers' goods or other producers' goods. Producers' goods exist in every system, no matter how primitive or advanced.
The first producers' goods were no doubt clubs to attack game or stones
to crack shells. Puny humans would barely survive without such goods,
but with them they perform miracles.

The discovery of the sixteenth century was, as Keynes put it, the
discovery (or perhaps rediscovery) of compound interest. He once calculated that every £1 that Sir Francis Drake plundered from Spain and
brought home to the queen in 1580 had become £100,000 by 1930,
and that the total was equivalent to the entire overseas wealth of the
British Empire at its height. Looking ahead, he indulged the hope that
the same process would solve "the economic problem" in another
hundred years or so (more than fifty of which have already gone by)
and that economists would then be "thought of as humble competent
people, on a level with dentists."[1]

Keynes was speaking of producers' goods bought with Drake's gold
and silver, and of the progressive investment and reinvestment of a part

of the proceeds of those goods in further producers' goods, and so on, for 350 years. The reinvestments were small, averaging about 3 1/4 percent a year; but the results were stupendous. Spain, in contrast, although her plunder from the Americas was vastly greater than Drake's plunder from her, used practically all her gold and silver to pay for consumers' goods, from castles in Iberia to armies in Italy and the Low Countries, with results that left her far in the British wake.

II

Just as there is nothing inherent in an object that makes it a good, there is nothing inherent in a good that makes it a producers' good. A hammer may be used in producing something for sale, in which case it is a producers' good. Or it may be used about the house or even become an object for collectors, in which cases it is a consumers' good. Or another time, a harried collector may grab a handsome specimen to drive a nail into something he intends to sell; then it becomes a producers' good again. A hen is a producers' good if her eggs are sold, but she herself may be literally consumed and so lay no more eggs. Even a steel mill may become a consumers' good; one near Völklingen in the Saar sheltered displaced persons for a time after World War II.

These classifications seem to reduce the real world to one of shifting and contradictory appearances. A hammer would seem to be both a consumers' good and not a consumers' good, which is logically impossible. But the object in question is not even a hammer in its sense qualities or in its shape (it might be a gavel), but in its use. The hammer is neither producers' goods nor consumers' goods—nor goods at all— except in the way it is used.

In the National Income and Product Accounts, a new single-family dwelling counts as a capital investment, no matter who pays for it or how anyone uses it. Some writers justify this sort of classification on the ground of the size or the durability of the house. But durability is an uncertain test: I have many books that are older than any house I have ever owned or lived in. Some go still further afield and classify consumer durables and even clothing as "savings." It is true that my dinner jacket is older than most houses on my street and, given the amount of wear it gets, may well outlast them. It is also true that it cost me less when I bought it than a replacement would cost me today, but this difference is savings only in the huckster's sense of "Sale! Up to 50% Savings!" I did not buy it for any productive purpose. Nor did I buy it for a speculative purpose, and I'd have been disappointed if I had, for in the absence of an established market for secondhand clothes, the cost of selling it would have eaten up the putative "profit." On the other hand, if I were a headwaiter, the dinner jacket might be a necessary uniform and so productive.

The danger in all nonfunctional classifications quickly appears when we look again at the question of compound interest. Castles in Spain were big-ticket items and durable, and the grandees who built them saved or borrowed money for the purpose. But the castles were consumers' goods; they were not used to produce anything except plunder and extortionate rents, both of which are, literally, counterproductive. In contrast, the British steadily ploughed 3 1/4 percent of their earnings back into the shops for which Napoleon scorned them, and into mines and railways and factories and ships, all of which, in turn, produced further goods. The Spanish investments satisfied the durability definition; the British investments satisfied functional definitions. There is a practical difference.

We must not conclude, however, that there is a standard percentage of income that an economy should invest, year in and year out. Here again, it proves impossible to avoid passing judgment. The 3 1/4 percent rate of British imperialism may for some purposes have been too high, for others too low, though we can be pretty sure that it was more suitable than the near-zero Spanish rate.

In studies of the distribution of wealth the faulty classification is misleading. As Lester Thurow points out, "Standard economics . . . assumes that people accumulate wealth solely to provide future consumption privileges," but great wealth results in economic power, "which entails the ability to order others about." Most Americans have little or no net wealth, and even the middle class have most of their wealth in the form of their homes. Since the recent inflation has greatly increased the value of residential housing, the distribution of wealth seems more equitable than formerly. But home ownership conveys little economic power, and Thurow shows that about 40 percent of all fixed nonresidential capital is controlled by only 482 families and individuals. Thus very few can order very many about.[2]

III

Producers' goods are things that have been saved. Agriculture is impossible unless seeds are set aside, reducing current consumption to ensure future consumption. In addition, labor must be devoted to making tools, building fences, turning pots for storage; and all these activities reduce the time available for idleness, recreation, and other forms of current consumption. In an industrial society, it is plain that power looms produce more cloth per man hour than hand looms, and that power looms are bought by men who have saved money or can borrow money from others who have saved.

But saving is a consequence of production. Nothing can be saved until it exists. No artifact exists until it has been manufactured. Production is inescapably prior to saving. Even the standard agricultural model fails; seed corn cannot be saved unless it has already been harvested.

In a modern economy, the priority of production is even more striking. When a corporation plans a new product, contracts are entered into with a construction company to build a factory, with tool manufacturers for the necessary machines, perhaps with an advertising agency for marketing plans, and so on. The corporation also assures itself of a line of credit to meet payments on these contracts as they come due. The bank that grants the line of credit gets its affairs in order so it can do what it has agreed to do. The various contractors and subcontractors and their banks all go through similar motions. Aside from a down payment here and there, no money is paid over until quite a lot of time has passed and quite a lot of work has been done. In short, a great expansion of debt takes place, including the credit extended by the workers (who customarily wait a week or a month for their pay), that extended by merchants satisfying the demands of the newly employed workers, that extended by wholesalers and manufacturers restocking the merchants, and so on, via what R. F. Kahn called the multiplier.

The expansion comes about, not as a result of savings, but as a result of production put in process by the corporation. No amount of saving by bankers and potential workers and suppliers would, in itself, have called the new production into existence. Nothing would have been produced if the enterprising corporation had not decided it could make a profit on it and if the people and firms it dealt with had not had faith in its ability to do so.

IV

The modern mode of production differs from previous modes not in that it uses or exploits producers' goods (for all modes do that), nor in that it uses or exploits labor (for all modes also do that), but in that it is organized as a system of continuous and interrelated flows. Such retail trade as existed in Aristotle's time was frowned on by him because he could not see how a retailer produced anything. In the ancient and medieval worlds, enterprises were relatively discrete and ad hoc affairs, as the construction industry is largely organized to this day. If one wanted a pair of shoes, one went to a cordwainer and had a pair custom made; there was no store in which one could buy what one wanted off the shelf.

The cordwainer, to be sure, was a specialist in leather working, and the apprentices he employed were, so to say, subspecialists, one perhaps being more skilled at preparing the leather, another at sewing. The efficiency of the division of labor had, as we have noted, been early remarked by Plato; it, too, fails to mark the modern mode.

What was true of small transactions was true of large. The merchants of Venice organized each commercial voyage as a separate affair. Their personal experience taught them the sorts of goods most likely to be wanted on the Golden Horn, and they stocked their outward-bound galleys accordingly. Likewise they brought home the sorts of things they could sell quickly and profitably at the quayside. The system was a series of speculative ventures, making the most of ad hoc opportunities to buy and sell. Those involved were, as they called themselves, merchant adventurers.

Modern economy, in contrast, is a flow. The first modern business was probably the wool trade, a trade that peculiarly lent itself to such organization. In the first place, the wool itself was, comparatively, not perishable. At all stages—as raw wool, as yarn, as cloth—it could be fairly safely stockpiled; working capital was born. Each stage, moreover, required a special machine—a spinning wheel, a loom: fixed capital. The entrepreneur bought wool from the farmers, put it out for spinning and weaving, generally on his own looms, gathered the finished cloth, and held it for sale to merchant adventurers, or sometimes handled the distribution himself in an early form of vertical organization. The flow could be steady because the end product—clothing—was in universal and perpetual demand.

Yet no one knew, when the sheep were sheared, what would ultimately become of the wool, nor could the entrepreneur be perfectly sure he would find a ready market, at a price to cover his costs, when he collected the finished cloth from his weavers. The rationale of his enterprise required him to keep going. With flowing enterprise came increased uncertainty and possibility of profit. The medieval or Renaissance guild master manufactured his products to order, reducing uncertainty and possible profit to a minimum.

V

Every new enterprise must accumulate producers' goods in the forms of fixed capital and working capital. To buy them, it needs liquid capital—money. Every continuing enterprise has similar needs; machinery wears out and raw materials are used up. Investment in producers' goods is never ending. All these goods are necessarily saved in the sense that they are withheld from consumption. As fast as they are used up (or dissaved) in the production of consumers' goods, they must be replaced. If the enterprise continues, the saving does, too.

With a few notable exceptions, producers' goods, as well as consumers' goods, are now produced for the market, and the market is not cleared. A colonial ranch house, a jet liner, a specialized machine tool, an evening gown, may be custom made; yet most of the materials of which they are made have been produced to meet an anticipated general demand, not a special-ordering particular demand. No scavenger of aluminum cans scours another roadside because Boeing gets a new order for a 727. No farmer plants another row of beans because I get a job. No automobile manufacturer builds an extra convertible because I now can afford one, nor does a steel mill open an extra furnace to supply the auto company's sudden need. The aluminum, beans, car, and steel are being produced anyhow. The resources they embody are being saved anyhow, as is all work in progress.

Money—the liquid capital—is likewise being saved anyhow. An enterprise needs money to buy materials, to pay rent and interest and taxes and wages. That is what cash flow is all about. The enterprise manages to save or borrow the necessary money, or it goes out of business.

We come here to an important distinction. While almost all production requires saving in the form of liquid capital, not all liquid capital is spent on production. This is another point where the failure to define terms functionally has led economic theory and practice astray. In this instance, practically all schools have been misled.

Keynes is as least partially responsible for the turn the problem has taken. In the course of defining "income" and "saving," he constructs and solves a pair of simultaneous equations as follows:

Income = value of output = consumption + investment
Saving = income − consumption
Therefore saving = investment.[3]

As his equations, being written partly in English and partly in mathematical symbols, don't look quite like ordinary equations, so his famous further inference ("Saving is a mere residual") is not an ordinary mathematical inference. To the extent that the equations are mathematical, saving and investment are equivalent, and either may be called a residual.

In any case, Keynes quite properly supports his famous inference by referring to the real world, rather than to his quasi-equations: "A decision to consume or not to consume truly lies within the power of the individual; so does a decision to invest or not to invest. The amounts of aggregate income and of aggregate saving are the *results* of the free choices of individuals whether or not to consume and whether or not to invest; but they are neither of them capable of assuming an independent value resulting from a separate set of decisions taken irrespective of the decisions concerning consumption and investment."

We can, I think, accept this line of reasoning, which amounts to saying that we know what individuals choose to consume and invest because we know what they do consume and invest.[4]☆ But we are still not so clear as we might be about what is meant by "investment." Keynes unfortunately gives us pretty much of a portmanteau definition: "In popular usage it is common to mean by it [investment] the purchase of an asset, old or new, by an individual or a corporation. Occasionally, the term might be restricted to the purchase of an asset on the Stock Exchange. But we speak just as readily of investing, for example, in a house, or in a machine, or in a stock of finished or unfinished goods. . . ."[5]

We observe at once that this definition is not functional. We observe further that while it may have a sort of validity microeconomically, it is grossly misleading macroeconomically. An individual's income (or at least wealth) may be increased by "investing" indifferently in a share of stock, a house, or a machine, but not all of these assets produce goods or services that swell the national income.[6]☆ A house may be a producers' good or a consumers' good, depending on whether it is for sale or for rent or owner occupied. A machine is a producers' good, or it is scrap metal. But what is a share of stock?

A share of stock is a legal asset, a claim on future profits or income, a right (attenuated, to be sure) to participate in control, evidence of partial and restricted ownership. But it is neither a producers' good nor a consumers' good. It is not an economic good at all. The company issuing it may have used the money from the sale to buy a machine. The machine produces goods; the share of stock does not (nor does the money used to buy it). To argue otherwise, one would have to point to the goods produced by the share of stock (or the money), as distinct from those produced by the machine.

Nevertheless, trading in shares of stock (and other securities) figures prominently in the "investments" of individuals and of the economy as a whole. It is both a microeconomic and a macroeconomic phenomenon. It absorbs vast amounts of liquid capital, although this fact is obscured by the failure (which we noted in Chapter 5) to define money functionally. Yet no account is taken of it either in Keynes's quasi-equations or in the more austerely mathematical versions that appear in today's textbooks.

Relying on a portmanteau definition of investment and on the presumed identity of saving and investment, American economists have, for fifty years or more, through Republican administrations and Democratic administrations, steadily advocated what they conceive of as Keynesian policies, intended to encourage saving. There is more than a little irony here, for Keynes held that, except in conditions of full employment, saving "may reduce present investment-demand as well as present consumption-demand."[7]

Since it is plausibly contended that the rich are better able to save than are the poor, the top personal income tax has been cut from 94 percent (subject to a maximum effective rate of 90 percent) in 1945[8] to 28 or 33 percent today, the severely regressive Social Security tax has been increased, the states have come to rely chiefly on regressive sales taxes, and various schemes, like Individual Retirement Accounts, have been tried. At the same time, the corporate tax rate has been lowered and various inducements to invest have been offered. Despite all this, it is claimed that saving is inadequate in the United States, and our performance is unfavorably compared with that of other nations, particularly Japan.

This is not the place to inquire into the received method of calculating the rate of saving. It will be sufficient for our purposes to agree that American productive investment has languished in recent years. Once-proud industries have withered, fundamental research has faltered, the infrastructure is decaying, and the median family income has stagnated while the cost of living continues its implacable climb.

Let us try to discover what caused the damage.

10

SPECULATION
Why a Bull Market Is a Disaster

I

If you have saved some money (since you have it, it is saved) and want to use it to get more, you can buy a factory (fixed capital), goods to sell (working capital), stock (claims on future profits), bonds (which will pay fees for the use of your money). You can put your money where your mouth is at Las Vegas or Atlantic City or in any of several state-run lotteries or race tracks. You can buy gold or a bundle of stocks or a bundle of mortgages or a carload of pork bellies (without having a clear idea of what a pork belly looks like or why anyone would want one). You can buy unimproved land or improved land, rare stamps or toy soldiers, a real Monet or lots of pseudo-Monets.

If you're a red-blooded American, you will expect prices to go up, whereupon you will sell your purchases and reap a capital gain. Or if you are of a more somber turn of mind, you can sell almost anything short and hope to make your gain as prices fall. Alternatively, still expecting prices to fall, you can do nothing with your money, hoarding it (exercising liquidity preference) in anticipation of eventually buying something cheap.

With the possible exception of how you use the first two items in the first paragraph, you will have been speculating or gambling. In ordinary speech, speculation tends to be defined somewhere between

106

gambling and enterprise on a scale of relative riskiness. But betting on dice (which everyone would classify as gambling) is liable to risks that may be closely anticipated, while launching a new product (the quintessential example of productive enterprise) is likely to be very risky indeed. In the publishing business, most new books lose money, though this is not the deliberate intent of either authors or publishers. If no one takes risks of the latter sort, nothing is done; there is no economy to analyze. Riskiness is a tangle, not a continuum.

Instead of relative riskiness, I have proposed the following criteria:[1] Gambling is risking wealth in a zero-sum game. If some players win, some other players must lose the same amount. The winnings and losings (after properly allocating taxes and the house's cut) add up to zero. Speculation differs from gambling in that it is not a zero-sum game. It can happen that all speculators win (though some may win more than others), that all lose, or that some win while others lose; and the sum of the winnings may be quite different from the sum of the losings. Speculation is, nevertheless, like gambling in that it produces nothing but rearranges—often to the great profit of the rearrangers— wealth that already exists. Enterprise is unlike speculation in that it uses wealth to produce new wealth, but it is alike in that it is not a zero-sum game. (If it were, it would be impossible for the economy to grow.) In a healthy economy it is possible for all reasonably astute producers to profit, at least to a degree. Prosperity in one business does not have to be counterbalanced by depression in some other; on the contrary, prosperity tends to spread.

II

Gambling, speculating, and enterprising all require money on a continuing basis. No sooner does one lottery pay off than its successor begins selling tickets. No sooner does the ball settle in the roulette wheel than the croupier calls for bets on the next spin. First and last, many billions are perpetually tied up in gambling of one sort or another (and we are speaking here only of legal gambling).

The sums invested in speculating are vastly greater. On a quiet day, over two hundred million shares will change hands on the different stock exchanges in the United States, to which must be added the option trading on the futures exchanges. All of this must be financed.

Almost all of this trading is of old or "secondhand" securities and has no necessary effect on the enterprises that gave rise to them. It is not denied that there may be indirect effects, as in events like the Campeau fiasco or in the way (absurdly exaggerated) in which the existence of a market for old investments may encourage the purchase of truly new issues. But the direct and ordinary effects are nil. It ordinarily makes no difference to an enterprise whether its stockholders are short term or long term, wise or foolish, genteel or riffraff. Nor does an enterprise ordinarily profit or lose from fluctuations in the market price of its securities. Although a price rising faster than the market average may make further financing easier to arrange and may also enhance the prestige and salaries of the firm's executives, the firm itself gets its money from each initial sale of its securities and is thereafter largely indifferent to what happens to the securities as old investments—except as a takeover or buyout becomes a possibility.

It is safe to say that practically the entire activity of the stock exchanges is devoted to speculation. There seem to be no statistics available on the proportion of exchange activity that concerns truly new enterprise, but even counting all new stock issues (and most of these merely refund old investments), it appears that the proportion is well under 1 percent. This speculative bias is likewise true of what preens itself as investment banking. Taken all together—stock exchanges, commodities markets, and investment banking—this business is very large. It is probably what President Calvin Coolidge had in mind when he said, "The business of America is business."

Exchanges of old investments necessarily cancel out. By definition, no new thing is involved; so whatever old thing someone buys, someone else has to sell. But the economy is not static, and the markets are not static, and something makes the exchanges worth the bother in the actual situation. That something is money.

Although no new thing is involved, the general level of the stock market—and of other markets, as well—can rise, because additional money goes into speculation.

III

The stock market is sui generis, neither exactly like an auction, nor exactly like an ordinary market where the producing economy buys and sells its wares. In an auction, whether for a bankrupt's final trinkets or for a sublime Old Master, the supply is limited. There is usually one and only one example of whatever is on the block, and there will be no more, at least not on this occasion. The demand, too, is limited; each prospective bidder has a strategy in mind and a final bid in mind. The bid, of course, has a dollar figure; so it seems not unreasonable to conceive of the auction as a contest or balance between a supply of money and, say, an Old Master.

Yet this is not quite right. All the bidders have more assets at their disposal than they're willing to venture on this sale. They may have many millions more. These extra funds affect the bids in the most casual ways. Because I have some pocket money to fool with, I may bid a couple of dollars for a plaster Venus de Milo with a broken clock inset in her belly, as a joke. Joke or not, my bid represents a demand for that supply of Venus. It is not money balanced against Venus, but demand for Venus against supply of Venus. I'd not make a similar bid for a kewpie doll; my fancy doesn't run that way.

Taking pocket money and available assets and all, the cumulated purchasing power at any auction—rural or sophisticated—might be called the money supply of the event. But most of it doesn't participate. Sometimes it may have nudged along the bidding, but it never nudges to the very limit of the supply.

The supply of stocks on the exchanges is also limited—fixed by the rules of the exchanges and the actions of the corporations' directors. The available supply at any given moment is much smaller than the authorized or issued supply, for many blocks of stock are not for sale at any price, and many more not for sale at any immediately likely price. On the other hand, when computer programs are churning the market, the same block of stock can be sold and resold many times in a few minutes, in effect increasing the supply of stocks, in the same way that high money velocity is said to increase the effect of the money supply.

Given the relatively fixed supply of stocks and the relatively fixed supply of money, we here come close to the classic formulation of the price level being determined by the money supply. The players certainly run from one fashionable stock or group of stocks to another, so that the price level is not so smooth as a millpond. On the other hand, the various stock indexes provide levels of sorts, and in bull or bear markets pretty much everything tags along.

Although it is theoretically possible for the general level of the market to rise merely because of a reduction in the supply of available stocks, a bull market cannot be sustained without a persisting influx of money. Likewise, a panic will greatly increase the supply of available stocks and will speed up the trading, so that a crash could theoretically occur without money leaving the market. Nevertheless, when such a panic subsided and the supply was reduced to normal levels, the market would quickly rebound to its prepanic level unless money had actually left it.

Needless to say, there is more to the stock market than the number of shares available. First, there are the "fundamental" values of the corporations that issue the stocks. It is reasonable for increased dividends or increased retained earnings to stimulate demand for a particular stock; but during the bull market from 1982 to 1987, the Standard and Poor's index of 400 industrials rose almost twice as fast as corporate profits after taxes. Second, and in recent years more important, the Federal Reserve Board's shifting maneuvers seeking to control the money supply, and necessarily affecting the interest rate caused reciprocal shifts in the value of every income-earning asset. The resulting volatility encouraged speculation. Neither of these factors is large enough to underwrite a bull market, and neither makes much difference in a crash. For such great movements, the market needs money coming in—or going out.

When money leaves the market in a crash, as in 1987, it simply disappears. If it went into cash, we'd see an instant doubling and redoubling of M1. If it went into productive new investment, we'd see a sharp rise in output. If it went into the bond or money market, we'd see a sharp fall in interest rates. If it went into commodities or real estate, we'd see sharp rises in those markets. If it went into consumption, we'd see a sharp rise in retail sales and, presumably, in consumers' prices. If it went, in some marvelously balanced way, into all these things, we'd see a sharp rise in GNP. If it went abroad, it could only be to places isolated from international finance. But after a crash we see none of these results. The money vanishes.

On October 20, 1987, as a free-fall threatened, Chairman Alan Greenspan announced: "The Federal Reserve, consistent with its responsibilities as the Nation's central bank, affirmed today its readiness to serve as a source of liquidity to support the economic and financial system." Thus a full-fledged panic was averted, but evidently the readiness was all. All four money measures fell, on a seasonally adjusted basis, from September to October, while in November M1 fell further, and M2, M3, and L went up only $2.4 billion, $15.0 billion, and $13.9 billion, respectively.[2]☆ (These comparatively small increases cannot, of course, be totaled, since the latter of each ordered pair includes the former.) If they were the result of the Federal Reserve Board's offer, they were new money, not money that had somehow safely escaped from the market, and anyhow they represented only a small fraction of the amount lost in the crash.

IV

It is not possible to say absolutely how much money disappears in a crash. Estimates of the losses in 1987 seem now to have settled at around a trillion dollars.[3]☆ Whatever it was, a vast sum simply vanished. It fell into a black hole, never to be seen again. Some people and some institutions had it one day; no one had it the next. The market was not a casino; the winnings were a long way from equaling the losings.

Yet the macroeconomic effect seems to have been slight. From this it is reasonable to infer that given the way the producing economy is organized—especially the way its rewards are distributed—it had no use for all those hundreds of billions of dollars. At the very least, we can say that the producing economy did not actually have the use of those hundreds of billions, whether it could have used them or not, and that the so-called recovery or expansion went on its sluggish way as though that money did not exist.

It is also reasonable to infer that the people who lost that money, whether as individuals or as managers of institutions, had no better use for it than to put it into the speculating economy.[4] We could of course argue about particular cases, but by and large this was true; and it certainly was true that they made no better use of it in fact. Many were no doubt foolish, but many others carefully considered the existing opportunities for productive investment and for consumption and rejected them for the stock market, perhaps as a lesser evil.

The uses to which they could put their money are after all limited. It could go into consumption, hoarding (or liquidity preference), new productive enterprise, or existing securities. If money goes into consumption, it causes the producing economy to expand; if it is invested in productive enterprise, it reduces the rate of interest the producing economy must pay to finance current business or expansion. If, however, it is held liquid or invested in existing securities, it is thereby denied to the producing economy and plays no part in it. Thus, as money flows into the speculating economy, the producing economy loses the increased sales or more manageable financing it might otherwise have enjoyed.

It loses nothing it actually is making use of, and this fact helps explain the producing economy's relative imperviousness to the 1987 crash. The producing economy had not used the money that went into the bull market and so was not affected when the money was lost. What the producing economy lost is merely what might have been. The loss or deprivation came at the very beginning and continued to grow as long as the bull market continued.

V

What might have been is lost forever. The jobs that never opened up, the goods that never were made and enjoyed, the services that were never performed—these were forestalled or aborted by the speculating. Their ultimate loss or nullity is what Wall Street cost the nation, and the world. The crash was incidental; the bull market itself had already done the damage.

The immediate sources of the lost money were the double-digit interest rate, which was encouraged to soar on the theory that the way to control inflation is to control employment, and the "supply side" tax cuts of 1981–82, which were mistakenly supposed to stimulate saving and investment. The theories behind the two sources were in conflict, but they share responsibility for the trillion-dollar increase in the national debt, which is roughly equal to the estimated loss in the market crash. These confused policies gave a trillion dollars of American money to people who couldn't use it; these people entrusted it to Wall Street; and Wall Street flushed it down the drain.

Whatever the immediate and intermediate sources of the money that was lost, its original source was the producing economy. Goods were made and sold and services performed, and people were paid for them. The pay took the forms of wages, salaries, interest, rent, profit, and taxes (because government produces goods and services, too). Ideally, those payments should have gone back into the producing economy for more goods and services. But several hundred billions of dollars of the payouts did not.

Some of these billions stayed out because of liquidity preference. As for the rest, it went into the speculating economy for the reasons we've already mentioned: The people who had it had no use for it, and the producing economy had no use for it. These reasons are, of course, flip sides of the same coin. The producing economy could have used the money if more people had bought its products, but several million of them didn't have money enough to do so. The tax decreases and the interest rate increases had given too much money to the wrong people. Other people could have spent the money on the products of industry, and industry could have expanded to give many of these people jobs. The industrial expansion could have brought money back from speculation.

The speculating economy exists and grows because the producing economy (including the public sector as well as the private) does not or cannot use all the wealth it produces. The public sector is myopically starved by a doctrinaire bias against public works and services, and there is not enough effective demand in the private sector to encourage investment. When present capacity can produce more than present consumers can afford to buy, producing more is folly. As both cause and consequence, we have a maldistribution of both income and taxation that gives many people more than they know what to do with, leaves vastly more people with less than they need for lives of decency and dignity, allows the decay of public necessities and amenities, and simultaneously drives the federal budget into deficit.

While a bull market drains money from the producing economy, a crash does nothing to restore it; it merely destroys the money that had been drained away. A bull market serves no purpose whatever. It creates nothing and reproduces nothing. The employment it provides performs no service for the public good. The money it sucks in it wastes. The market's claimed function of financing productive enterprise may be facilitated by liquidity; it is destroyed by volatility.

VI

Why should speculative frenzy get under way in the first place? Society certainly needs markets for old investments so that institutional endowments and pension and insurance funds can at least be suitably liquid. Yet these exchanges are not necessarily frenzied. What makes them become so?

The answer is usually given in psychological terms. Certain people are said to be speculators by nature (Keynes thought this true of Americans), and at times a speculative fever does seem to grip the land. The fever may be related to sunspots or to fear of war or to satisfaction with election returns. Sunspots aside, it will be remembered that the market broke in September 1939, and that it frequently rises after an election, no matter who wins. Such fluctuations are trivial; something more substantial than whim is surely at work in any sustained rise. An explanation will be found in a high interest rate, a volatile interest rate, or of course a combination of both.

A high rate of interest forces investors—whether individuals or corporations or "institutions"—to hunt for projects that turn around quickly. If the interest rate is 5 percent, the interest costs of a project that matures in six months are 2 1/2 percent or a little less, while those of a project that matures in five years are 27.6 percent. The latter is daunting enough; but when the rate is 10 percent, the five-year interest cost is equal to 55.3 percent of all other costs, or 35.6 percent of all costs, including interest. In contrast, a stock market manipulation that can be accomplished in, say, a week can earn at the rate of 10 percent if it gains as little as 0.2 of 1 percent on the money ventured. In the last quarter of 1987, almost half the *daily* shifts of the market were greater than 2 percent.[5]

Such considerations (which include no allowance for entrepreneurial profit) go a long way toward explaining the reluctance of American industry to invest in long-term development. Japanese managers are more far sighted than American managers, not because of differences in education or temperament or diet, but because the Japanese interest rate is less than half the American.[6] As long as the U.S. interest rate remains high, even a crash like that of 1987 does little to modify the systemic bias in favor of speculation.

A volatile interest rate obviously multiplies opportunities for trying to guess which way the rate is likely to jump. Whether the economy is likely to prosper becomes a secondary consideration, as is shown by the regularity with which, over the past decade, the market has risen on what ordinarily would be thought to be bad news (such as a fall in employment). A volatile rate also opens sudden gaps between the stock and the futures markets, thus sucking in vast sums whose investors hope to profit from the gaps.

That speculation is relatively short term is certainly of its essence and helps account for its perennial attractiveness. Speculation is a quicker way to make money than is production because it has no production time. Even when one buys land, expecting a town to expand eventually in a certain direction, one can sell out at any time if disappointed by the rate of expansion or if another speculator wants a piece of the action. Speculators can make much money fast, and a short-term investment must be concerned with the diurnal vagaries of the market. Today the vagaries are based on various statistics, periodically compiled and released, among them the money supply in its several forms, the budget deficit, the trade deficit, unemployment, inflation, and corporate plans. Probably less attention is paid to the last than to the others—perhaps because the last can be changed by human beings on their own say-so, while the others seem somehow impersonal. These others, moreover, dictate certain responses to followers of conventional economics—particularly to the governors of the Federal Reserve Board, who can be expected to try to make conventional adjustments in the money supply, hence in the interest rate, and hence in the capitalized value of assets. Long-term investment has to be based on both the future of the economy and the future of a particular industry. Although correctly foreseeing great postwar business activity and prosperity, one would have been a fool to invest in a photostatting business with Xeroxing on the horizon.

VII

Obsessed by fear of inflation, and eager for doctrinaire reasons to exercise control of the money supply, the Federal Reserve Board managed to free itself in 1951 from its 1942 agreement with the Treasury to stabilize the prices and yields of government securities, with the incidental effect of holding all interest rates down (the prime in those years remained at 1.50 percent). Thereafter the Reserve steadily (and unsuccessfully) attempted to control inflation by inflating the interest rate.

Following the appointment of Paul A. Volcker to the chairmanship in the summer of 1979, the Board decided to worry primarily about the money supply, allowing the interest rate to soar erratically. There is no doubt that the policy was designed to do what it ultimately did do: damp down enterprise and throw people out of work. The *New York Times* reported that when Volcker was asked whether tightened monetary policies (which the Board was pursuing) and tightened fiscal policies (which he advocated) would lead to recession, he replied, "Yes, and the sooner the better."[7] A decade later Volcker advised Zdzislaw Sadowski, president of the Polish Economic Society, that "of course" Poland must go through a recession.[8] Standard economics has no cure for inflation other than a recession, and no preventive of inflation other than stagnation. In either case, widespread unemployment is the main ingredient of the regimen.

Not only does speculation survive in conditions that damp down enterprise, it actually thrives in such conditions. Speculation, which usually depends on rising prices, is itself a stimulant to price rises. A rising interest rate requires price rises to pay the bankers' bills. A rising interest rate therefore fuels the inflation it was supposed to dampen. Thus the immediate effect of the 1979 decision to encourage the interest rate to surge was a simultaneous surge of inflation. It took four years of depression and all the suffering that that entailed to bring inflation down to a rate that, being the lowest in ten years, elicited much self-congratulation but was actually substantially higher than the trend of the decades before the Federal Reserve Board began to worry about the money supply.

VIII

Although it is a perversion of sound public policy to encourage speculation, it is nevertheless true that some sorts of speculation are inevitable and even useful in our world of uncertainty. Being unable to foretell the future, a business firm necessarily guesses when it orders capital goods for future delivery. When the goods come in, they may be worth more—or less—than the contract price, and the firm will accordingly realize what amounts to a speculative profit or loss. To minimize such swings, a firm will sometimes hedge by speculating in stocks, commodities, whatever. Thus, if the firm fears the delivered goods may turn out to be less valuable than the current price, it will sell speculations short. Then, if prices do fall, the money gained by the short-selling will offset the money lost on the capital goods. Of course, if inflation is anticipated, the buyer of capital goods is unlikely to hedge against that; but then the seller may hedge by hoping that an increase in the price of the securities he buys will offset increased costs of manufacturing the capital goods he sells.

It should be added that hedging, in spite of its occasional usefulness in helping individual firms to moderate profit swings has little or no effect on the prices firms charge and consequently little or no effect on the price level. On the other hand, by increasing the amount of money devoted to speculation, hedging participates in the general deleterious effect on the economy. This participation is true also of speculations in foreign currencies and also of collections of art and artifacts, whose prices are supported in large part by the expectation that they can eventually be sold or even given away at a handsome profit underwritten by misguided provisions of the inheritance tax and the charity deduction.[9]☆

Whenever the monetary authorities attempt contraction of the money supply, speculation will drain money from both production and consumption. Whenever the monetary authorities encourage a volatile interest rate, speculation will be stimulated and enterprise will suffer. Whenever the monetary authorities allow loans to support margin trading on the exchanges, speculation will be encouraged and enterprise will suffer. Whenever the taxing authorities give favored treatment to capital gains, speculation will again be encouraged and enterprise will again suffer.

It would be foolish to try to prevent all kinds of speculation, not because people are psychologically addicted to it, but because the uncertainty of our lives makes it inevitable. At the same time speculation can and should be controlled. The most effective control is to take the profit out of it. This can easily be done by capital gains taxation starting at 100 percent on sales of assets held less than one year and declining slowly to the same rate as on regular income on sales of assets held ten years or longer. Needless to say, this proposal is contrary to the voodoo economics currently popular in the United States.

11

PROPERTY

The Labor Theory of Right

I

Profit is the economic reward of enterprise, as wages are the reward of labor, interest the reward of lending money, rent the reward of lending land or utilities in the broadest sense. Profit, whether personal or corporate, is what is left after expenses have been paid. This simple definition, which is not esoteric but conforms with the actual accounting practice of actual business, will bear close attention, both for what it says and for what it does not say.

What this definition says is that profit is something other than wages, interest, or rent. It does not say that profit has any analyzable cause or any assignable amount. It is merely the remainder, at any given point, of the income from the sale of the enterprise's products, less their costs of production.

Profit is systematically different from interest, though the two are often confused. Interest is a fee paid according to contract for the use of money. Profit is the uncertain return of enterprise—that is, of making or doing something. When an entrepreneur provides his own money (or when a firm finances this year's expansion out of last year's profits), it may happen that an explicit charge is not made for the use of the money. It may also happen that an entrepreneur does not charge the enterprise for personal services rendered. In these situations, wages as well as interest become commingled with profits.

Enterprise always has something left over—it may be loss or it may be gain—because the future is unknown and unknowable. No matter how carefully we plan, we must, in the end, be more or less surprised. This is not merely a statistical result, as is the fact that half of the parties to a bet must be disappointed. Nor is it merely an empirical observation of the outcomes of the best-laid plans of mice and men. More important than statistics or empiricism, the systematic uncertainty of the future is a requirement of responsible action. If Pandora's box had not kept the future hidden, the present, too, would have been foreordained; life would have been a walking shadow; and there would not even have been a meaningful way of claiming that it was meaningless.

Insisting that something is always left over, we do not have to—indeed, we cannot—know where that something comes from. Our definition posits no specific source for profit. In some cases profit may be the result of chance or of a risk well run; in others the chance falls the other way. Sometimes it is the consequence (which for some enterprises may be favorable) of war or pestilence. Sometimes innovation is richly rewarded, and sometimes it is cruelly punished. Sometimes vigor achieves wonders; at other times what was hoped to be vigorous action proves to have been the rushing in of fools. Whatever we may decide, after the fact, to have been the source of a particular profit, an enterprise has no way of systematizing all sources of future profits and losses. Whatever is systematically accounted for is thereupon allocated and charged to wages, interest, or rent. Profit or loss will still be left over.

II

"Normal profit" is an informal concept regularly used in business.[1] Though informal, the concept has a great effect on the price level and on the state of the economy in general. It is not a determinate figure; statistics do not explain it. Rather, it is a determining figure; it sets a goal, a target, a standard by which prospective enterprises are judged. It is not an absolute standard like, say, the amount of radiation a human body can tolerate at a certain point. It is, instead, a rate, a percentage—which is understandable because its opportunity cost is a rate, the interest rate.

Though related to interest, normal profit is not, as the interest rate is, a contractual rate, but is a hoped-for rate, based on experience or history and subject to great fluctuations depending on the prevailing morale of society. A society or a firm marked by creative energy and good will will set the rate very low, while one racked by pessimism and financial greed will set it very high.

A high normal profit tends to impede enterprise because fewer enterprises will be judged likely to earn so much. Not only will fewer new businesses be started, but many existing businesses will contract their operations, shutting down those "profit centers" that seem unlikely to earn that normal profit.

If you expect it to be difficult to make a profit, you will make your task harder by demanding a higher rate. A higher normal profit will require higher prices, which will tend to reduce sales, which may cause diseconomies of scale, which will adversely affect total profits and, probably, the achieved rate of profit, too.

Adam Smith argued that increased profits have a geometric effect on prices, as opposed to an arithmetic effect of increased wages. But actual profits are merely what's left over after bills are paid and receivable collected; so they are affected by, but cannot affect, actual prices. Normal profits, on the other hand, being calculations made before the project begins, do have the effect Smith noted.

When wages are increased, it is by an absolute amount—so much an hour—but normal profits are increased a differential amount—such and such a percentage of costs, including wages. This percentage applies to every firm in the chain of production, from raw materials to final sale, and the increased normal profits of every firm lower in the chain are included in the base of higher firms. "The rise of profit," Smith concluded, "operates like compound interest. Our merchants and master-manufacturers complain much of the bad effects of high wages in raising the price, and thereby lessening the sale of their goods both at home and abroad. . . . They are silent with regard to the pernicious effects of their own gains."[2]

III

Since profits result from enterprise, profits should go to enterprise. As all modern economies have developed, however, profits accrue to capital, which is merely one of the factors of enterprise. This is obviously true of capitalism, and it is true of communism as well, where the means of production, which is another name for capital, are the property of the state, not of the enterprises that do the producing.

It is easy to understand how these arrangements came about. Until very recently, all enterprises were conducted by individuals or small groups of individuals who had, in one way or another, amassed the wealth used in their businesses. Whatever land they used was also owned by them. And they themselves directed the enterprises and in many cases performed all the work involved. Consequently it was reasonable for the profits to go exclusively to them; and when it was a question of selling the business, the decision was theirs and the rewards were theirs. Today, however, though individual enterprises in the classic manner are large in number, they do a small proportion of the business of the country, reap a minuscule share of the profits, employ a tiny minority of the workers, are typically not in manufacturing, and generally have short and erratic lives. Makers of better mousetraps are largely figments of nineteenth-century romantic imagination.

The modern corporation is itself the entrepreneur. It may have started as a one-man show, and it may continue under the dominance of one man. But he does not own it, and the profits go to those who do. The owners, moreover, and only they, have the right to sell the corporation or any part of it and to take for themselves the entire net proceeds of the sale. This is an unreasonable state of affairs, because, as everyone knows, the legal owners of a modern corporation have practically nothing to do with it. The legal fiction has it that the stockholders elect the directors, and that the directors appoint and oversee the officers who conduct the daily business of the corporation. In practice, unless a hostile takeover is in progress, officers generally select and dominate the directors, who are routinely elected by those stockholders who bother to return their proxies.

Not only do the stockholders have practically nothing to do with the corporation, they never wanted to have anything to do with it. They merely wanted to make an investment or to speculate on a takeover or merger. They had somehow come into some money, and they wanted to place it where it would be reasonably liquid and also have a chance of returning something more than bank interest. The invention of the limited liability company was a blessing for such people, and the blessing was magnified by the creation of efficient securities markets. Since, with few exceptions, shares are "fully paid and nonassessable," those who hold them need not worry about the company's debts, nor need they fear the loss, even in the extreme case, of more than they paid for the stock. And since they can sell out at any time, they need not fuss about providing alternatives to company policies they find unsatisfactory. Instead of trying to organize opposing points of view, they can sell out and register their meaningless disapproval in that way.

No matter what careless or even deliberate horror is perpetrated by their company, the owners accept no responsibility. They would not, they insist, have become owners if responsibility had been expected of them. How could they have known that the gasoline tank of the Pinto was unsafely designed? How could they have known that DES might cause cancer? How could they have known that exposure to asbestos could lead to leukemia twenty years later? And if there had been some way in which such knowledge could have been available to them, what could they as individuals, each with a few shares or even a few thousand shares, have done about it? There was no way in which they could effectively participate in the daily operations of Ford or Lilly or Johns Manville; and on the other side, the managements of those companies would claim that they could not operate with such participation. Aside from the confusion that would result, what could then be done to protect trade secrets (whatever they may be)?

What we have said so far is neutral as to persons. The personal ownership of consumers' goods presents no great problem; whoever consumes them thereby owns them. You can't possess the bread that I eat, and you have no desire to possess my toothbrush. I may be indebted to you for the cost of the bread or the toothbrush, but the bread and the toothbrush, themselves, are mine.

In general, there is no doubt that at least some consumers' goods can be personal property, although the rights they consist of may be limited or modified in various ways (for no right is absolute), and the limitations and modifications may change as the world changes. The great prob-

lems concern the ownership of producers' goods, because that ownership includes the right to control production. Those who own producers' goods have control of their fellows in a vital way.

IV

Property is not a thing but a bundle of enforceable rights.
In the beginning, rights are enforced by one's strong right arm, and
property is accordingly what a person can physically take possession of.
"An Englishman's home is his castle," expresses the idea, which was,
over the centuries, elaborated by the common law. Adam Smith called
this right "value in use," which he distinguished from another right,
"value in exchange."

The recognition of exchange-value is indeed a characteristic of modern capitalism. In the United States it is scarcely a hundred years old
and is not yet fully understood. In *Legal Foundations of Capitalism*,
one of the neglected great books, John R. Commons wrote, "Finally,
in the first Minnesota Rate Case, in 1890 the Supreme Court itself
made the transition and changed the definition of property from physical things having use-value to the exchange-value of anything."[3] Prior
to that decision the courts would enforce only one's right to hold
property. The question did not come before the Supreme Court until
the Thirteenth Amendment ended property in people and the Fourteenth Amendment extended responsibility for civil rights to the states.
In the Slaughter House Cases of 1872, the Court, in a split decision,
held that, under the law, property was merely use-value. The contrary
view was presented powerfully in dissent but did not finally prevail until
eighteen years later.

Exchange-value makes property an idea, not a fact. It is what people
think they can do with it that determines it. Its setting is historical. It
looks to the future. It is an opportunity for doing. It is also a problem,
the consequence of a past doing. Less abstractly, if I have worked to
build up a bookstore, I can work to continue it or expand it or even
sell it, but I can scarcely turn it into a filling station. Past doing makes

present and future doing possible; it establishes opportunity but not formless or unrestricted opportunity.

Exchange-value is the capitalization of expected profits, not of realized profits. Past profits are spent, just as past costs are sunk; future costs and future profits are what rule. As property becomes idealized in this way, it comes to include what Commons called good will, which is not merely reputation based on past performance but a system of continuing relationships. A business is a going concern or it is nothing. If I auction off my goods and chattels, I do not establish a continuing relationship with the buyers or even with the auctioneer; my auction is not a business.

The organization of a business counts for more than its physical assets. Tools and machinery, factories and warehouses can be bought outright, or their services can be rented. It is not different with good will, which is frequently the real object of takeover and buyout contests. Without the brand names, RJR Nabisco's factories and warehouses would scarcely have been worth what was paid for the company in 1989. Good will can be rented as well as bought, as when large sums are paid to advertising agencies for discovering and dramatizing the secret built-in goodnesses that identify products, when enormous sums are paid to electronic and print media for access to audiences they have built up, and when further sums are paid to athletes and other celebrities for endorsements. Even good organization can be rented, as witness the burgeoning business of consulting. The owners and purveyors of these capital goods and services, regardless of whether they created them or developed them or inherited them or merely found them, are paid for their use or purchase at market prices, which like all market prices are quite independent of the goods' origin, difficulty of manufacture, and so on.

"Owning capital," Joan Robinson said, "is not a productive activity."[4] Extending her remark, we can say that neither ownership of capital, ownership of land, ownership of labor power, nor ownership of money is a productive activity. Ownership of these goods and services is not the enterprise and so is not entitled to the profits of the enterprise, but only to the profits of the goods and services themselves, that is, to purchase prices or fees for service. It may happen that any of these various owners participates in a given enterprise, but only workers necessarily do so. From the point of view of the enterprise, managers (who are paid salaries and bonuses) and even directors (who collect fees for service) are employees, grander perhaps but not essentially different from laborers on the factory floor.

V

The foregoing considerations lead to what I call the Labor Theory of Right. Because labor, whether current labor or past labor, is the source of economic goods, many have attempted to find in labor the source of value. These attempts have failed, as we have seen, but the impulse behind them was sound. It is by labor and only by labor that we produce goods and come to possess them. Nothing exists except in conjunction with human activity. Whatever is made is made by the hand of man or woman—literally manufactured—and whatever services are performed are performed by men and women. Labor is primary, though not the source of value. Instead, labor is the source of right.

Even conventional theory is ultimately based on the Labor Theory of Right. Whatever one owns came into existence—not as a mere object but as an economic good—as a result of labor. Its production entailed the use of producers' goods, but they in their turn are the result of labor, and they came into one's possession as a result of labor, whether one's own or someone else's. Land and natural resources remain natural objects unless cultivated or collected. Thus the entitlement of land and capital to participate in profit depends, even as understood by apologists for the present system, on the fact that they are the embodiment of past labor. The entitlement of current labor is immediate; the workers are present, and the sweat glistens on their brows. But the entitlement of the owners of capital is secondary; it depends on the fact that their capital was itself once a direct entitlement of labor. Thus their entitlement cannot rise higher than that of labor, which is its source. What is past, what is even dead and gone, cannot take precedence over what is now and is continuing.

Abstinence, the classical basis for the rights of capital, is not the exclusive province of stockholders and bondholders. The workers' abstinence is no less severe; they stay on the job instead of going fishing or lying in the sun. Some workers may not absent themselves from felicity to the satisfaction of some observers. The same can be said of some holders of portfolios.

Nor is risk taking an exclusive function of capital. Life is risky, and no life more risky than that of propertyless working men and women. The stockholders' risk is obvious; they may lose their shirts and have to work to get others. The laborers' risk is not less real for being possibly less dramatic; they devote time and sometimes money to learning a skill that may become worthless if the enterprise fails. They are also more closely committed to the enterprise (even when they hate it) than are the stockholders or bondholders. It is more difficult for them to pull out at the first sign of faltering, for jobs are hardly ever easy to find, and they cannot handily move from town to town in search of work. The stockholders or bondholders have only to call their brokers. Finally, the workers may be ruined by the company's decision to move from one locality to another, while the stockholders may gain from such a shift.

The right of labor to participate in profit is bolstered by the implications of any employment contract. As we saw in the little hiring scenario in Chapter 5, it is in the nature of things necessary either for employers to pay their employees in advance or for employees to do a job before they are paid for it. The latter option being the custom in our system, the employees of any business have their earnings for half a pay period on perpetually revolving interest-free loan to the business. As a result, the business can make a corresponding expansion of plant or inventory or marketing services. In short, its capital is increased by this contribution of labor as effectively as it is by the cash contributions of capitalists.

Thus there is no right that capitalists can claim that laborers do not have a claim to. If capitalists have a right to control enterprise, so do laborers. If capitalists have a right to receive profits—or suffer losses— so do laborers. So far, the right of one is not stronger than the right of the other. A good society, however, will recognize the wisdom and justice of Jefferson's dictum: "The earth belongs to the living and not to the dead."

VI

Rights exist only as they are asserted. No right exists merely because it is asserted, but no right exists unless it is asserted. The assertion of a right is an act of will, and the recognition of a right, as by law, is an act of will in which everyone participates as a member of society. The failure to assert a right is also an act of will, as is the failure to accept responsibility; and the failure of the law to assign a responsibility is a failure of the will of the society.

Il gran rifiuto of today's economic life is the stockholders' assertion, supported by the law, of ownership rights and their simultaneous refusal, also supported by the law, of all ownership duties whatever. Classical entrepreneurs were proud of their enterprises. They were textile manufacturers, dry-goods merchants, railroaders. No one claims that such commitment was or can be a certain preventive of abuses of all kinds—abuses of workers, of investors, of the public—but it does clear a ground of responsible action for those with the will to occupy it. To be a conglomerate person is to be nobody in particular, with no commitment to anything in particular except the bottom line, the bottom line or a speculative killing being in fact the only excuses for the conglomerate.

To be a portfolio holder is to be even less significant, especially since so much of today's typical middle-class portfolio is made of mutual funds, money-market funds, insurance policies, and the like. Although the funds' shareholders regularly receive reports of the securities their funds own, it is safe to say that they could not name many of them and are unlikely to know more about any of them than may be compressed into a paragraph of a broker's newsletter. They have nothing to do with the success or failure of their funds and far less to do with the companies they partially and indirectly own than the proverbial office boy.

The attenuation of ownership has reached a point where between one-third and one-half the shares of most of our large corporations are owned by "institutions"—not only mutual funds, but insurance and pension funds, charitable endowments, churches, colleges and universities, public service foundations, and private trust funds generally. At first glance one might think that the vesting of ownership in such responsible hands would make for stability. Quite the contrary. The managers of the funds are indeed responsible, but theirs is a fiduciary responsibility, which constrains them to accept whatever offer promises the highest immediate gain for their beneficiaries. If they do not they may find themselves defendant in a suit for damages. Thus it can happen that the trustees of a corporate pension fund that owns some of the corporation's stock will vote those shares in favor of a takeover, and the takeover will result in the beneficiaries' loss of their jobs and possibly of the pension rights that presumably were being protected. Nor are the managers of mutual funds less likely to jump for the quick buck, for their performance will be judged by what they have done this day or this quarter. Neither trustees nor managers can afford to be bothered by what may happen to the companies they have temporarily invested in. And individual stockholders, too preoccupied with their own affairs to take an intelligent interest in their companies, are no different.

This triumph of finance over enterprise is inexorable so long as ownership carries no responsibilities. Irresponsible owners are classical economic men par excellence, and they will go where they can get the most of what they are interested in, which is money. They will consequently put pressure on brokers to find for them companies that will slake their thirst; brokers will pressure investment bankers to float the issues of such companies; investment bankers will pressure commercial bankers to give priority to such companies; and all pressure will be brought to bear on the management of every public company to do whatever needs to be done to increase the bottom line.

That frequently the easiest way to increase the bottom line is to go, as they say, the merger-and-acquisition-and-diversification route is only the most visible outcome. Such maneuvers generally can increase the bottom line only by "rationalizing" the merged companies—which means closing plants and firing people. In such circumstances, loyalty is comprehensively destroyed. No one is or can afford to be loyal to the enterprise—not the owners, not the fiduciaries, not the financiers, not the suppliers, not the management, not the work force, not the customers. Nor are owners, fiduciaries, financiers, suppliers, managers, workers, or customers encouraged to be loyal to each other.[5] This atomization of concern is doubtless a major cause of the widely deplored decline in standards of workmanship. It certainly is a major cause of increased speculation on Wall Street.

VII

Marx had an apocalyptic vision of a final battle between capital and labor, but it didn't come to pass on any of the several occasions when he expected it in his lifetime, nor is there reason to expect that the struggle will end of itself. To be sure, there is no lack of peacemakers ready to demonstrate that capitalists and workers need each other, nor is there a lack of more or less grudging acceptance of that mutual need. Otherwise the economy would not work at all. But there are times when the mutuality disappears. These are, typically, times of change, when a business is faltering, or, contrariwise, when a technological leap forward seems possible or desirable.

In depressions or recessions some capitalists lose some money, but many workers lose their jobs. This outcome is so commonplace that no one even thinks to defend it. I doubt that it can be defended. If both capital and labor are essential to production, by what right are things more worthy of protection or conservation than people?

As for technological advances, they have always been resisted by workers. Yet Britain could not have achieved its first breakthrough if landowners had not enclosed the commons and driven tenants off the land to make way for sheep. Later, if the Luddites had had their way, the Industrial Revolution would have been aborted; and if the followers of Captain Swing had prevailed, the denizens of the cities could not have been fed even as well as they were.

As economists and editorialists scold, automobile workers resist giving up their jobs to robots. Labor-saving machines are opposed as labor-eliminating devices. Why can't these people see that new robotic industries will make new jobs, just as automobile making turned out to employ many times as many people as harness making? Why should anyone in his right mind fight to preserve mind-deadening work on the old-fashioned production line? What is so great about conditions in Southern textile mills that leads people to want to keep them going in the face of cheap imports from the Orient?

Society is certainly better off with more mechanization, more robotization. It is a blessing that the bulldozer and the earthmover have supplanted those who used to "push-a, push-a, push on the Delaware-Lackawan'." It is a blessing that the backhoe has made "ditchdigger" an obsolete term of opprobrium. It is a blessing that the dishwasher has replaced the scullery maid. Not only is such progress irresistible, it is largely beneficial.

But there is trouble in paradise. The trouble is systemic. The individuals who are displaced by progress are systematically denied the benefits of progress. The working class or the worker-as-function may be better off in the famous long run, but the individual workers will often lose not only money but job, career, independent livelihood, sometimes forever. None of this necessary. It is a result of the faulty design of the modern corporation.

VIII

The irresponsibility of stockholders has been widely noted, and much ingenuity has been lavished on proposals to correct the situation. Some of these notions try in one way or another to make it easier for dissidents to be elected to the boards of directors, thus presumably encouraging stockholders to pay attention. Others would mandate representatives of "the public" on the boards, thus trying to make the boards responsible to somebody, regardless of the fact that the stockholders are responsible to no one.

Such schemes are doomed to failure, not because they are necessarily wrong-headed, but because no one actually wants them. A few enthusiasts now busy themselves in attending and speaking up at stockholders' meetings, but investors with prudently diversified portfolios could not possibly master the intricacies of the businesses they partly own. They realize they could not; so they sensibly find better things to do with their time. Public board members would not be in much better case. They could not expect to make a career attending board meetings, nor could they realistically expect to learn enough about any company to be useful. The most likely outcome is that they would be co-opted by their genial colleagues; and if they should entertain ideas at variance with those of the rest of the board, they would find it difficult to overcome the pressures of small-group psychology, especially as the public to whom they were supposed to be responsible would not only be largely indifferent but would have no way of supporting or rejecting or learning about the board members' ideas.

More important, the public's interest in any particular company is abstract and can be satisfied by general laws. The public is reasonably concerned that the corporation pay its taxes, abjure fraud, respect its workers, not harm the environment, and refrain from skittering hither and thither in search of weak regulation and lower taxes. These ends could and should be served otherwise. There is, however, no rational possibility of framing a law requiring stockholders to assume any responsibility that they could not in practice discharge—one, moreover, that neither they nor the corporations they invest in want them to have.

Why, then, should stockholders, who refuse the duties of ownership, be protected in the rights of ownership? There is actually only one reason: They now enjoy those rights. Abstinence and risk taking they share with bondholders and employees; management they leave to a special kind of employee. What is left is possession, and that is nine points of the law. The tenth point, however, is rationality, and movement should be in that direction.[6]

IX

In his book *Beauty Looks After Herself,* Eric Gill wrote that a slave does what he has to do when he is at work and what he wants to do on his own time, while a free man does what he wants to do when he is at work and what he has to do on his own time. On this basis, most men and women are slaves, though in bondage only to themselves. The reasons for this are various, and they are by no means all economic.

The economic reasons flow largely from the authoritarian and megalomaniac structure of most contemporary business enterprises. Small is indeed beautiful. This is not because small is more efficient than giantism. Maybe it is, and maybe it isn't. The beauty of smallness is in the eye of the producer, not necessarily of the consumer. A small company can be a better place to work than a large one. Small institutions can allow more scope for individual assertiveness and creativity and responsibility of all kinds than large ones do. But there is no necessity about this. Her people and her institutions made Athens the school of Hellas, as Pericles said; the less-distinguished neighboring city-states were less remarkable but not because they were larger or smaller.

The beauty of smallness is that it diffuses power, not that it expands competition. Neither competition nor its mirror image, cooperation, is an end in itself. Competition is the sanitized descendant of Thomas Hobbes's war of all against all, and cooperation is the prudent alternative to that war.

Theory has it that competition spurs workers to greater productivity and entrepreneurs to cheaper and more plentiful products. Without this spur, it is said, the world would stumble, while with the spur the economy leaps from triumph to triumph—and not just the economy, because statesmen and artists and scholars compete for fame, as workers and entrepreneurs compete for money.

This is a pretty story, often told, and there is much truth in it, but it has an ugly side. As early as Ricardo, it was argued that competition drives wages down to the subsistence level and keeps them there. The competition of entrepreneur against entrepreneur prevents even the tender hearted from paying more, while the competition of worker against worker prevents even the stout hearted from holding out for more. This is the Iron Law of Wages, which prompted Carlyle to call economics the dismal science.

Not only does competition have an ugly side, it also turns out to be diffuse and shapeless. One can, for example, read only so many suspense novels in a year; so a given suspense novel obviously competes with all the other suspense novels in print. But it also competes with true spy stories, with movies, with a TV on the installment plan, with other forms of entertainment, with forms of quasi-entertainment (like a new gadget for an automobile), and ultimately with everything on the market. At any given moment, whatever a consumer spends on one thing cannot be spent on something else. This fact emboldens apologists for big business to argue that even oligopolies must operate in the market as if so-called perfect competition obtained. If automobile manufacturers tried to gouge consumers, it is explained, the latter would run their old cars a while longer and spend their money on something else.

There is some truth in this tale, too. But if everything competes with everything, there is no need to worry (as some, like Friedrich Hayek, do) about an end to the "competitive system."[7] What exists anyhow, regardless of what anyone does, needs no defense and indeed admits of none. Consequently it is understandable that the courts have been unable to settle on a clear approach to antitrust law.[8] A prime example of the absurdity of trying to use competition as a touchstone for the organization of business is the provision of the Clayton Act that a company may engage in certain business practices otherwise defined as unfair if it can show it does so to meet competition.

Similar difficulties and absurdities would arise if cooperation were substituted as the touchstone. We are all interdependent, and so cooperation is as universal as is competition; there is honor even among thieves. Courts devoted to the idea of cooperation would, in addition, be bewildered by the ancient common-law notion of conspiracy, particularly a conspiracy in restraint of trade.

X

The invisible hand was supposed to drive prices down and quality up. Galbraith has taught us not to expect the market to work that way in the world of big business, which he calls the planning system.[9] But it doesn't work as it is famed to do even in what he calls the market system.

In the textbook business, which is minutely fragmented and fiercely competitive, competition frequently has the effect of pushing prices up rather than down. As an apposite example, we may consider one of the biggest submarkets of the textbook market—the freshman principles of economics course. Fifty years ago the texts for this course looked like ordinary books; you could hold them in one hand while you read them; and you could carry them to class without backache. Then one of the publishers got the idea of dressing up his entry with a second color and a larger paper size, which would sometimes make the graphs a bit easier to understand and might make the whole thing look livelier—more like a magazine. The innovations would have approximately doubled the printing costs if the publisher had not dramatically increased his market share. The increased attractiveness increased sales, which permitted longer press runs, which helped hold the price down. But of course the

other publishers quickly copied the innovations, with the result that
each publisher soon had roughly the same market share as before. Press
runs were necessarily reduced to those of precolor days; so unit costs
went up. As costs went up, so did prices. It cannot be pretended that
students' understanding of economics has improved proportionately.

Such a competitive dance is performed in many another industry,
forcing prices up rather than down, reducing the variety of goods
offered for sale, and generally (as a book of business advice once had
it) selling the sizzle rather than the steak. This outcome is a puzzle to
classical economists, but it can be readily explained. The explanation
does not, I hasten to add, turn on the slyness of the competitors, who
are no worse and no better than anyone else.

The explanation does turn on one or two facts about the industries
involved. In the textbook business, for example, demand is restricted.
There are only so many students taking freshman economics in any
given year; so there is nothing any publisher can do to make much
difference in the size of the market. Students who have one textbook
have no use for another at any price. The students, moreover, themselves have restricted options. Assuming that they're going to study at
all, they can buy a new copy of the textbook, or they can buy a
secondhand copy, or they can borrow their roommate's copy. They do
not have the option of substituting something else. If the assigned text
is Mansfields's, they can hardly make do with Samuelson's, and they
certainly can't substitute *The Norton Anthology of English Literature*,
no matter how great a bargain it is.

Faced with this restricted market, publishers have correspondingly
restricted options. If they want a larger share of the market, they can
seek it by lowering their price or "upgrading" their product, or both.
A little business experience will convince them that price lowering, by
itself, is seldom the solution of choice. Henry Ford almost ruined his
company by sticking doggedly with his Model T long after Chevrolet
had come out with a somewhat more practical, more comfortable, and
more stylish competitor at a higher price. At the other end of the
business scale, restaurants find it profitable to serve extra-large portions
at extra-large prices. The gourmands among their customers will hap-
pily eat what's put before them, and the gourmets will be delighted to
take home a doggy bag full of expensive morsels for their pets (or for
their own next-day's supper). In all these instances, producers have

found again and again that while price may be a factor, it is by no means the most significant factor in the competition for market shares.

A restricted supply will similarly upset the classical theory that competition invariably benefits consumers. In spite of the frenzy of the fall of 1983, there was not, it turned out, a substantial shortage of Cabbage Patch dolls. Competition forced retailers to bid the price up in order to get something to draw customers into their stores; consequently a little shortage became, as a result of competition, a temporarily big one. Something like this happens almost every Christmas without hurting anyone very much. (There is one case in which almost everyone is hurt, and seriously, and that is the case of banking.)

The failure of competition to perform as theory says it does is no surprise to anyone, not even to classical economists. Examples of the failure are too many and too obvious, but they are blandly countered by the proposition that the public gets what it demands. No one really believes that, and the proposition cannot be proved or disproved on its own terms. The theory says that competition gives the public what it demands; therefore what the public gets is what it demanded. This form of reasoning is known as *petitio principii*, or begging the question, or assuming what you pretend to prove.

XI

If the invisible hand actually did turn unregulated competition to beneficent ends, the ancient rule of caveat emptor should perhaps be resuscitated. Professor Herbert Stein, formerly chairman of the Council of Economic Advisers, once made a widely retailed mot to the effect that people of liberal mind trust anyone over eighteen to vote for president of the United States but don't think the common man or woman capable of buying a bicycle without do-gooding governmental intervention.

But a purchase is not a one-way transaction; I don't get a bicycle for nothing. When I buy one from Professor Stein for $199.99, I give him two hundred-dollar bills, and he gives me a penny and the bike. Professor Stein says that I, the emptor, should make myself a self-reliant expert on bicycles before I trade in his shop and that if what he sells me proves dangerous or shoddy, it's my fault, not his.

If so, why shouldn't caveat emptor be balanced by caveat venditor? If he can (unintentionally or maybe not) sell me a dangerous or shoddy bicycle at my peril, why can't I pay him with counterfeit hundred-dollar bills, at his peril? Or a rubber check? Why shouldn't he be required to make himself a self-reliant expert on these matters, and not go running to the sheriff for help?

Obviously it's no answer to say that counterfeiting is against the law. That law could be repealed, just as the Federal Trade Commission can be hamstrung. Nor is it any answer to say that check bouncing is cheating and so immoral and bad for the soul; the same can be said for selling dangerous bicycles. Nor is it any answer to say that government regulations impose an intolerable burden of paperwork on the bicycle business. The legal requirement that I have enough money in my account to cover my checks means that I must balance my checkbook, and that's an intolerable burden of paperwork, if you ask me.

Paper money, personal checks, and credit cards have been good for business. They make business easier to transact. Seller and buyer don't need to wear out their teeth biting coins. Within broad limits, they can trust what is proffered. They can trust, because this is in general a trustworthy society. And it is a trustworthy society in part because the sanctions of the criminal law enforce the trust.

If recipients of rubber checks had to rely on the civil law, they'd be faced with endless delays and absurd costs. They would spend hundreds or thousands of dollars, not to mention hours of court appearances, to get a judgment that they'd still have difficulty collecting. They couldn't afford such costs, so they couldn't afford to accept checks, so they'd have to restrict themselves to much slower and smaller cash-only business. The threat of criminal penalties, enforced by the state, deters check cheats and makes it possible for merchants to trust the rest of us, to the merchants' benefit and ours.

What's sauce for the goose is sauce for the gander. I'd be readier to buy Professor Stein's bicycle if I knew it's safe and I'd be surer it's safe if I knew the law would crack down on him if it weren't. I can't afford to sue him for damages unless I've been catastrophically hurt, which neither of us wants to happen. Since he really does not intend to cheat me, and I really do not intend to cheat him, we'll both be better off if we know the law will call those who do cheat to account; we'll both be better able to trust each other.

Perhaps more important, if the law made it possible for me to trust what is offered for sale, I'd no longer have to make dubious reliance on brand names as guarantees of product quality. Then Lewis Mumford's vision of the efficiency of parochial production might become a reality, and so might E. F. Schumacher's vision of the beauty of smallness. Then, too, Ralph Nader would at last be recognized as the champion of the free market.

XII

The great refusal of the stockholders has an apparent parallel in the reluctance of the generality of workers to participate in management. The parallel is only apparent. The stockholders refuse to play a role that is now legally theirs, while the workers are slow to fight for a role that is rightfully theirs.

There are many reasons for this. In the history of American labor relations, workers have been able to improve their lot primarily through tradewide and industrywide unionization. Given what must be reckoned a persistent bias of the courts, the workers have been at the scarcely restricted mercy of the bosses. Their survival has depended on their solidarity with one another, rather than on the prosperity of the firms they work for. Even profit sharing has been looked at askance and usually rejected as a disguised form of the speedup.

Employee ownership is not without its supporters. In the 1920s Edward A. Filene, searching for a way out of the misery of early-twentieth-century industrialism, became a strong advocate. Accordingly he tried to establish a form of employee ownership in his Boston department store, but was disappointed to discover that most of the employees were not interested or were overawed by a few of their more energetic fellows.

In spite of many such experiences, enthusiasts for employee ownership claim that self-interest will make the employees work harder, and that employee-owned firms will therefore outperform conventional corporations if not drive them out of business.[10] Nothing like this has happened. Self-interest remains undefined; and some employee-owned firms are efficient; some are not. Efficiency is not the issue; justice is. It is desirable to be efficient, it is vital to be just.

12

PRODUCTIVITY

*Why Micro and Macro Don't
Always Mix*

I

Though the gross national product is a comparatively new idea, and though statistics relating to it have been systematically collected for not much more than fifty years, the term "GNP" has passed into the common vocabulary, where it is frequently invoked as an infallible guide to proper policies. The idea is, however, of severely limited usefulness, and its misuse confuses and misleads public action.

It may be helpful to cite a few examples. A recent budget for the United States space shuttle and related activities was $6.9 billion. The same amount of money could have paid for roughly 100,000 units of public housing, whose construction, incidentally, would probably have employed more workers than the shuttle. It is a matter of judgment whether more communications satellites are more in the public interest than more housing; but the GNP is of no help in making that judgment, because the two programs have closely similar effects on the GNP.

Again: The Johns Manville asbestos products swelled the GNP three ways: first, when the products were manufactured and installed; second, when doctors, nurses, hospitals, pharmaceutical manufacturers, lawyers, judges, and insurance adjusters were employed because of the resulting cancers; and third, when workmen were employed in removing the asbestos installations. Anyone with his eyes solely on the GNP would be delighted with these results, but they were catastrophic for many individuals and wasteful for the society.

Again: Mark Twain dramatized the irrelevance of the GNP in his quip about two women who "earned a precarious living by taking in each other's washing." If a woman renounces home washing and takes a job in a commercial laundry, she thereby increases the GNP. She may also enlarge her life and increase her contribution to society, but whether she does so or not will not be discovered by examining the GNP.

Again: In the 1970s Brazil was widely hailed as a wonder-working economy because of the rapid increase of its GNP. A decade later, however, it was evident that the apparent prosperity had had only adverse effects on the lives of the squatters in the hillside *favelas* behind Rio and the sugar workers in the northeastern provinces. Strict attention to the GNP had misled the world's bankers, who consequently sponsored an economic as well as a social failure.

Again: If you are a manufacturer of a detergent or of anything else for a broad market, you will find the GNP irrelevant or misleading. Your proper concern will be whether there are enough people employed and well enough paid to buy your product. And if you are a purveyor of diamond bracelets, you will base your output on the number of millionaires, not on the GNP.

There is nothing in the foregoing that is not well known, and the examples could be endlessly multiplied. Yet economists and businessmen and public officials maintain their faith in the GNP. Measures that would protect us from pollution of our environment and damage to our health are routinely opposed because they would, it is said, decrease production. (Ironically, those who oppose conservation generally call themselves conservatives.) The habit of thought is pervasive; even so-called liberal economists tend to talk of a trade-off between a healthful environment and production, and Third World public officials protest that they cannot "afford" to be concerned with health or safety.

Such trade-offs are only too obvious in one-company towns where the single factory is a gross polluter of air and water. When threatened with laws requiring it to clean up its operations, the company counterthreatens to shut down the plant altogether and thus destroy the town's excuse for existence. The threat and counterthreat indicate an incompatibility of microeconomics, the economics of the individual or firm, with macroeconomics, the economics of the nation or society.

II

The division between microeconomics and macroeconomics is well established. It was not always thus. The names of the divisions do not appear in the first edition of *Oxford English Dictionary*, published in 1933, or in the second edition of *Webster's New International Dictionary*, whose last issue was copyright in 1953. Now, however, college courses routinely appear under one rubric or the other. What has been put asunder is not easily joined or rejoined.

Indeed, they cannot be joined so long as economic activity is taken to be the maximization of material gain by the individual, the firm, and the nation. That the material interests of these parties are not always identical or even parallel is too obvious to discuss and consequently is not discussed except in homilies of the sort that everyone recognizes as self-serving. When the boss harangues the workers with the thought that they're all players on the same team, the latter are forewarned of a policy likely to benefit someone else more than it benefits them. When President Eisenhower's Secretary of Defense "Engine Charlie" Wilson, former head of General Motors, piously proclaimed, "What's good for General Motors is good for America," everyone laughed, and the laughter did not need explanation. When private citizens closet themselves with Form 1040, or corporation financial officers with Form 1120, neither takes seriously the form's inspiring prefatory message from the commissioner of Internal Revenue.

It is worthwhile to stop a minute and note that the foregoing are all examples of the fallacy of composition, which is so frequently encountered in economics discussions that it may be called the economics fallacy. The error lies in assuming that what is true of every member of a logical class is true of the class itself, or vice versa, that what is true of a class is true of each of its members. For other examples: since every event has a cause, it is illicitly concluded that the universe—that is, all events together—has a cause. Or in economics, since individuals can become rich by hoarding, the nation will be more prosperous if consumption is discouraged.

The division between macroeconomics and microeconomics is more than rhetorical. Standard microeconomics holds that the purpose of business enterprise is profit maximization, and it follows as a principle of successful business management that it's sensible to cut your losses. Any fledgling MBA has a quick eye for seeing how any firm's activities can be divided into semiautonomous "profit centers" and a quick ear for hearing which profit centers are now yielding a desired rate of profit, which ones can be made to do so, and which ones are hopeless. Those in the last category may in fact be profitable; they are just not profitable enough. The minimum acceptable rate of return is the money-market rate. If you can get, say, 10 percent just by lending your money to someone else, why should you go to the bother of running a business that earns less than 10 percent? Or if you do, in the course of your business, borrow money from banks (which is one thing banks are for), and if you pay a rate of little better than that 10 percent, you're obviously not doing very well with a profit center that doesn't earn more than you pay.

So you are advised to sell the weak profit center if possible, otherwise to liquidate it. You will probably have to take a loss, but at the current corporation tax rates, about a third of your loss will be paid for by the government via the reduction of your income and hence of your tax bill. The funds thus freed can then be applied to the promising profit centers, or put into the money market, or used to reduce your corporate debt. However you use the funds, the net profit of your company will be improved.

Consider a profit center that is earning 4 percent on invested capital of a million dollars, while the firm's target is 14 percent. Even if the weak profit center—workers, customers, inventory, plant, and all— were abandoned as a total loss, the aftertax result would be that about a third of a million dollars would be available for use in the centers that earn 14 percent or more. Fourteen percent of a third of a million dollars is $46,667, while 4 percent of a million is only $40,000.

Such vandalism, which is sometimes hailed as "creative destruction,"[1] is bad enough in the arena of microeconomics. The workers and the customers are injured, and the inventory and plant—and the work that went into them—wasted in a world of shrinking resources. The injury and the waste are far greater when macroeconomic problems are approached in the same way. It is said that just as in a firm there are many profit centers, so in the nation there are many firms. On this analogy it is widely thought that national policy should be directed toward encouraging strong firms and weeding out weak ones.

Analogy is a seductive form of argument that at best is only suggestive. In the present instances, there are two crucial differences between the analogies and the actual world. The first is that what is weeded out by the proposed policies are not tares among the wheat but human beings—people, men and women, fellow citizens. The second is that there is no way, in the actual world in which we live, for new industries, no matter how promising, to replace old industries, no matter how unfruitful, in the twinkling of an eye. The replacing can be done in an equation, on paper, in an instant; but in the real world it takes time. The real world is a world of human beings who exist in time and only in time. Things done or made take time, and the less primitive they are, the more time they take.

Moreover, the write-off against taxes that provides much of the incentive at the micro level does not work at the macro level. A corporation can shift much of its loss onto the other taxpayers, but the national wealth must suffer the entire loss of any destruction.

It would have been absurd to imagine that the Lockheed or Chrysler plants could have been immediately—or ever—converted to producing electronic devices or processing information or whatever industries were expected to take their place. Yet ordinarily responsible citizens did in fact allow themselves to brush aside the facts that tens or hundreds of thousands of fellow citizens would have had their livelihoods destroyed, and that millions of dollars' worth of plant would have been laid waste as effectively as if it had been bombed. All this destruction would have been in the supposed interest of some new industry that no one could even name. The proposed destruction might have been acceptable—you can't make an omelet without cracking eggs—if anyone had had in mind how and how quickly the displaced people and plants could be restored to usefulness. But no one has the right to bet other people's lives on the hope that something will turn up for them in the long run.

Nor are such macroeconomic effects valid even in the timeless world of classical economics. If the gross national product is the sum of individual productions, then the national total is diminished whenever any of the factors of production is withheld or disbarred. The national product is greater if people are making automobiles inefficiently than if they are doing nothing. It is greater if they are raking leaves than if they are doing nothing. Something is more than nothing, so every additional thing produced increases the gross national product.

Thus profit maximization on the part of a firm may result in diminishing the gross national product. This result is quite independent of the harm done to people. Microeconomics can be—and often is—at war with macroeconomics. This apparent paradox is yet another example of the fallacy of composition. What is good for General Motors is not necessarily good for America, and this is no paradox but a well-understood matter of common observation.

III

The incompatibility of microeconomics and macroeconomics is particularly stark in discussions of what is called productivity, a problem said to underlie the special problems of the nation's competitiveness in foreign trade and hard-core unemployment at home. The United States is said to be losing out to Japan in a number of industries because of falling, or at least not steadily increasing, productivity. And the influx of women, blacks, Hispanics, and young people into the labor force is said, for a variety of invidious reasons, to lower the average competence of the labor force.

At first glance, this account certainly seems plausible; but starting with the very definition of productivity, there are difficulties abounding. There are, to be sure, several ways of defining productivity. They all, however, are of the same general form as the most common one, which takes the GNP for a given period and divides it by the number of hours worked in that period. That the GNP is an unreliable figure we have already said. In the present instance, it must be noticed that the figure of the GNP is stated in terms of money, that the United States GNP is stated in dollars, and the Japanese in yen; and that any comparison of the productivity rates of the two countries therefore turns initially on the exchange rates of the currencies. If the dollar is overvalued, as it was conceded to be in the early, and perhaps again in the late, 1980s, the United States productivity rate will be understated in relation to that of other countries—in this case Japan's.

Putting this initial consideration aside (no doubt refinements can be introduced into the calculations to minimize the distortion), let us look at the consequences of stating productivity as a function of "hours worked." On this basis people say that attention to clean air and safety decreases productivity and should therefore be avoided. As Professor Paul Davidson points out, "Since clean air has no market value, it shows up merely as an additional cost without any concomitant increase in gross national product. Thus if the Japanese are worse polluters of the environment than the United States, then, all other things being equal, the productivity measure shows that the Japanese are 'more productive' than the U.S. workers." In the same way, it is solemnly averred that that productivity is increased by keeping millions of people unemployed.

Consider what happens to productivity when a skilled journeyman carpenter increases his output 50 percent by taking on an unskilled apprentice go-fer. You might think that increasing production would increase productivity, but you'd be mistaken. If the journeyman's original output is x and "hours worked" is y, his original productivity is x/y. After he takes on the apprentice, their joint productivity becomes $1.5x/2y$, or $.75x/y$—a decrease of 25 percent.

The conventional method of calculating productivity is plainly absurd. Are there other ways? Tinkering with the numerator will make no significant difference. It's all the same, whether output is stated in dollars of value added or utils of satisfaction or foot-pounds of work or numbers of doors hung. So long as the denominator is "hours worked," the consequence of hiring the apprentice will be a 25 percent drop in productivity.

Turning to the denominator, we see that "hours worked" is only superficially homogeneous and so is not a satisfactory unit anyhow. As we noted in Chapter 7, Marx thought himself justified in assuming "that the labour of the workman employed by the capitalist is unskilled average labour."[2] If this was a valid assumption in his day (and probably it wasn't), it certainly is not in ours. Our go-fer apprentice would not

know what to go for (and so could do no work) without the journeyman
to direct him. Their skills are, as skills, incommensurable.

The problem is one of relating the different skills—the different
kinds of hours worked—to each other and thus devising a truly homogeneous unit. As it happens, Keynes tried to solve the problem, although productivity in the modern sense was not an issue for him.
Instead, he felt need for a "labour-unit" in his theory of employment.
He wrote that "in so far as different grades and kinds of labour and
salaried assistance enjoy a more or less fixed relative remuneration, the
quantity of employment can be sufficiently defined for our purpose by
taking an hour's employment of ordinary labour as our unit and weighting an hour's employment of special labour in proportion to its remuneration; i.e. an hour of special labour remunerated at double ordinary
rates will count as two units."[3]

Returning to the productivity problem, we see that if the ordinary
money-wage is, say, $10, this may indeed be a truly homogeneous unit,
but it is merely a multiple of a homogeneous unit we already had ($1)
and tells us nothing new. It does, moreover, transform the pretended
productivity ratio into a routine cost ratio. Depending on our choice
of numerator, it will give us the labor cost per unit of output or per total
output, which we may compare with the raw-materials cost or the
interest cost or the advertising cost or any other cost that attracts our
attention. Or we may find it useful to compare the money-wages of
management with those of middle management or of tub-pickers and
keypunchers. We may even, if we refrain from taking the results too
literally, compare our ratios from year to year or between our firm and
our competitors. Cost ratios like these are valuable tools of business
management and control, but they are quite different from the conventional notion of productivity, which is, after all, an undefinable concept.

From the point of view of the national economy, the question is,
How great is the national product? When we ask this question, we see
that every contribution, no matter how little, no matter how clumsily
or lazily produced, will swell the total. As my grandmother used to say,
every little bit added to what you've got makes a little bit more. The
nation does not become stronger or richer by keeping any potential
worker unemployed. The conventional notion of productivity is here
irrelevant.

From the point of view of the separate enterprise, the question is, How much does it cost to produce the product? When we ask this question, we see that, again, the conventional notion of productivity is irrelevant. In our carpenter example, a contractor would not hesitate to hire an apprentice to assist the journeyman, provided the apprentice's wages did not exceed the money value of the increased output. A sensible contractor would certainly also explore other ways of reducing his costs or increasing his output. Perhaps his bottom line would be greater if he provided his carpenter with better tools rather than with more assistance. Perhaps the profit would be greater if he found a cheaper carpenter or squeezed the wages of the one he has. Perhaps he would be better off by following the Japanese practice of subcontracting wherever possible, thus passing off to the subcontractor the search for ways to reduce costs. Whatever his solution to his problem, our contractor will be concerned with money costs and money profits. He will, at various times, compare his sales income with his advertising costs, his administrative costs, his inventory costs, his research costs, his postage costs. He will try to control all of these, exactly as he tries to control his labor costs, which depend more on wage scales than manhours. The number of man-hours it takes to produce his product will be important or interesting only to the extent that it affects costs, and the effects will not always be in the same direction.

The conventional notion of productivity is an attempt to solve an economic problem without money. It does not work. Not only must costs be stated in terms of money; products must be so stated also. A steel mill may be able to say it employs so many man-hours to manufacture so much steel of such-and-such specifications, but that is only half of production as an economic problem; the other half is whether that much steel can be sold at a given price. Most businesses are more complicated, anyhow. A modest book publisher, with a thousand or two titles of all sizes, shapes, and descriptions in print, can put a meaningful figure to its output only in terms of money. As for the national output, no one could add tons of steel, numbers of pickup trucks, copies of unsuccessful novels, bushels of tangerines, and gallons of martinis consumed at three-martini lunches without getting a headache.

You can't add apples and oranges, but the nation must add them to arrive at the national product, and so must the individual enterprise to determine its profit. Moreover, the product or profit, when stated in dollars, is seen to be subject to the entrepreneurial fiat that set the prices. Not only does the price determine how many items can be sold, it determines the total income from the product (or, if you prefer, the income per item) and therefore the productivity (if it were sensible to calculate this by dividing product by man-hours).

A significant fact about any productivity index, whether of labor or of capital, whether carefully designed or sloppy, is that it is a ratio, a fraction. There are two ways to increase the value of any fraction: you can increase the numerator (2/3 is greater than 1/3) or you can decrease the denominator (1/2 is also greater than 1/3). In microeconomic terms, you can increase a firm's profitability either by increasing sales or by decreasing expenses. In times of recession or depression, surviving firms will generally choose the latter option and will pay particular attention to holding down wage levels and especially to pruning the labor force wherever possible.

As President Coolidge is said to have pontificated, "When many people are out of work, unemployment results," and this truism points to another conflict between microeconomics and macroeconomics. For unemployment caused in the way we have described is plainly in the interest of the firm and equally plainly contrary to the interest of the nation, and the attempt to bring them together at this point is another example of the fallacy of composition. If maximization of material gain is the goal, it will always be in the interest of the nation to increase output, while it is often in the interest of the firm to decrease employment and output.

Finally, it should be emphasized that "productivity" is supposed to measure the efficiency of the economy, including the adequacy of the infrastructure, the quantity and quality of the industrial plant and distribution system, and the effectiveness of management, as well as the skills and dedication of the work force. The last is not infrequently the least significant factor in the determination of output—especially when output is low. Unfortunately, however, since "hours worked" is the denominator of the productivity ratio, it is the factor that casual commentators tend to talk about. In short, the term is theoretically flawed; and even if it weren't, it would still be misleading.

IV

It is obvious that whatever I do will have some effect on the firm for which I work, that whatever the firm does will have some effect on the national product, that whatever the nation does will have some effect on me and my firm. It is equally obvious that these effects are not all always in the same direction or of comparable strength.

The direction and importance of the effects depend on the purpose pursued. If health is my concern, healthy working conditions and a healthy general environment are in my interest. And in the other direction, since the nation is concerned for the health of the population as a whole, it will be in its interest to control the pollution emitted by factories and to try to eliminate communicable diseases. There is no conflict among these purposes; they all work together. Purposes with a similar unity of effect would include education, efficient communications, safety from violence—welfare in its ordinary sense. Often there are local conflicts that can be compromised; thus, an improved highway may require taking a person's home by eminent domain, and the compensation offered by the state in a given instance may not be reasonable, but there is no difficulty with the principles involved.

With the maximization of material gain, as we have seen, the situation is quite different. Person, firm, and nation may be, and often are, at cross purposes. Nevertheless, in modern times the maximization of material gain has been thought the proper objective of economic activity. In pursuit of that objective, conservatives have emphasized the creative power of individual energy, and liberals have emphasized the organizing power of the state.

As a practical matter, the conservative-liberal confrontation was considerably papered over during the past hundred years, and especially during the quarter century following World War II. An extraordinary increase in output lent plausibility to the metaphor President John F. Kennedy borrowed from Prime Minister Winston Churchill: "A rising tide raises all boats." Although the relative shares of the national product scarcely changed, the absolute increase in the total—from $209.8 billion in 1946 to $1,077.6 billion in 1971 (even in so-called constant dollars the increase was 135 percent)—allowed almost everyone to benefit dramatically. The subsequent years, however, saw the boats rising unequally, with many sinking.

That some of the exaggerated inequality was deliberately brought about only confirms the judgment that in terms of material gain, microeconomics and macroeconomics are not systematically connected. There was no reason for the record-breaking 735,000 individuals and firms that in 1983 were petitioners in bankruptcy to be cheered by the so-called recovery of that year. There was no reason for the 320,000 new millionaires of the years 1976 through 1980 to be upset by the stagflation of that period.

There is no reason for starving people to be cheered by a rising GNP. For starving people to be reconciled to their fate, they would have to be shown not only that the national prosperity was enhanced by their starvation, but also that their sacrifice was the salvation of their fellow citizens and of the nation that nurtured them. Such a showing can be made to a soldier in time of war. But no one pretends that such a showing can be made in economics at any time.

V

It should not surprise us to have to conclude that if maximization of material gain is the objective of economic activity, no unification of microeconomics and macroeconomics is possible. Maximization of gain is an undefinable and meaningless concept.

But if economics is a division of ethics and justice is its goal, the two subdisciplines come together readily enough. Indeed, they must come together, because they cannot then maintain themselves separately. Ethics is neither an exclusively private affair nor an exclusively social affair; it involves both individual and society because they define each other. Not only do individual and society define each other, but the mutual definitions are framed in ethical terms. The state requires certain actions and forbids many actions, all in the interest of maintaining just and civil relations among its citizens. The citizens demand that the state do this.

What just and civil relations may be is a historical question. The standards were developed in time and exist in time. More important, they are historical because the future is uncertain and unknowable. The "separate but equal" doctrine of *Plessy* v. *Ferguson* seemed wise and just to most people in 1896; it turned out to have unjust consequences and was overturned in *Brown* v. *Board of Education* in 1954. Every individual action and every social institution is inexorably subject to similar revision.

13

INTEREST

And the Parable of the Talents

I

Money functions or serves as it is used in buying, selling, and contracting for goods and services, and in storing wealth, and only as it is so used. Money declares or publishes or makes possible comparative prices, both present or spot prices and future or forward prices, and only money does this. To engage in economic activity, one must put money in one's purse. Just as war is too important to leave to the generals, money is too important to leave to the bankers.

The services money performs command a fee, which is interest, just as workers are paid wages for their services and landowners exact rent for the use of their property. In all these cases whatever performs the service is eventually returned to its owner, unless it is destroyed or damaged (whereupon the owner has a claim on the person responsible). Interest, wages, and rent are paid for the service, not for what performs the service. With ordinary commodities, it is the other way around.

Interest, wages, and rent are all contractual payments, whether explicit or implicit. An agreement is reached on a service to be performed and on the payment that will be made for it. When a loan is discounted, the interest is paid before the service is performed, and similar arrangements can be made with wages and rent. In either case, the services of money, labor, and land are all continuing services, and the contracts governing them necessarily look to the future.

The rate of interest in any given contract depends upon the borrower's and the lender's judgment of the value of the services (assessments of transactions costs, of the risk of nonpayment, and of inflation or deflation are of course also involved). The interest rate is, in short, determined in the same way other prices are determined. Without, I think, any exception, the economists who have written on the theory of interest have tried to validate it (or, in the cases of Aristotle and St. Thomas, to invalidate it) on some special ground, usually psychological. Nassau Senior established his reputation with the notion that interest rewards abstinence; Alfred Marshall, observing that rich lenders are not necessarily abstainers, defined it as the reward for waiting; Keynes called it the reward for not hoarding; and Irving Fisher gave it a psychological base in impatience.[1]

Any of these explanations may be true in one case or another, but they are no more determinate than Bentham's felicific calculus, and they do not advance understanding. It is not important, even when true, that borrowers are impatient and lenders patient. The same distinction can be made between employers and employees, between renters and landlords, and between buyers and sellers of any commodity. I hire someone to mow my lawn, partly because I am lazy and partly because I am impatient to get it done and claim to have other things to do. I rent a house because I'd have to wait too long if I first tried to accumulate enough to buy one. I buy a hat because I don't know how to make one. None of this matters. One retains the services of a moneylender exactly as one retains the services of a laborer or a landlord, with this vital exception: money and land can be alienated, but labor cannot.

There is a money market, better organized than, but not unlike, the labor market and the real estate market. What is done in these three markets is more significant of the sort of people we are than are the doings in the various markets for goods, because money, labor, and land are involved in every economic transaction, while no one has to have a new hat.

As we have noted, an economy with comparatively high interest and low wages (consequences of high normal profit) is one marked by cynicism and greed. A cynical and greedy society will make inadequate use of its labor and inappropriate use of its money and so will be less productive than it might have been. Its speculating economy will outweigh its producing economy.

Money is not an ordinary commodity like bread. The practical consequences of this domestic consideration can be quickly shown. If bread is, for whatever reason, overpriced, only the bread bakers languish. We can always eat cake. If, however, money is overpriced—that is, if the interest rate is too high—bankers may prosper rather than repine, for the increase in the rate may offset, or more than offset, a possible fall in the demand for loans. But the rest of the economy will surely languish.

II

Corporations have cash flows in both directions. A little experience enables corporate financial officers to operate on a day-to-day basis, estimating fairly closely how much they will take in, and planning quite precisely how much they will need to pay out. Whatever cash they accumulate in excess of these diurnal needs represents wasted opportunity unless they immediately put it out at interest.

Obviously, this sort of activity, which is at least moderately nerve-racking, is scarcely worth the bother when interest rates are low. It was not extensively practiced in the early post–World War II years, when the prime rate was 1.50 to 1.75 percent. Corporations then routinely deposited their temporarily unneeded cash in their checking accounts, which drew no interest. Banks liked that and depended on it.

Gradually, however, interest rates rose. This was largely the doing of the Federal Reserve Board, which was possessed, then as now, of the notion that inflation was an imminent threat. Then as now, the threat was to be exorcised by restricting the money supply. By the end of the 1950s, the prime rate had gone to 4.48 percent; two decades later it was up to 12.67 percent; in December 1980 and January 1981, it topped out at 21.5 percent. As a result of this surge in rates, there were several tremors in the banking world that went by the name of disintermediation crises. The septusyllabic adjective meant that banks, regulated as they were in the interest rates they could pay, were pushed out of the intermediate position between their biggest depositors and their biggest borrowers, who found ways of getting together more directly to meet their complementary needs. The former depositors thus got a bit more for their money, and the former borrowers had to pay a bit less for theirs. Then in the late 1970s, personal depositors rushed to the new money-market mutual funds. The banks suffered and the thrifts suffered severely.

These crises could obviously have been met in either of two ways. Either the Federal Reserve Board could have pushed interest rates back down, or the regulations (most of which had been prompted by the bank failures of the Great Depression) could have been lifted. Needless to say, the bugaboo of inflation and surviving hatred of the New Deal and aversion to regulation and eagerness for high interest rates made the outcome practically inevitable. The negotiable certificate of deposit, introduced in 1960, allowed banks to compete in the money market on the basis of price. In 1970, interest-rate ceilings were suspended for time deposits of more than $100,000; by 1982, the minimum was down to $2,500, allowing banks to compete freely for all but the smallest depositors, whose business was increasingly handled on a fee-for-service basis. In the meantime, Regulation Q was rescinded, NOW accounts allowed banks to pay interest on checking balances; state usury laws were suspended; FDIC insurance was extended; banks were permitted to sell insured money-market funds; there was a general relaxation of restrictions on branch banks; and by 1984, the New Deal reforms were in a shambles.

III

Interest, high or low, has a continuous proportionate inflationary effect on the price level; it is also a floor below which commercial interest rates cannot long fall. Indeed, since it usually costs banks a point or two to do business, the rates they charge tend to be that much higher than the rates they pay. And this floor is maintained by the competition of the banks with each other and with the kinds of businesses (insurance companies, stockbrokers, even retail merchandisers) that have been permitted by deregulation to perform banking functions.

Competition is by no means a universal good, and in the case of banking it is almost a universal disaster. Ordinary businesses compete with each other more at the selling end than at the supply end. Their competition at the selling end forces them to exert downward pressure on the prices they pay for their supplies. In the case of banking, the shape of competition is significantly different, because its supply— money—is different. A bank's first problem is to attract deposits, and the most effective solution is to raise the interest it will pay. Raising the rate is especially important to meet competition from money-market funds and Treasury bills. A complementary solution is to open branches where depositors (and perhaps borrowers) are. Today, major intersections are more likely to have four banks than, as formerly, four filling stations. The same search for funds (together with the delights of not even vestigial regulation) encourages the expansion of international banking.

All of this is expensive. Competition forces banks to pay higher and higher interest rates and to offer more and more expensive services. As the bankers say, their cost of funds increases; so of course the rates they charge borrowers must increase, too. Deregulation has ripped off the ceiling over interest rates and has put in its place an unstable floor under them—a floor, moreover, that has at least a tendency to levitate. Because of this wobbly floor, the Federal Reserve Board has less power to push rates downward (assuming that such an idea ever crossed their minds).

IV

Having attracted deposits, the deregulated banks, now thinking of themselves as businesses like any other, are faced with the other half of the ordinary business problem, namely, how to sell their expensive product at a profit. Some of the solutions are worth glancing at.

Perhaps the most important, at least in the short run, is the encouragement of speculation, whose deleterious effects we have already discussed. New kinds of speculation are constantly invented. In the 1980s, leveraged buyouts absorbed a lot of money at high rates, without in any way increasing production.

Perhaps more important in the long run is the encouragement of agribusiness, resulting directly in heartbreaking bankruptcies in the farm belt and indirectly in possibly permanent damage to the ecosystem—a vital subject beyond the scope of this book.

Unquestionably important in its effect on the state of the world is the development of international banking, especially the frantic competition to see who could press the most money on Third World and Communist Bloc nations. As Richard Lombardi has shown, the big banks, bemused by the silly saying that countries don't go bankrupt, sent vigorous loan officers criss-crossing the world with literally billions of dollars to lend. These loan officers were in effect salesmen; they had quotas like salesmen; they were rewarded on the basis of the amounts of money they contrived to lend; and they were not always careful in investigating the uses to which the money was to be put.[2]

In spite of excited stories in the daily press, the trouble with these loans—the trouble from the point of view of the banks, that is—is not that there is scant prospect of their ever being repaid. The trouble is that the interest—generally at rates floating well above domestic rates—cannot or will not be paid. The banks would be perfectly happy to roll the principal over and over and indeed have done so, if only the interest would keep rolling in forever and ever. If they didn't roll the principal over but somehow collected it, they would have to go to the expense of finding another borrower to press it on.

In all their selling, especially in the foregoing examples, the banks are forced by competition to concentrate their efforts on those situations in which they can hope to enjoy economies of scale. Once you have an organization capable of handling a corporate takeover, you hunt for more and bigger takeovers to support your organization. Likewise, a farmer willing to buy and equip and mortgage thousands of acres is more interesting to you than a lot of people looking for (as a bestseller published in the Great Depression had it) five acres and independence. And of course it's easier to persuade a possibly rapacious Third World official to build an expensive state-of-the-art sugar refinery than it would be to find and finance several smaller and more practical projects.

V

Whenever economies of scale are significant, they become a force for concentration. In the modern banking system, this concentration appears not only as centralized control but also as shared exposure. Only a score or so of the largest banks can afford to play a substantial role in international finance, where interest rates are highest, and where the demand for loans is insatiable. The demand was magnified in the 1970s as the price of oil increased under the management of OPEC. The banks competed to offer the Arabs high interest rates for their winnings, which were then "recycled," also at high rates, in loans to the countries that had been hit hard by the OPEC price increases.

This recycling has made the United States and other major Western countries unwilling partners of the big banks, whose failure will not be allowed to occur for fear of disrupting all aspects of international trade. But the partnership is broader than that. For the thousands of smaller banks have been lured—or forced by competition—into a more explicit partnership with the big banks. As the cost of funds has increased for all banks, the smaller ones have had to emulate the big ones by making at least some loans at very high interest rates. This is not merely a search for profits but a struggle for survival. They have managed to survive partly by buying pieces of the foreign loans from the big banks and partly by depositing large sums with the big banks. As a result, the failure of a big bank could bring down not only its commercial depositors, but also its small-bank clients, whose larger commercial depositors would in turn be ruined. And the blight would spread. It is for this reason that the threatened failure of Continental Illinois caused so much concern.

Because of the high cost of funds, a bank could be forced into insolvency by refusing to make large loans at high interest. The risk in such loans is ultimately great, but the risk of not making them is immediate. Hundreds of thrifts, of course, were bankrupted by this dilemma. It is probably safe to say that very few loan officers are intentionally sloppy; they are forced to be so by competition. If they aren't sloppy, someone else will be, and they will be out of business.

VI

In recent years, the monetary authorities have excused their actions by pointing fingers at the high United States deficit, which will, they claim, result in increased inflation. It is therefore worth stopping a moment to consider the causes for and the effects of the exponential surge of the federal deficit in the 1980s.

According to projections made by the Congressional Budget Office, the tax and spending laws that were in effect on January 1, 1981 (that is, at the end of the Carter administration), would have yielded a *surplus* of $29 billion in 1989. But even the austere laws that were in effect nine years later were projected to result in a 1989 deficit of $92.5 billion.[3] The principal causes of this spread were the tremendous increase in military spending, the vast and varied tax cuts of 1981, the "revenue neutral" tax cuts of 1987, and the high interest rate.

Military spending has the virtue that Keynes noted in pyramid building, that there is no end to it.[4] It is also stimulative. In this it is like any government expenditure and indeed any increase in aggregate demand. Businesses produce goods if they foresee a demand for them; so public expenditures, being both large and visible, are especially stimulative. Although we could have wished for a better use of our money, the military buildup was, together with the slight relaxation of monetary controls in the summer of 1982, decisive in the business recovery that started a few months later.

The tax cuts had a different effect. They were intended to stimulate the "supply side," on the theory, whose fallacy we have discussed, that saving leads to investment. Accordingly, the 1981 personal income tax favored all the rich; the 1987 tax favored all the rich who had no shelters; and the corporate tax favored the prosperous, the hope being that those who didn't need money would save it.

This hope was disappointed, and for a simple reason. Since the federal budget was already in deficit, the tax cuts necessarily increased that deficit. The increased deficit had to be funded; that is, bonds to cover it had to be sold. And to whom were they sold? To those who had money, of course, and these were, in general, those who had benefited from the tax cuts. The upshot was that the rich and prosperous were given money with which to buy government bonds. In effect, they were given the bonds, although of course some used their windfall in other ways. The maneuver accomplished as extraordinary a transfer of wealth—and that to people already wealthy—as America has seen.

This was not all. Since the Federal Reserve Board was keeping the interest rate high, the new bondholders were given a handsome rate of return—14 or 15 percent or more, running thirty years into the future. Before long, the interest payable on the federal debt was greater than the deficit, and the compounding of that interest more than offset savings that might be made elsewhere in the budget. In consequence, the only way of reducing the deficit, as repeatedly demanded by the Federal Reserve Board in the 1980s, was by raising taxes, which, by reducing aggregate demand, would have had a further depressive effect on the economy—except in the politically unlikely case that the increased taxes fell on those who had benefited from the 1981 and 1987 cuts.[5]

This dilemma could have been avoided if the tax cuts had gone to those who would spend them. It could have been avoided if the Treasury and the Federal Reserve Board had cooperated in holding down the interest rate, as they did during World War II. As it happened, however, both fiscal and monetary policies were misdirected.

VII

The high interest rates resulted in a "strong" dollar. Foreign investors—especially Japanese and German—were attracted to American securities, partly because of the favorable rates, and partly because of America's size and political stability. Bidding for dollars with which to buy these securities, they forced the exchange rate of the dollar steadily upward. From a low of $0.83 in 1979, the multilateral trade-weighted value of the dollar (March 1973 = 1.00) rose to $1.32 in 1985, an increase of 69 percent.

"Strong" is of course a strong word, and politicians boasted of their prowess in making the dollar stronger. The Federal Reserve Board characteristically approached the question first from the point of view of inflation. A month after his induction as chairman of the Reserve

Board, Volcker appeared before the House Committee on the Budget. "Another obvious result of our distressingly poor price performance," he testified, "has been the recurrent weakness of the dollar in foreign exchange markets." The weak dollar, he argued, was itself inflationary, "partly because of the direct effects on costs of imports and partly through the reduced competitive restraints on prices of domestically produced goods."[6]

Volcker's argument was plausible, but its actual consequences were disastrous. The strong dollar strongly compromised America's ability to compete in international trade. Whereas the weak dollar had made our import costs high and our export prices low, the strong dollar did the opposite. Imports, from Mazdas to Madras shirts, became cheap, but we found ourselves priced out of our foreign markets. The Reserve gained what was at best a minor advantage in its perennial wrestle with inflation, but the economy paid for it with major damage to our exporting industries and a stubbornly persisting foreign trade deficit. In the process, upwards of two million Americans lost their jobs.

The Reserve came to put more emphasis on the cause of the strong dollar—the high interest rates that attracted foreign purchasers of American securities. Without them, it was said, the budget deficit could not have been financed, or it could have been financed only by crowding American business out of the money market. Again the argument was plausible, and the actual consequences disastrous. In 1989 the on-budget interest cost was $180.5 billion, or almost $30 billion more than the budget deficit for that year. And of course, if historically quite reasonable rates on government bonds (say 2 percent) had been in effect from 1978 through 1989, the federal debt would have been at least $750 billion less, and there would have been no need even to think of attracting foreign investors to buy Treasury bonds.

Since the interest rate is, both in our theory and in practice, the independent variable, while the supply of money, however defined, and the demand for money are dependent variables, it is clear that the deficit has nothing to do with crowding out: Businesses are certainly deterred from borrowing by high interest rates, but these are not the inexorable consequence of impersonal economic laws but rather the intended result of the deliberate policies of the monetary authorities themselves.

Even on the Reserve Board's own theory that the money supply (M1 or M2) is the independent variable, the policies have been grievously mistaken. Over the two decades from 1963 to 1983, M1 in relation to GNP fell 39.3 percent, and M2 fell 24.4 percent. (Both have risen since 1982, the rise helping to account for the recovery that started in that year.) The history of those decades was such that a rational monetary authority would have pursued a policy of expansion rather than contraction.

Most important of the reasons for expansion, the labor force increased enormously. First, the post–World War II baby boom was fully operational by the end of the period, adding millions to the national work force. Second, the antidiscrimination measures of Lyndon Johnson's Great Society, together with a series of Supreme Court decisions responding to suits brought by the NAACP Legal Defense Fund and others, made it possible for millions of blacks, although still handicapped, to enter the nonagricultural labor force. Third, the modern women's movement, launched by Betty Friedan in 1963 with *The Feminine Mystique,* resulted in the self-authorization of the intention of millions of women to escape from what they saw as the stultifying conditions of housewifery. Fourth, the 1970s saw the return to civilian life of close to a million Vietnam veterans and war-industry workers.

There was, of course, some overlapping. It is possible to be a black, a woman, a war veteran, and a member of the baby-boom generation, all at once. Nevertheless, the labor force as a whole increased from 73.8 million men and women in 1963 to 124.3 million in 1988. That is an increase of 50.5 million workers, or 68.4 percent.

Finally, this period saw the consolidation of a long revolution in the way business is conducted. Until the time of the New Deal, it was common to see signs in shops reading "In God We Trust. All Others Pay Cash." To be sure, there was money available for speculation, but it was available only to the well-to-do, and only the well-to-do had charge accounts, which they were expected to settle monthly. It was not possible to cash a check except where you were personally known, and not always there. Mortgages were for five years, or often for only one; they were renewed if your standing remained good, but they were not automatically renewable. Credit was tight, but not much was needed to float the economy.

A second way of doing business lasted from the start of the New Deal to, roughly, the Eisenhower administration. At the start of the period,

Sears, Roebuck and Montgomery, Ward shipped only COD or when payment accompanied order, and Macy's still advertised "6% Less for Cash," but these were merely among the last to give in. The FHA and the VA guaranteed mortgages for twenty years at 4 percent, with only 10 percent down (later such mortgages were available for thirty years, with no down payment). Automobiles and washing machines and radios and furniture were sold on the installment plan. More people had checking accounts, and almost anyone could cash a check almost anywhere locally. Quite a lot more money was needed to float this economy than had been needed for the previous one, but the government kept the interest rates relatively low, and the money was available.

The third way of doing business, characterizing the period we're now in, might be called the credit-card way, although credit cards themselves account for only a small portion of consumer debt. In any case, almost anyone can buy almost anything almost anywhere on credit. This of course means that sellers have to wait for their money. And the wholesalers then have to wait, and then the manufacturers, and then the producers of raw materials. Where trade a half century ago was largely current, it is now largely afloat. The need for money is enormous.

In addition, it turns out that this way of doing business is explosively dynamic. Just as the New Deal shift from one-year mortgages at 6 percent to twenty-year mortgages at 4 percent resulted in a housing boom, the credit-card shift has brought forth a fantastic expansion of all sorts of consumers' goods and consequently in the whole economy. In the quarter century ending in 1988, consumer credit outstanding increased from $81 billion to $727.8 billion, and home mortgage debt went from $278 billion to $2,056.6 billion.

All these factors—the increase in the labor force, the need for capital investment, and the demand for everyday credit (not to mention the vast but uncharted growth of the underground economy)—should, on any theory, have prompted a rapid expansion of the money supply.

The Federal Reserve Board and the banking system as a whole—not any Congress nor any president—made the present deficit inevitable and ostensibly unmanageable. Private enterprise would not have been crowded out of the money market by sky-high interest rates if the banking system had behaved rationally.

The interest rate is not a fact of nature or an act of God. It is a function of government. Since interest is a function of government, it is a duty of government to regulate it. In the United States, this is mainly the job of the Federal Reserve Board, which for forty years and more has been idiotically trying to hold down the cost of living by increasing the cost of doing business.

VIII

While it is generally recognized that a severely restricted money supply will support high interest rates or push them higher, it is also widely contended that an increased supply would result in even higher rates. The conventional theory is that fear of inflation would bring this about, because it would be anticipated that too much money would be chasing too few goods.

According to the theory, bankers and others with money to lend are unwilling to make loans unless they are reasonably sure of getting not only their money but also their purchasing power back. Assuming that their desire to do so may be contemplated sympathetically, there remains the question of how they are going to manage it if the Reserve lowers the interest rate, this being, as we have seen, the way to try to expand the money supply. In the conventional theory, if the lenders don't get a high money rate of interest, they don't lend. That is not so smart. One is reminded of the slothful servant in the Parable of the Talents.

While lenders' strikes regularly plague small and weak countries and can have partial success even in a country as large and rich as France, it is scarcely possible to imagine one in the United States unless the monetary authorities cooperate (as they did, especially from the fall of 1979 to the summer of 1982 and continued to do, though less firmly, thereafter). Lenders could not bring it off by themselves. They might try to send their money overseas—a flight from the dollar. Much could be done (given the will to do it) to impede such a flight; but it would not in any case be an unmitigated disaster, since a weaker dollar reduces imports and stimulates exports and so helps close the balance-of-trade gap.

From the point of view of prospective lenders the major result of a fall in interest rates is a run-up of the stock and bond markets, because a fall in the interest rate increases the capitalized value of every income-earning asset. Prospective lenders who sit on their money during such goings-on will suffer great losses. They may not like the prevailing interest rate, but their choice is between that rate and nothing at all. Convinced though they may be of future inflation, persuaded therefore that the low money interest rate makes the "real" interest rate even negative, they can do nothing with their money unless they accept the money rate. If, like the slothful servant, they bury their money and so preserve it, they will merely forgo all interest, no matter how unreal it seems to them. Inflation or no inflation, the most successful investing (or speculating) strategy is the one that winds up with the most money. That amount of money may have less purchasing power than what one started with, but it certainly has more purchasing power than a smaller amount would have. A negative "real" interest rate, in apparent contradiction of the laws of mathematics, proves to be greater than zero.

In a confrontation with rational and determined monetary authorities, money can run to speculation, consumption, or investment in productive enterprise, but it can't hide. Speculation can be inhibited by sound taxes and banking regulations, and it often carries its own inhibitions in the shape of high carrying costs and unorganized markets. And no one should object to consumption or productive enterprise, for the lower interest rate should have been managed precisely to increase aggregate demand and stimulate investment.

The money interest rate is what matters to both lenders and borrowers. The so-called real rate, no matter how it may be calculated, does not appear except as a result of the calculation. It is called real, but it has no actual existence. Inflation presents moneylenders with a serious problem, but they have no more right to be protected from its consequences than do the people who are doing or have done the work of the world. Conservatives are quick to claim that it is inflationary to give cost-of-living adjustments to workers or retirees. It is, as we shall see, far more inflationary to encourage moneylenders to tack an inflation adjustment onto the interest rate.

The so-called real rate is like the other alleged realities we have encountered: self-interest versus enlightened self-interest, market value versus labor value, actual dollars versus constant dollars, money wages versus real wages, nominal GNP versus real GNP. Economists have wasted much time and confused much thought with their propensity to see the world as a dualism, in which, as Charles Peirce said, appearance and reality are like a freight train held together by a feeling of good will between the engineer in the cab and the brakeman in the caboose.

IX

One of Keynes's central ideas was that in a healthy economy, prices, including interest rates, are "sticky." A sticky price is not merely slow moving, it is historical, being based on the past and looking forward to the unknowable future. Without such stickiness, it is difficult, if not impossible, for businesses to undertake projects that require a long time to bring to fruition, and industry therefore stagnates. This effect can be observed in the contemporary and much-deplored concentration of corporate officers' attention on the quarterly or monthly bottom line.

Much of the trouble in the present economy has been due to the fact that interest rates, over the past several decades, have been far from sticky. Their volatility has encouraged speculation and discouraged enterprise. The imposition of stickiness, therefore, should be one of the objectives of reform. Since another of the objectives should be a substantial lowering of interest rates, policymakers are faced with a dilemma. If rates are lowered overnight, the principle of stickiness will be grossly violated, and the economy will be thrown into confusion. But if rates are not lowered overnight, unemployment will continue to be high, and we shall be continuing the injustice of forcing the disadvantaged to pay the cost of the high rates.

There are two main weaknesses in the present Federal Reserve System: (1) Not all forms of banking and quasi-banking are under the system's control, and (2) the system itself is not under political control. The independent status of the Federal Reserve makes it almost impossible for the United States to pursue a coherent economic policy. It was, in the first place, unwise in the extreme to place so much power in the hands of an insulated body, and the Reserve has shown itself again and again and yet again unable to use its power except to the grave detriment of the nation and of the world.[7]

The Reserve's great power is almost exclusively negative. It can set the discount rate and the federal funds rate very high and thus discourage or inhibit borrowing, but if it sets the rates low, it can't guarantee that the rates will be put to use. It can deplete the banks' reserves and thus constrict the money supply as tightly as it pleases; but even though it should remove the reserve requirement altogether, it can't make people borrow. The Reserve has great negative power. It can snub the economy down, bring it to a halt, even force it to back up. But the Reserve's theoretical power to expand the money supply can only lead the economy to available funds; it cannot make anyone use them.

Congress and the president, on the other hand, have positive as well as negative powers. They can increase the money supply by running a deficit. The deficit is paid for with bonds (or, it may be, by coining money); so the government itself can do the borrowing that expands the money supply even when the private sector is laggard. And Congress and the president could contract the money supply by eliminating the deficit, either by not spending so much or by taxing more. They could, in fact, run a large surplus and make money very scarce indeed, and the interest rate very high.

It might thus appear that Congress and the president have all the necessary power, both positive and negative, and that the Federal Reserve Board is merely a quaint survival from a more innocent day, useful for its clearinghouse operations and, from time to time, as a lender of last resort. Unfortunately, the powers the Reserve does have are fully adequate to cause appalling grief, as is starkly visible in its 1980s record. Ironically, it has been warmly praised for its actions, thus confirming Keynes's wry observation that in finance it is more praiseworthy to fail conventionally than to succeed unconventionally.

For fail the Federal Reserve certainly did. Acting with the intention or pretension of controlling inflation, the Board caused a long and deep recession, threw 4 million men and women out of work, denied employment to millions of others, fastened impossible debt service on Latin America and Africa, destroyed our international trade, changed us from the world's largest creditor to the world's largest debtor, and saddled the federal government with debt service that is now double the annual deficit.

Did the Federal Reserve do all that single handed? Not quite all. It had, throughout, the solemn support of the rest of the banking community, and it could count on the creative policies of the Reagan administration to give it occasions for its actions. But the actions of the Federal Reserve were essential for the disasters I have named.

On the other side of the ledger is the claimed success in throttling inflation. I shall look into that part of the record in later chapters. Here, it is enough to note that the Federal Reserve has been ostentatiously battling inflation for more than forty years, and that despite all the famous victories, the inflation rate now is four or five times what it was when the fight started.

It is also claimed that the named disasters would have been worse if the Reserve hadn't kept a tight rein on money. It's hard to see how. Would unemployment have been higher? Would the South American and African debt service have been harder to handle? Would a weak dollar have weakened our foreign trade? Would our federal debt service have been greater? The answer, in all cases, is surely negative.

Only the naive will fancy that it will be easy to get the banking system under rational control. It can scarcely be expected that today's rogue bankers will go gentle. At the very least, they will make ingenious and determined efforts to find loopholes comparable to those exploited over the past forty years, and there might even be a surge of high-level loan sharking. Such efforts could be contained if all branches of government—legistlative, executive, judicial, and the citizenry—could disabuse themselves of the notion that banking is a business like any other.

Banking policy must be judged not on the prosperity of the bankers, not on the GNP, not on a low interest rate. A high GNP and a low interest rate are desirable not in themselves, but only as contributors to the proper economic objective of free and full employment in a just society.

14

INFLATION I

The Myth of the Full-Employment Trade-Off

I

During the last nine years of his life Joseph A. Schumpeter worked on the posthumously published *History of Economic Analysis,* a remarkable work of some 1,200 pages that he almost, but not quite, finished. Schumpeter had studied, practiced, and taught law in Egypt, Austria, and the United States before becoming involved in politics at the end of World War I. He was for a brief time Austrian minister of finance and subsequently president of the Biedermann Bank until it collapsed in 1924. He then taught economics at the University of Bonn before going to Harvard, where he remained from 1932 until his death in 1950.

These biographical details are suggestive in relation to a surprising fact about Schumpeter's monumental work. Although he discusses in great detail the work of all the major economists and almost all those of the second, third, and even fourth and fifth ranks (the index of authors runs to twenty-one double-column pages), there is no entry in the subject index (which runs to thirty pages) for "inflation." Given the cacophony that has oppressed us in recent years, his silence is deafening. Here is a tremendous scholar who, as government official, banker, and teacher, was in the thick of one of the great hyperinflations of all time, and he finds nothing worth noting on the subject in the writings of the great and near-great economists from Aristotle to 1950. He has a great deal to say on monetary theory and on business cycles (he himself wrote a massive book on the subject), but nothing on inflation as such.

The foregoing anecdote strongly suggests that inflation as we know it is a comparatively recent phenomenon, dating roughly from World War II. This is the first thing to understand about it. Before the second half of the twentieth century, there were price dislocations aplenty. Price increases were characteristic of the boom phase of the business cycle, and the bust phase had contrary dislocations. What went up, came down. Whether the cycle was one of forty or fifty years, as Kondratieff thought, or something of shorter duration, it was a cycle, and inflation was followed by deflation as day the night, whereupon the sequence repeated itself. The Great Depression convinced many that Marx was right, and that the vibrations of the capitalist system would shake it apart. Much attention was therefore paid to proposals for damping the vibrations down, leading Keynes to remark, "The right remedy for the trade cycle is not to be found in abolishing booms and thus keeping us permanently in a semi-slump but in abolishing slumps and thus keeping us permanently in a quasi-boom."[1]

Inflation was not a primary concern of Schumpeter's generation, not only because their attention was distracted to the business cycle, but also because prices, from the Industrial Revolution to the end of the nineteenth century, had been trending steadily downward.[2]☆ In recent years, of course, they have been trending steadily upward. We have had five recessions of varying severity in the past quarter-century, and through them all prices have kept going up. The business cycle used to be marked by a harrowing deflationary phase. We have suffered none of that. In the recessions there has been some moderating of inflation, but there has been no overt deflation, at least not in the industrialized world. When we congratulate ourselves on licking inflation, we mean merely that we have (we hope) slowed it down.

The second thing to understand about inflation is that hyperinflation is special and different. Its conditions and consequences are special, and there is no reason to believe that it grows out of inflation as we know it. In every case of hyperinflation, the afflicted country is saddled with massive foreign debts denominated in foreign currencies. This was true of the Weimar Republic, and it is true of Argentina, Brazil, and Mexico today. The Weimar hyperinflation was quite quickly stopped because payment of the war debts was delayed, restructured, and ultimately forgotten. Latin America's hyperinflations will continue until the creditors face the fact that the debts will not be repaid.[3]☆ The United States debt poses no such threat to the nation. It is denominated in dollars. Even if a large portion of it is held abroad, it remains under American control, because it is payable in dollars under American control.

The third thing to understand about inflation is that it is not solely a monetary problem. Money is certainly involved in it, as money is involved in every economic question, but the familiar example of a country that overnight makes every dollar worth two dollars is not an example of inflation. Prices may be set at any multiple of the present prices; and if all prices are changed by that multiple, no one is hurt, and no one gains.

In the many historical instances of debasing the currency, two sets of prices are not changed: contracts for the payment of debts and contracts for goods to be delivered at a specified price. When a nation debases its currency, all debtors and most speculators are delighted and all hoarders and creditors and some entrepreneurs are dismayed.[4]☆ What has been upset is not the value of money (as we saw in Chapter 5, money has no "value"), but contracts. Inflation is a disturbance of the price system, of the relation of one price to another. It is peculiarly historical. High prices are not a sign of inflation. Higher prices are. Higher than what? Higher than yesterday's. And lower than those anticipated for tomorrow.

Perhaps the most important thing to understand about inflation is the vacuity of the popular cliché that it is "too much money chasing too few goods." Examples abound of insatiable demands arising for particular goods at a particular time and place. The excitement of an auction can lead to extravagant prices. More seriously, when the wheat crop—or the distribution thereof—failed in pre–Revolutionary France, desperate need bid the price of bread up catastrophically. But there was not "too much money" chasing that bread. On the contrary, people were impoverished as they sold everything they had at distress prices in a frantic effort to raise money for food. In ancient Egypt, Joseph's foresight in the seven fat years enabled him, in the lean years, to squeeze the people and reduce the country's freeholders to sharecroppers. He could scarcely have done this if the pharaoh's subjects had had "too much money."

The modern economy is so large and substitutes are so plentiful that it is difficult for any person or group of people to corner a market as Joseph did; yet the economy is so interdependent that trouble anywhere tends to spread. The gas lines at the beginning of OPEC were only a temporary annoyance, but petroleum enters widely into industry and agriculture, and the rise in its price contributed to rises in all commodities, especially those produced by corporations that value their supplies and inventories on the last-in-first-out basis. Just as there was panic filling of gasoline tanks by motorists and of oil tanks by homeowners, so there was panic stockpiling of all supplies by manufacturers and of all merchandise by retailers. An expected general shortage of commodities resulted in temporary and localized actual shortages. But the general shortage never ensued. In fact, the stores were full of goods, and business was sluggish, because prices jumped faster than people's ability to pay. There was not, at any time in the movement, too much money chasing too few goods. If you can't afford to pay the prices asked, it is silly to claim you have too much money.

Nevertheless this cliché is the explicit or implicit rationale for many doggedly pursued public policies, many of which, as we shall see, are not even well designed to satisfy these fallacious premises.

II

There are two received theories of the inflation that has been a fact of economic life since the end of World War II. The first blames the phenomenon on high employment and wages. The second, which I shall discuss in the next chapter, looks to high interest rates to control it.

Practically all economists, businessmen, bankers, politicians, and journalists are united in endorsing the doctrine that high employment makes for high inflation. Their unanimity is very curious, first, because few, if any, other economics propositions command such universal assent; second, because it is among the most unequivocally dismal notions in all this dismal science; and, third, because there is no evidence whatever to support it. I don't mean that no evidence is offered; I mean that the evidence offered is false or irrelevant or both.

If the proposition weren't so dismal, it wouldn't be worth troubling about. But look at what it means: It assumes that inflation is the worst economic misfortune that could befall us, and it asserts that in order to avoid—or simply to control—inflation, we must prevent several million people from having jobs. Even if all these millions were fully qualified and fully motivated, they would still be unemployable, given the inexorable working of the system.

Journalistic reports of the thoughts of mainstream economists might lead one to believe that when they talk about 6 percent of the work force being unemployable, they mean that all those millions are too little educated, too stupid, too sick, or too pregnant to participate in the modern economy. But that's not exactly what they mean.

One problem that would remain, even if all the unemployed were fully qualified, is friction in the economy, that is, time lost as workers are between jobs. Again there's misunderstanding (and some economists misunderstand themselves), for it often sounds as though there were several million people out there whimsically flitting from job to unemployment insurance to job for no reason at all. There are no doubt some such free spirits, and they'll always be good for political anecdotes; but the real friction results from business coming and going.

In 1987, said to have been a year of prosperity, there were more than 60,000 corporate bankruptcies in the United States. Most of them were very small, and some of the larger ones were simply for the purpose of restructuring, which in this context generally meant breaking a labor contract. Nevertheless, the total assets involved exceeded $36 billion, and it is safe to say that a couple of million people lost their jobs during the proceedings.

Always there are "efficient" mergers, which are efficient because they fire "redundant" workers. And there's all the seasonal unemployment—clerks and warehousemen let go after the Christmas rush, farm workers between seasons, production people laid off during model changeovers. And there are all the customers' men dropped after a market difficulty, and all the others who lose their jobs when their companies' business temporarily slows, and those whose jobs disappear when their companies relocate for tax reasons—or in search of cheaper labor. It's easy to see how there could be much waste in the economy.

Continuing the friction metaphor, economists claim that increasing the rate of employment will increase the friction, thus causing the economy to heat up, inflation to run away (the metaphor becomes a bit mixed), and everything to grind to a halt. What they mean is that unless 6 percent of the work force is unemployed, workers will be able to bargain more effectively for higher wages, thus pushing up costs and, *a fortiori*, prices. Certainly they learned from Marx's metaphor of the industrial reserve army that a whiff of unemployment tends to chill the ardor of workers' wage demands. But despite their mathematics, the economists do not know, and cannot know, how great a rise in inflation (if any) will be caused by a given fall in unemployment. One may be a function of the other, but whether it is or not and whether the possible function is large or small, are strictly empirical questions. And the factual evidence that we have is a long way from supporting the economists' theory.

In 1988, when inflation was running at about 4.5 percent and unemployment at about 5.4 percent, there was much satisfaction with these figures and also much concern that higher inflation was imminent. Yet following World War II, there had been twenty years in which unemployment was at a lower rate, twenty-six years with lower inflation, and no fewer than sixteen years when both inflation and unemployment were lower. Not only that, but in the year of lowest unemployment, inflation was lower than in all except four of the forty-odd years in question. In the year of highest inflation, unemployment was higher than in all but seven of the years. These figures certainly do not support the doctrine of a trade-off between inflation and employment.

That may be said to be the small picture. A bigger picture is represented by the runaway inflations of our time that are regularly flashed on the screen to scare us into doing something drastic about inflation now, before we all have to get wheelbarrows to carry our worthless money to market to buy a loaf of black bread. Besides the Weimar Republic runaway, the prime example is Latin America today. If the doctrine were sound, those countries should have expected to have full employment and overheated economies to start their runaways. Exactly the contrary, though, was the case. Each one suffered from appalling unemployment, and Latin America still does, without in any way impeding or controlling the inflation. These examples do not support the doctrine, either.

To round out the empirical record, we may note that today, of all non-Communist industrialized nations, Switzerland has both the lowest unemployment and the lowest inflation, while Japan is next lowest in both categories.

Since the facts so flatly contradict the theory, how did the theory get started? Its roots are very deep, reaching down to the "law of diminishing returns," first formulated by Anne Robert Jacques Turgot in the eighteenth century and subsequently accepted without question by economists from Jean-Baptiste Say on the right to Karl Marx on the left, and even by John Maynard Keynes until late in his career.[5] It is certainly plausible. Just as agricultural costs rise when production is extended to less favorable land, so it seems that industrial expansion should require the use of less and less suitable materials and less and less efficient workers.

Plausible or not, the modern world—especially the capitalist world—doesn't work that way. Unlike eighteenth-century agriculture, the industrial economy is not a closed system, with a finite amount of land, but an open system, based on credit, and open to the future. Business is not a succession of mercantile adventures, each of which terminates as a market is cleared, but an ongoing concern. The world is more prosperous than it was in Turgot's day because of economies of scale, incessant innovation, and the creativity of money.

The law of diminishing returns nevertheless continues to be an article of faith among neoclassical economists because it is essential underpinning to marginal analysis and general equilibrium theory. Also, in 1958 the law was joined by the Phillips curve, which seems to demonstrate a reciprocal relation between unemployment and inflation in Great Britain in most years from 1862 to 1957, just as the law might predict.[6]* In the United States, the decade of the 1960s produced an almost perfect Phillips curve ending in a vertical ascent, leading some to infer that if unemployment fell to 4 percent, inflation would rage indefinitely.

This inference is so satisfyingly dismal that belief in it has become a test of orthodoxy, despite the fact that the preceding and succeeding decades produce graphs that might very well have been traced by a seriously deranged butterfly.[7]*

In short, there is no relevant evidence reliably connecting high inflation and full employment. We have not, after all, ever had full employment except in wartime, when inflation of civilian prices is to be expected because production of civilian goods is necessarily curtailed. On the other hand, we have many times had inflation in peacetime.

Strictly considering the data in hand, it is not logically possible to say that high unemployment has a particular effect, one way or the other, in initiating inflation; there are undoubtedly plenty of additional explanations to be adduced. The incontrovertible point, however, comes at the other end, for massive and growing unemployment has uniformly and miserably failed to slow down runaway inflations wherever they have appeared.

III

Mathematically, it is impossible for too much money to be chasing too few goods, provided that the goods that workers produce are at least equal in value to their wages. Since private-sector output is currently about 1.3 times wages and salaries, this condition would seem not too difficult to meet. On these premises, perfectly full employment (not 4 percent unemployment or 6 percent unemployment) cannot be inflationary. Indeed, any unemployment whatever will have an inflationary effect because the unemployed will be receiving some sort of relief, thus increasing the money in circulation either directly or indirectly, but will be producing no goods for money to be spent on.

It is safe to say that no one—especially no conservative—accepts the foregoing reasoning; yet it is a logical implication of Say's law, which is widely accepted—especially by supply-side conservatives—as a guide to public policy. Say wrote, "[T]he only way of getting rid of money is in the purchase of some product or other. Thus the mere circumstance of the creation of one product opens a vent for other products."[8] The usual, more aphoristic, formulation of Say's law is "Production creates its own demand." The policy recommendation that follows seems obvious: "It is the aim of good government to stimulate production and of bad government to encourage consumption."[9]

The trouble with Say's law is that empirically it is insupportable. If it were valid, a universal glut (that is, goods no one could afford to buy) would, as he said, be impossible, and inflation would, as we have seen, be next to impossible. But there certainly have been depressions, and there certainly is inflation. Something is wrong with his analysis, and anyone who has ever, as polemicists used to put it, met a payroll knows what it is. It is a distinct possibility that you can't sell all of what you make. Sometimes you can't sell any of it. Mathematically, production creates its own demand; actually, it does not.

What is true of the demand for products is also true of the demand for labor. It may be that my skills are so specialized—or so minimal—that there is no demand for them at any price. It may be that business is so sluggish that a universal glut really happens, in which case it would be folly for an entrepreneur to hire me to produce more. Keynes's quarrel with classical economists turned on his insistence that involuntary unemployment can and does occur. Millions of citizens in all lands can testify that he was right.[10]

IV

In the real world, where business is actually done, time is always a factor.[11] Everything takes time, and so everything requires planning for the future. Retail stores buy ahead for delivery in a few days, weeks, or months. Manufacturers work even farther ahead in buying raw materials and much farther ahead in ordering new machinery. All of this ordering takes the form of contracts with prices stated. Prices are stated in terms of money.

This is the way business is actually done and the way it is inevitably done, because the future is systematically unknown. However rational one may be in one's expectations, one would be foolhardy to order machinery without knowing its price, especially since one usually has the option of buying secondhand machinery or a whole plant at some known current price. On the other side, one would be foolhardy to manufacture specialized and expensive machinery without an order in hand. To get the order, the machinery manufacturers must set the price; and to set the price, they must be confident that they will have a competent work force at settled wages. And this will also be true of all the subcontractors on whom they must rely. It is therefore not at all in the interest of business that wage scales should fluctuate widely in search of a supposed equilibrium.

Wages are consequently the subject of contract negotiations and are not always left to the vagaries of the hypothetical market. The market being bypassed in this manner, the doctrinaire objections to government interference in that market disappear, and it becomes possible to consider the government's being at all times the employer of last resort, offering decent wages, regardless of the presumed necessity of the work done, though it would certainly be good public policy to try to arrange work as useful as possible. Given the present deterioration in public facilities, there is plenty to be done.

The objection to having people on relief do useful work comes not from those on relief but, very properly, from those presently employed, who understandably fear political pressure to reduce their own pay to the relief level. This fear would disappear if relief work were paid regular wages, rather than subminimum wages, and relief workers could then be given useful rather than "noncompetitive" work.

Some emphasize the hurt to society when people, whether willfully or not, live without working. Others emphasize the hurt to individuals who are not permitted to make a contribution to—or to enjoy the privileges of—society. Both hurts are severe and unquestioned. Yet they are permitted to exist, to continue, to grow. Sometimes, as in the United States in the early 1980s, they are deliberately exacerbated.

A people-oriented political economy would take direct action on this problem; a pseudo-science approaches the problem indirectly. In the direct approach, the government creates the needed jobs. Where direct action has been tentatively tried, as in the early New Deal, the cost of the program was not substantially greater than the cost of inaction. The deficit in 1933, the last Hoover budget, was $2.6 billion, while in 1939, the last prewar year, it was $2.8 billion.

Of course there was waste. There is waste in private industry, waste in private homes; life is wasteful. It is safe to say that the Pentagon now wastes more in a week than Dr. New Deal did in the entire eight years before being replaced by Dr. Win-the-War. But that is not the point.

Nor is it relevant that most of the nongovernment art of that period, like most of the WPA art, no longer satisfies our aesthetic taste. The point is that millions of people were enabled to preserve their self-respect.

In the meantime, thousands of schools, libraries, hospitals, post offices, dams, and other public buildings were built. Electricity was brought to the farms. A start was made on public housing. Thousands of miles of highways were constructed. Thousands of square miles of public lands were improved by the CCC. Hundreds of pictures were painted; scores of plays were produced; uncounted amounts of literary and historical material were collected, preserved, and made available for study; fifty or more guidebooks were published, many of which have not been superseded a half century later. And millions of men and women were enabled to make a contribution to society. The extent of these contributions is obscured by the statistical quirk whereby those who worked for the WPA, CCC, NYA, and the rest of the so-called alphabet soup are counted as unemployed.

What the government does or does not do is crucial for the prosperity and the morale of the people—not just those involuntarily unemployed, but all the people. The government is literally the employer of last resort. It may fail at its task, leaving the rejected citizens with nothing to turn to, and the government with nothing to show. It may succeed in ways that, for various reasons, foreclose development. Egyptian necropolises, Greek acropolises, Roman circuses, medieval cathedrals, all were magnificent public efforts, inevitably flawed. As for us, it is an open question whether we shall prove capable of anything more glorious and more liberating than a plethora of shopping malls.

There is no denying the probability that full employment would allow many people to make wage demands and improve their position. Nor can it be denied that the position of many people should be improved. The present price system would be upset; and even for those with increased money wages, the "real" wages might prove less than expected, because a measure of price inflation would ensue. The major shift, however, should come against the interest rate. This would be merely the inverse of what has been happening for forty years.

In contrast with the cost of money, the cost of labor has been a remarkably steady factor in our economy. This cost may be determined by dividing the total wages and salaries of all nongovernmental employees by the GNP (*ex* governmental expenditures).[12] In the thirty years from 1960 through 1989, this figure has fluctuated narrowly between 79.0 percent (in 1970) and 70.7 percent (in 1965), and in only four of these years did the figure rise or fall by more than two points.

It is not, however, incised in granite that labor's share should be 75 percent, rather than much more or much less. A further caveat should be entered: When we talk of compensation of employees we lump together the multi-million-dollar salary of the *Fortune* 500 CEO with the fringe-free hourly wage of the part-time handyman setting out geraniums at the corporation's suburban headquarters. There is reason to believe that, especially in the past fifteen years, the salaries at the top of the pay scale have grown astronomically (and the take-home pay has grown faster yet), while hourly wages at the bottom have actually fallen, in so-called constant dollars, by 10 percent.

15

INFLATION II
The Bankers' Classic COLA

_____ I

David Ricardo was insistent on what is known as the wage-fund theory, which holds that a business has a certain fund out of which it pays its costs and its profits; consequently, as Ricardo wrote, "There can be no rise in the value of labour without a fall of profits."[1]☆ This theory continues to be supported by strong gut feelings in many corporate board rooms, but Schumpeter dismissed it with the observation that "high rates of profit and high wages normally go together."[2]

Yet Ricardo was right—or almost right. His mistake—very common in his day and not uncommon today—was in confusing profits with interest rates. Interest rates and wages are indeed in conflict with each other, because both are costs of doing business. No business can exist without labor, and no business can exist without explicit or implicit interest costs. Both interest and wages are contracted costs agreed to before sales are known, while actual profits, as we have previously noted, are a residual.

Actual profits are a residual, but what I have called normal profits are a determining factor in business estimates and have the interest rate as an opportunity cost. The interest rate thus has a double effect on business plans. In general, a project will not be undertaken unless expected sales are at least equal to the sum of labor costs, materials costs, marketing costs, interest costs, and normal profits. (Whether fixed costs are considered will not affect the point before us.) Since in the actual world prices are set, not in an auction, but as a result of estimating and planning, labor costs and the double factor of interest costs and normal profits are in the wage-fund relationship with each other. If prices are held steady, these rival costs cannot both go up. If either goes up, the other must come down. If one goes up while the other holds steady or if both go up, the selling price must go up or the project must be abandoned.

On the basis of the foregoing, we should expect a positive correlation between high interest rates and inflation, the former being a cause of the latter. It is, however, widely believed that high interest rates stop inflation rather than contribute to it. The belief is so settled that everyone expects as a matter of course that the Federal Reserve Board will raise the interest rate whenever it is imagined that inflation threatens. If any doubt of the efficacy of this program is expressed, it is quickly squelched by reference to the unquestioned fact that inflation rates and interest rates were lower in 1986 than in 1980. (It is nevertheless true that inflation ran at a lower rate than 1986's in thirteen of the previous years after World War II. The 1986 "triumph" was scarcely remarkable.)

In the past forty years, there have been two periods of relative stability. In 1952–56, the Consumer Price Index fluctuated between 1.9 percent and minus 0.4 percent, while the prime was 3.0 and 3.77 percent. And from 1961 through 1965, the CPI inched up from 1.0 percent to 1.7 percent, while the prime was steady at 4.50 percent, except for 1965, when it was 0.04 point higher. Politically speaking, the first period embraced the last year of President Truman's term and the first four years of President Eisenhower's, while the second period included the last year of President Eisenhower's presidency, all of President Kennedy's, and the first two years of President Johnson's.

We might debate whether the low CPI of these years caused the relatively low prime, or vice versa; but neither way do the figures support a doctrine that relates a high prime to a low CPI. Indeed, if there is any correlation between prime and CPI, it is that they go up and down together. From 1949 to 1967, the CPI increased less than 3 percent in every year but one, and the prime was under 5 percent in every year but the last two. In the twenty years following 1968, the

CPI increased more than 3 percent in every year except one, while the prime was above 6 percent in every year except two.

Some might be tempted to argue that the Federal Reserve Board was not resolute in restricting the money supply, and that it subsequently was forced, as the sports announcers say, to play catch up. The record, however, is that M1 as a percentage of GNP fell from 28.2 percent in 1959 to 14.5 percent in 1981. The fall was remarkably steady, with only three upbeat years and only one year in which the fall was more than 3 points. But starting at 15.2 percent in 1982 (the year in which the Reserve is supposed to have got control of inflation) the figure rose to 16.8 percent in 1986, the year of lowest inflation in twenty-two years.

If M1 is the money supply (and it was in fact the quantity that the Federal Reserve claimed to control during these years), it was, as a percentage of GNP, cut almost in half in the years when inflation was growing, but increased with the decline of inflation. The experience with M2 has been different and essentially flat, with a low of 58.8 percent of GNP and a high of 66.4 percent, but its second highest point (66.1 percent) came in 1986, the recent year of lowest inflation.

In short, the empirical record does not support the theory that a high interest rate controls inflation and it directly contradicts the theory that inflation is controlled by contracting the money supply.

II

There is every reason to expect a high prime to cause a high CPI. First, let us make a minor observation. The inflation rate is not a figure you read off an instrument like a barometer. It is a statistical construct, and one of its factors is the interest rate. This is an arbitrary effect, and one that could be arbitrarily eliminated (though the rate at which homeowners and other consumers can borrow is indubitably an element in their cost of living); but it stands as a real fact in the real world.

Second, let us repeat the much more important observation that speculation is vastly stimulated by volatile and rising interest rates. It was said in the 1980s that if high interest rates had not been available to bring in foreign money, federal borrowing as a result of the budget deficits would have crowded producers out of the market. But as we saw in Chapter 10, speculation can always crowd out production, and that is what happened during the long bull market of those years, despite the foreign money.

There is, third, a much more serious effect than either of these. If you're running a business, and your friendly banker says he wants 20 percent to renew your 10 percent loan, your first defense is to cut the payroll, and your second is to raise your prices. Moreover, the loan isn't the only thing that bothers you, because the opportunity cost of investing in your business rises with the interest rate; so you must raise your normal profit, which increase runs geometrically through the economy, raising prices as it goes.

Of course, it happens, sooner or later, that high prices, high unemployment, and low wages have their adverse effects on business. Sales fall, and payrolls are squeezed further. Unions fear to strike. But since wages have only an arithmetical effect on costs, the net pressure on prices will still be upward as long as interest rates remain high. Even a very severe recession will at best only slow inflation; it will not stop it as long as interest rates remain high. And this is exactly what happened in the 1980s. After the brief fall to a tolerable level in 1986, the CPI resumed its rise.

If the Federal Reserve controlled inflation in the early 1980s, it did it by so increasing one of the costs of doing business (interest) that a worldwide recession was induced. The claim is made that this had to be done in order to break what was called the wage-price spiral. And what was the vice of the spiral? If it had not been broken, it would, they say, have so increased one of the costs of doing business (labor) that a worldwide recession would have resulted.

One could dispute the relative inefficiency or the relative injustice of the two recession-inducing measures, but on the premises there is no essential difference between them. They both work by escalating the costs of doing business. But that is only theory. No one knows whether a wage-price spiral would actually cause a recession because such a spiral has never run its course. On the other hand, everyone knows—or should know—what happens when you push up the interest rate. There is a further irony here. The Federal Reserve Board has interfered grossly and grievously with the free market in order to save it. And what was the free market being saved from? It was being saved from a free market in wage rates.

III

The other popular theory of inflation (too much money, too few goods) is fallacious in ways we've already discussed. Yet, letting that pass, one wonders how raising the interest rate, or allowing it to rise, could be thought appropriate to the problem. A high interest rate no doubt chills the ardor of borrowers and thus may hold down the amount of money in circulation. Not all borrowers, however, are equally chilled. Speculators, as we have seen, find high rates stimulating.

Consumers are said to try to maintain their accustomed or desired standard of living. They will shoulder heavy debts at usurious rates to do so. Thus their readiness to assume mortgages at more than double the legal maximum interest rate of a few years ago; thus the cavalier expansion of credit-card borrowing; and thus the failure of high interest rates to impede the chase for goods. In fact, since high rates have proved acceptable to consumers, the consumer-loan business has become so attractive to banks that the paradoxical probability is that high rates have resulted in more money chasing goods, not less.

The famed bottom line, on the other hand, enforces a more circumspect demeanor on businesses, few of which find it profitable to expand when the cost of financing is in the double-digit range. Many find it impossible even to continue. Consequently, high interest rates, which have only a minor effect on demand, may have a major effect on supply. Whether or not there is more money in the chase, there are fewer goods in the running. Putting it more generally, there are fewer goods than there would have been otherwise.

The interest rate is a special cost of doing business. It is a pervasive, invasive cost. It is an inescapable cost. Even if one does not need to borrow, one does need to weigh the opportunity cost of investing one's money in one's business instead of lending it out. Interest and normal profit are opportunity costs of each other. Like normal profit, interest is a rate, a percentage, and hence an exponential factor in the cost of doing business. It is not a one-time factor, as is each separate increase in, say, the price of oil or the hourly wage rate. It exerts a steady upward pressure on costs, and hence on prices. Thus interest is ipso facto inflationary. It is also necessary; it is the cost of investment. In a noninflationary economy or a healthy business, it is less than the profitable output that results from investments.

The interest cost is the only cost that has this tireless effect. We used to hear much about a wage-price spiral, but a wage increase in the automobile industry (for many years the pundits' whipping boy) works its way only slowly through the economy. Initially it affects only the price of automobiles, and it never brings about a uniform wage scale. Wages of grocery clerks remain low, and all wages in Mississippi remain low. A boost in the prime rate of a prominent bank, on the other hand, immediately affects the rates charged by every bank in the land; and while it is possible for borrowers to shop around a bit for a loan, they find that rates vary within a very narrow range.

IV

People with money to spare, as we have noted, are said to be enticed into lending it by the prospect of getting their money back at a stated time with stated interest. What they want back is not the money, but the money's purchasing power, and in inflationary times, the only way to get back the same purchasing power is to get back more money. Hence the Bankers' COLA or cost-of-living adjustment.

Of course, bankers don't call it a COLA. They have, in fact, been unremitting in propagandizing the notion that COLAs are bad and inflationary and greedy and likely to cause the downfall of the Republic. The COLAs they talk about are those that appear (or used to) in labor contracts, where they are manifestly an increased cost of doing business, and those that appear in Social Security and other pension payments, where they are manifestly an increased cost of government. (An unmentioned COLA is the indexing of the income tax.)

As this is written, the propaganda against COLAs (coupled with high unemployment and underemployment) has pretty well knocked cost-of-living clauses out of labor contracts. The Social Security COLAs are somewhat more secure because there are more worried senior citizens than there are enlightened union members. Even so, the steady drumbeat from investment bankers (when they take time from promoting LBOs, which they evidently don't think inflationary) has put the American Association of Retired Persons on the defensive.

It is curious that the Bankers' COLA is accepted as a natural law, discussed matter-of-factly in the textbooks, while the others are deplored as the work of greedy special interests out to line their own pockets at the expense of the nation and its God-fearing citizens. For the life of me, I can't think why Social Security COLAs are inflationary, but Bankers' COLAs are counterinflationary.

Although the only actual interest rate is the money rate, bankers and their monetarist theorists talk of "real" interest plus a premium for inflation. Let us take them seriously. If there were such an identifiable premium, it would be a COLA in everything but name. If there were an identifiable real interest rate, it would be the rate in effect in a stable economy.

The economy has gyrated considerably in the past forty years, but there have been the two relatively calm periods mentioned above. In 1953–55 the prime was between 3.02 percent and 3.67 percent. In 1961–65 it was essentially unchanged at 4.5 percent. While a case might be made for the lower figure (which is, after all, still higher than the rate in effect when the foundations of the modern economy were laid), let us give the bankers the benefit of the doubt and call 4.50 the "real" rate and everything above that the Bankers's COLA.

As this is written, the prime stands at 10 percent, so the Bankers' COLA is now 5.5 percent or higher. But this rate is only the COLA cost of some new loans; it does not include the COLAs in continuing interest payments on outstanding loans from prior years. Many of these are low, for some happy people are still paying off 4 percent mortgages. And many of them are enormous, for in 1980 and 1981, the prime reached 21.5 percent (currently the all-time record), and Treasury bonds, which have no risk factor, reached 15.75 percent (which some will still be paying in the twenty-first century).

In 1988 the monthly average domestic debt of nonfinancial sectors in the United States—everything from Treasury bonds to your bank credit card balance—was $8,994.5 billion. The interest paid on that debt was approximately $942.8 billion. which is an average rate of 10.48 percent. So in 1988, the Bankers' COLA was between 5.98 percent (if the "real" rate was 4.50 percent, as it was in 1961–65) and 6.71 percent (if the "real" rate was 3.77 percent, as it was in 1956). In dollars, the 1988 Bankers' COLA was between $537.9 billion and $603.5 billion.

Again, let's give the bankers the benefit of the doubt and take the lower figure. A few comparisons may help put that $537.9 billion in perspective. It is more than fifty—repeat fifty—times the Social Security COLA that bankers in particular like to talk about. Using figures in President Bush's first budget, we find that it is more than five times the projected deficit for fiscal year 1990, it is more than five times the entire cost of Medicare, it is one and three-quarters times the entire cost of the Department of Defense. It is greater than giving every working man and woman in the land, from part-time office boy to corporate CEO, a 20 percent raise—and there'd still be some $75 billion left over to pay the unemployed $10,000 each and every one.

When we talk of Bankers' COLA, we are talking of an enormous charge the economy pays because of misguided policies of the Federal Reserve Board. The Reserve no doubt sincerely believes it is controlling inflation, but its policies are actually a stimulant to inflation. This will always be the case because the outstanding domestic indebtedness is greater than the GNP. If the Bankers' COLA were the same as the inflation rate, the cost of the COLA would still be proportionately larger than the cost of inflation. If (as is frequently, if not generally, the case) the Bankers' COLA is greater than the inflation rate, the cost of the Bankers' COLA is exponentially greater than the cost of inflation.

Interest charges are a large and growing component of the cost of living.[3]* In 1947, this component was 4.81 percent of the total. (Needless to say, I am not here talking about the interest rate—the prime was 1.50 percent in 1947—but about the percentage of the consumers' dollars that goes to pay interest charges.) From the 1947 figure of 4.81 percent, this percentage climbed steadily—to 5.94 percent in 1957, to 7.68 percent in 1967, and to 10.16 percent in 1977. Then in the years of manic obsession with inflation, it soared, reaching 18.88 percent in 1987. When this rise is compared with the relative stability we have noted in total wages and salaries, we have serious reason to doubt the conventional theory of inflation. To continue to believe that high wages cause inflation and high interest rates cure it is to echo Martin Luther's cry in *The Bondage of the Will*: "Since that cannot be comprehended, there is room for exercising faith while such things are preached and openly proclaimed."

Since the Bankers' COLA costs the economy more than inflation does, it is evident that there would be no inflation if the COLA did not exist. Other things being equal, there would be no deficit either.

Very great changes would follow if the Bankers' COLA were eliminated. Reducing the interest rate to its "real" level would tend to stimulate investment in productive enterprise, with a consequent growth in employment. It would probably trigger a one-time surge in the stock and bond markets, followed by a gradual falling off of speculation as productive investment possibilities opened up.

As things are now, however, the Bankers' COLA is an incubus of unconscionable weight depressing the economy. That this is so is revealed by the statistics whose subject is people rather than things. The median family standard of living is falling, even with two-wage-earner families more common than formerly. The number of people living in poverty is growing; and within that group, the number of those who work full time but are still poverty stricken is growing even faster. The rate of unemployment—even counting 37 million part-timers (25.3 percent of the labor force) as fully employed and not counting at all a million people too discouraged to seek work—is shocking.[4] These are marks of deflation, of recession, of bad times. That our overall appearance is one of inflation is almost exclusively attributable to the Bankers' COLA.

The alleged prosperity in this country—indeed in the world—is largely confined to those who have managed to make the Bankers' COLA work for them. The little protection that the retired, who can no longer defend themselves, derive from the Social Security COLA actually helps keep the economy going. Where would the Sunbelt states be without it?

V

Every American boy or girl who paid even the slightest attention in school knows that mercantilism was a bad idea. It bled the colonies for the benefit of the homeland, and consequently the colonies revolted. Those who listened a little longer also know that the mercantilist striving for a "favorable" balance of trade meant exportation of consumable goods and importation of precious metals, a policy that is ultimately self-defeating because, as Midas found out, gold is not good to eat.

As an example of mercantilist foolishness, Fernand Braudel tells us that in 1703, toward the start of the War of the Spanish Succession, the English were advised to send "grain, manufactured products and other goods" from home to their troops fighting in the Low Countries. They could have bought these supplies easily and presumably more cheaply on the Continent, but the government was "obsessed by the fear of losing its metal reserves."[5] Any follower of Adam Smith or David Ricardo can see that this policy led England to waste real wealth (usable goods) and save nominal wealth (unusable metal).

In the world of theory, the mercantilist passion for a favorable balance of trade seems indefensible. It is surely more sensible to secure what you can use than to squirrel away what is of little or no use in bank vaults. But as Braudel reads the historical record of the actual world, he is forced to recognize that the mercantilist policy was in fact successful. "In any case," he writes, "every time we have to deal with a *comparatively* advanced economy, its trade balance is in surplus as a general rule."[6] Flying in the face of classical economics, the more advanced economies exported usable goods and imported gold and silver.

The classical theory fails here (as elsewhere) because it is both ahistorical and asocial. It describes an instantaneous slice of a world without time, and it concerns things, like the GNP, not people, like you and me. Criticism of the English policy of 1703 silently assumes that purchasing war matériel overseas would have had no effect on English farms and factories. The assumption is that the goods purchased on the Continent would have been added to those produced at home and that the English wealth would have risen accordingly. But in the real world,

English farmers, deprived of part of their market, would have cut back production expenses (which is here another name for employment). And English manufacturers of soldier suits and the like would surely not have continued producing them if the government didn't buy them. Their employment, too, would have fallen. These drops in employment would have meant a decline in the English standard of living. The mercantilist policy preserved that standard of living (such as it was); the classical theory would have reduced it.

In the infrequently noticed catchall Chapter 23 of *The General Theory*, Keynes includes some "Notes on Mercantilism . . ." He observes that a favorable balance of trade, by bringing in gold and silver, increased a country's money supply, which forced down the interest rate, which stimulated investment.

Investment is not stimulated—not stimulated rationally, that is—for its own sake. From the point of view of the investor, the purpose of investment is to produce goods that are in demand and can be sold at a profit. From the point of view of the nation, the purpose of investment is to provide employment for its citizens and to produce things that are wanted. Since employed citizens are able to make purchases—create demand—these two purposes can work together, though they do not necessarily do so.

In the early modern world of the mercantilists, the interest rate was, as Keynes said, held down indirectly (and probably unintentionally) by fostering a favorable balance of trade. To have a favorable balance of trade, a country must export more goods than it imports. To export more goods, it must produce more goods. To produce more goods, it must employ more people. The secret of mercantilism's comparative success lies in the increased employment of labor.

For the power of labor is very great. Even putting to one side the facts that capital is the result of past labor, and that natural resources can be exploited only by labor, labor power is our ultimate power. The laziest, least competent, least efficiently applied labor can today produce far more than it needs to sustain itself.

Our agriculture and forestry now produce more food than we should or can eat, more than enough natural fibers to clothe us, more than enough lumber to house us, with 3 percent of our labor force. Since even at our shabbiest, we allow almost no one to fall through the safety net and actually starve or freeze to death, it is plain that we do not need additional workers to provide for their own subsistence. Therefore, the output of every previously unemployed worker we manage to put to work will raise our standard of living a bit more above subsistence. And we can do this without importing gold or silver to control the interest rate. We simply have to have the cooperation of the Federal Reserve Board.

VI

Our half-century-long preoccupation with inflation is evidence of a profound confusion of American will and thought—indeed, the confusion has been practically worldwide. Inflation is not an evil in itself; some evils may follow in its train, but no particular evil necessarily does. Evils, moreover, are always specific, not general, and are therefore open to specific treatment, while the chosen attacks on inflation have systematically damaged all aspects of the economy, with the exception of speculation.

In the public discussion of inflation, the evil that used to have most attention was the erosion of the standard of living of retired people and others living on a fixed income. Here is a specific evil that can be assessed and a cure proposed. In fact, this evil was assessed; cures were proposed; and the cures, the first of which has been in effect since 1966, have been remarkably successful. In 1966 Medicare began to protect the aged from one of the most crushing burdens of old age and to provide millions with health care that otherwise would have been denied them; in 1972 and 1973, automatic cost-of-living adjustments were legislated for Social Security payments. Since these COLAs were tied to the CPI, and since the CPI was skewed because of the weight it gave to the mortgage rate, and since the elderly are in general not borrowers anyhow, there is no doubt that many retired persons were better off in 1980 than they had been ten or more years previously. That was, after all, the intention. To be sure, a great hue and cry, led by a committee of investment bankers, persuaded the nation that the elderly had it too good, and managed to raise Social Security taxes and to lower benefits. That is not the point. The point is that the urgency of doing something about inflation was said to turn on damage done to the elderly. Given the damage, something was done about it. If what was done was considered too much (or too little), that only reinforces the argument that specific cures can be devised for specific ailments. There was no need to adopt monetary policies that ravaged the economy of the nation and of the world to address the problems of a small (though growing) segment of the population.

The recent attacks on Social Security have traded on the confusion that has existed since the program's New Deal beginnings. From the start, Social Security has been partly an insurance (or endowment) program and partly a welfare program. Social Security taxes are a form of forced premium payments; yet the benefits are not strictly proportional to the premiums. The attacks on the program have concentrated on its insurance aspect. The "bankruptcy" of the program was deceptively foretold. To avoid this alleged bankruptcy, taxes were raised and benefits reduced.

This was all very well, but it was flatly subversive of any attempt to solve the problems of those living on a fixed income. In the eight years after the Federal Reserve Board allowed the interest rate to rise unimpeded, the CPI went up 56.6 percent. Such an increase is of course devastating to people living on fixed incomes. One may wonder how, in the face of these figures, it can be argued (as it is argued) that the elderly are now better off than those still of working age. The principal answer, of course, is that wages—especially hourly wages—have fallen in constant dollars in the same period. It is not that the retired are better off but that those working are worse off.

It is sometimes said that the long-term or secular rate of inflation is 3 percent, and excited self-adulation results whenever it is approached. But even at that rate, the consequence in eight years would be a 26.7 percent increase in the cost of living. Policies—of whatever sort—that bring inflation down to its long-term rate may mitigate but cannot solve the problems of people who live on fixed incomes. If solving those problems is a sincere objective of a policy, they must be addressed directly, as they were in 1966, 1972, and 1973. Our experience since those years shows that such direct action, emphasizing the welfare aspect of Social Security, can be successful.[7]

Of course, many have scruples against promoting the general welfare and so want to emphasize the insurance aspect of Social Security. They cannot then honorably use the plight of the elderly as their reason for supporting draconian measures against inflation, because the draconian measures hurt the elderly along with everyone else. They may have other reasons for supporting draconian measures, but the plight of the elderly cannot reasonably be one of them.

To be sure, the elderly are not the only people living on fixed incomes. There are the widows and orphans, over whom many tears were shed in the opposition to New Deal controls of the stock exchanges and the banks. Crocodile tears aside, this problem is admittedly wider than that of Ferdinand Lundberg's sixty American families of great wealth. Addressing the wider problem, it might be urged that the welfare aspect of Social Security be broadened to cover such of the citizens as are not now covered. Beyond this, it must be acknowledged that people who live on fixed incomes—whether the result of savings or of inheritance—have no greater claim to immunity to the vicissitudes of life than do those who work for a living. As it happened, the programs that were undertaken in the announced intention of controlling inflation in fact caused—and were intended to cause—widespread unemployment. At the same time the soaring interest rate—which was deliberately encouraged to soar—offered opportunities for aggrandizement to banks and to individuals with access to money. In short, the policies actually adopted have favored unearned income over earned income; that is, those whom Keynes, following R. H. Tawney, called functionless investors over those who do the work of the world.

16

INTERNATIONAL TRADE

How the Multinationals Are Different

I

The first requirement of international trade is that there be nations. If there were no nations, there obviously would be no trade among them.

The distinguishing marks of nationhood are sovereignty and citizenship. A neighborhood or a region has boundaries and inhabitants; but it is not a law unto itself, nor do its members have exclusive rights, privileges, immunities, and duties. A neighborhood cannot make war, nor can a region draft its occupants in its defense. A neighborhood may have customs and traditions, but a nation has laws and a history. A region may have economic advantages, but a nation assumes economic responsibilities.

Despite some who believe nationhood not to be necessary, we do actually have nations. Despite some who believe economics to be a natural science, nationhood does actually make a difference in business enterprise. Given these actualities, the task for economics is to discover what special considerations, if any, lead nations to trade with one another and what special principles, if any, govern such trade. It is not enough to show that, in general, international trade expands the market, encourages the division of labor, and permits economies of scale, nor is it enough to show that, in general, international trade is a civilizing activity. Such showings can equally be made regarding in-terregional or interpersonal trade. Moreover, showing that interna-tional trade is advantageous for Belgium or Ghana or Taiwan says little or nothing about its importance for a continental power like the United States.

At the outset, we may name three conditions that set reasonable limits to discussion of international trade:

First, if we are under no obligation to guarantee fellow citizens the right to a particular job in our nation at a particular wage, we are under even less obligation to guarantee foreigners a particular job here or in their homelands.

Second, if no one has a right to a particular job at a particular wage, no one has a right to a particular product at a particular price.

Third, if we have a nation, we have a duty to maintain it.

II

Ever since Adam Smith, economists have been practically unanimous in support of free trade. Writing in the year of American Independence, Smith declared that "Great Britain derives nothing but loss from the dominion which she assumes over her colonies."[1] The loss came not only from the cost of defending and administering the colo-nies but also from the higher prices that British exporters could charge because of their monopoly. Higher prices in the colonies induced higher prices at home; so all nonexporters suffered.

For Smith, foreign trade was of minor importance, anyhow. It served two main purposes: It enabled countries to exchange surpluses, and it facilitated the division of labor by expanding the market. In further-ance of these ends, he opposed the monopolies and restraints on, or inducements to, trade that were root and branch of the mercantile system.

Over the past two hundred years the domestic market in any one of a score of countries has become larger than the largest world market Smith could have imagined, and the division of labor has gone far beyond the eighteen operations in the manufacture of pins that he immortalized. More important, the merchant adventurers of his day have been supplanted by today's multinational corporations. Nevertheless, his arguments for free trade still circulate and in the United States have inspired a tradition running from John Hay's Open Door in China, through Cordell Hull's Reciprocal Trade Treaties, to the postwar General Agreement on Tariffs and Trade.

David Ricardo was perhaps of even greater importance than Adam Smith to the cause of free trade. In 1817 he advanced his famous Law of Comparative Advantage, which purports to demonstrate that international trade is mutually profitable even when one country is absolutely more productive in terms of every commodity traded.

On the face of it, this proposition seems implausible, but Ricardo explained it this way: Suppose that a certain amount of wine exchanges for a certain amount of cloth. Suppose that in England it would take a year's labor of 100 men to make the cloth and of 120 men to make the wine, while in Portugal the man-years required are 90 and 80, respectively. In these circumstances, it would be to Portugal's advantage to make only wine and to England's to make only cloth, with the countries then exchanging the surpluses. Portugal would multiply its wine output 2.125 times $[(90 + 80)/80]$, and England its cloth production 2.2 times, and since the cloth and the wine are equal in value, both countries would come out ahead.[2]

Ricardo was quick to concede that his law applied only to international trade. "Such an exchange," he observed, "could not take place between the individuals of the same country. The labour of 100 Englishmen cannot be given for that of 80 Englishmen, but the produce of the labour of 100 Englishmen may be given for the produce of the labour of 80 Portuguese, 60 Russians, or 120 East Indians. The difference in this respect, between a single country and many is easily accounted for, by considering the difficulty with which capital moves from one country to another, to seek a more profitable employment, and the activity with which it invariably passes from one province to another in the same country."[3]

Ricardo went on to declare that "feelings, which I should be sorry to see weakened, induce most men to be satisfied with a low rate of profits in their own country, rather than seek a more advantageous employment for their wealth in foreign countries."[4]

What Ricardo could not foresee, and what his modern followers have overlooked, is that the new multinational corporations fail to share the feelings of patriotism or indeed of prudence that he ascribed (somewhat naively even in the nineteenth century) to the capitalists of his time. Today capital flits freely from here to there, moving as indifferently from Schenectady to Singapore as it did in Ricardo's day from London to York.

This is not the only weakness of his law as a guide to modern policy. More important is the fact that although the law begins by considering data that would be historical if they were actual (the equivalent values of the wine and the cloth and the numbers of workers engaged in producing them), it ends by assuming that the industrial changes it recommends can be accomplished in an instant and without other consequence—in a word, ahistorically. The British vintners are immediately to become weavers and the Portuguese weavers vintners. The British wine presses are immediately changed into looms, and the Portuguese looms into wine presses. Such transformation was perhaps almost imaginable in the first quarter of the nineteenth century. Even then, if the transformations were not accomplished immediately, in a trice, both parties would have unemployed workers and unutilized factories, as well as shortages of both wine and cloth. The resulting suffering and waste would more than offset the promised 6 or 10 percent increase in output, which could be accomplished in many less traumatic ways.

Like so much of classical economics, the Law of Comparative Advantage is suited to a world without time, where everything happens all at once, or not at all. Also like so much of classical economics, it assumes full employment. If either England or Portugal has substantial numbers of unemployed workers, it would be more advantageous to train them as weavers or vintners, as the case might be, than to keep them on the dole while importing cloth or wine.

What generally happens today, however, is that First World countries like England tend to abandon the production of both cloth and wine and to import both from some country where labor costs are lower. The question then becomes, How will England pay for the imported cloth and wine? By exporting something else, most economists cheerily reply, but they tend to be bashful when asked what that something else might be. If because of their lower wage scales (or for any other reason) other countries can underprice England in the pro-

duction of every product you can name, why should they buy anything
at England's higher prices?

Well, it may be urged, England, limping into the postindustrial
world, can concentrate on service industries; and while some services,
like motorcycle maintenance and baby-sitting, are hard to export, financial services are easy. And in fact historians have made much of the
importance to the British Empire of "invisibles"—interest, insurance
premiums, royalties, profits, and employment for younger sons. Of
these, only the last did anything to solve England's unemployment
problem, and today it is already happening that financial companies are
having their computer keyboarding done abroad at low wages.

In any case, the invisibles can only help pay for visible imports. They
can't carry the whole load, or even a major share of it. All financial
services together, including exploitative profits, seldom amount to more
than 40 percent of the cost of a product, and frequently are less than
20 percent, thus leaving from 60 to 80 percent of the cost of imports
uncovered. In the glory days of the British Empire, these costs were
covered in the usual visible ways of manufacturing and exporting textiles and guns and steam engines and anything else anyone could think
of. This is no longer so easy for England to do, nor is it easy for the
United States. Japan can do it, but she is not hagridden by theories
about free trade.

The ultimate consequence of abandoning productive industry is
national stagnation and decline—decline of both power and standard
of living. It has happened before. In 1675, a Spanish nobleman, one
Alfonso Nuñes de Castro, wrote, "Let London manufacture those
fabrics of hers to her heart's content; Holland her chambrays; the
Indies their beaver and vicuña; Milan her brocades; Italy and France
their linens, so long as our capital can enjoy them; the only thing it
proves is that all countries train journeymen for Madrid and that
Madrid is the queen of parliaments, for all the world serves her and she
serves nobody."[5]

Don Alfonso understated Spain's contributions to the wealth and
happiness of mankind. She may have produced little or no cloth, but
she provided services—military services, administrative services, ecclesiastical services—to the New World, and also to the Two Sicilies,
to the Low Countries, to Burgundy, and to the Holy Roman Empire.
These services, valuable though they may have been (there has been

doubt on this point), were not enough to support the imperial style in Madrid. When the silver from the Indies ran out, Spain, for lack of trained journeymen, slipped into a slough of despond from which today, three centuries after Don Alfonso, she has yet to escape.

III

One of the puzzles of recent years, especially for conventional economics, has been the ease with which American industry has been penetrated and defeated by foreign competition from the counties we defeated in World War II and from less developed countries of the Pacific rim. Since the United States has a heavy investment in capital plant, both in total and per worker, and since the United States is relatively thinly populated, it has been—and still is—argued that the United States has a comparative advantage in capital-intensive industries and a corresponding disadvantage in labor-intensive industries. On the basis of these supposed advantages and disadvantages, it has been— and still is—argued that the United States should expand its capital-intensive industries and export their surpluses, while shifting out of labor-intensive industries and importing foreign substitutes.

The conventional theory is not only a policy proposal, it is also supposed to be a description of the real world, for the advantages and disadvantages should inexorably induce the described result. The trouble is that it does not work out that way. Professor Wassily Leontief made an extensive quantitative analysis that showed "that an average million dollars' worth of our exports embodies considerably less capital and somewhat more labor than would be required to replace from domestic production an equivalent amount of our competitive imports. . . . In other words, this country resorts to foreign trade in order to economize its capital and dispose of its surplus labor, rather than vice versa."[6]

Professor Leontief's explanation of his finding has possibly contributed to the talk we've been hearing in recent years about labor productivity. He felt that American workingmen were better educated and more interested than those of other countries; that even though they were generally paid much more and often had somewhat less capital equipment per worker, they were so efficient and ingenious "that in any combination with a given quantity of capital, one man year of American labor is equivalent to, say, three man years of foreign labor."[7] While recognizing that it would take some time for so-called backward countries to catch up, Leontief pointed out that the American position was not unassailable. He wrote, "[T]he factors, whatever they may be, which are responsible for the high relative productivity of American labor might soon become operative in other economies and thus accelerate the elimination of disparity between the effective comparative supply of capital here and in foreign countries."[8]

Professor Leontief was writing in 1953. In less than two decades, Japan had fulfilled his prophecy, to be quickly followed by other countries of the Pacific rim. In the same years, Italy came to dominate the shoe business, Sweden remained prominent in automobiles, and even Yugoslavia tried to make a mark. More recently, American agriculture, which had long tolerated minor wintertime imports from south of the border, has been challenged and sometimes overwhelmed even in its home market by produce from Mexico, Chile, Argentina, and Brazil. These are only examples of the great changes that have transformed the United States from an exporter to an importer.

There are three principal reasons for the changes. In the absence of any one of them the transformation could not have occurred. The reasons are entrepreneurial, financial, and wage related. They all fulfill themselves in many ways.

First, entrepreneurial. Much has been written about the Japanese collegial system. Big government gets together with big banks and big industry (there is no big labor in Japan) and decides what shall be done, and then does it. Sometimes a mistake is made, as when Honda was advised to keep its mind on motorcycles, but the general success of the system is there for all to see. Also there for all to see is the system's dependence on and exploitation of a hierarchical society. It is not a remarkably pretty system, but no one doubts that it has been a remarkably effective one. It has also been remarkably resilient in meeting competition from neighboring countries. Thus in its planning for recovery after the war, Japan recapitulated the history of the Industrial Revolution by first emphasizing textiles. In this they were soon challenged by their neighbors, whose labor costs were much too low to think of matching. Almost at once Japan gave up the ambition to sell textiles internationally. The home market was protected, but the international market forgone. All effort was, instead, shifted to optics, electronics, automobiles, and now computers.

The Pacific rim neighbors' challenge depended not only on cheap labor but also on a new entrepreneurial style—one which has also made inroads in other lines, principally electronics. The new style was, in fact, pioneered by Americans, but it has been developed with enthusiasm, vigor, and excitement, especially in Singapore and Hong Kong.

In the paradigmatic version, an American clothing company sends representatives to the style shows in Paris and Milan, where they buy models they think suitable for marketing in the States. They then take the models to Hong Kong or Singapore, where they work out modifications of the style, partly to appeal to American tastes, and partly to accommodate Oriental production capabilities. At this point a local entrepreneur takes over and subcontracts with others—to buy cotton, say, in Bangladesh; have it woven into cloth and dyed in Taiwan; cut to pattern in Hong Kong; basted in the People's Republic of China; and finished in Seoul.

Here, again, the path opened by textiles and clothing was soon followed by other industries. Parts for all kinds of electronic devices, from calculators to hearing aids, can similarly be broken down into subparts capable of being turned out by semiskilled workers with relatively inexpensive machines. It is Adam Smith's eighteen steps in the manufacture of pins all over again, but with the steps no longer concentrated under one roof but spread, higgledy-piggledy, over half the globe.

The entrepreneurs who organize these industries are young men— most of them, it would appear, Hong Kong Chinese—of boundless energy and enthusiasm, who make Western "can do" operators listless by comparison. Already they are supplying parts for Japanese TVs and cameras, and consider themselves capable of managing the whole thing. Industries that the West has lost to Japan may well be lost to Hong Kong before the island's lease runs out.

Despite its successes, what we may call the Hong Kong entrepreneurial style is inevitably in a subordinate position. The energetic young Chinese who organize the operations lack an essential ingredient of commercial independence: They have no access to the ultimate market. They can quickly cobble together a congeries of small shops to make almost anything you want in almost any quantity at a most attractive price. But they do not themselves decide what to make; and if they did, they'd have no way of selling it. They can go to General Electric and offer to supply parts or even the whole of a hearing aid or whatever, but they do not design the hearing aid, nor do they discover the Western demand for such a thing.

Consequently they are always at the mercy of the First World companies that do control the markets. These may be manufacturers who sell the imports under their brand names, or they may be retailing chains big enough to buy all the sports shirts or kitchen utensils or bicycles the entrepreneurs can supply. Needless to say, the entrepreneurs have some countervailing power. If Sears pushes them too hard, they can go to K-Mart; if Black & Decker seems unreasonable, they can offer their services to Stanley.

To eliminate this pushing and shoving (otherwise known as the competitive system), First World companies become really multinational and open factories abroad under their own names. The multinational style is particularly effective in Africa and South America, where local entrepreneurs are less frenetic, and of course in Europe, where there are markets to supply as well as skilled labor to exploit.

The multinational corporation is a financial institution as well as a manufacturer or retailer. It shows this side of itself first in its decision to expand abroad at all, judging as it does that this is a more profitable way to invest its money than domestic expansion would be. It shows its financial side next as it chooses locations for its operations, being attracted to countries that offer subsidies or tax concessions. It shows its financial side finally and most clearly as it invests in foreign companies.

When General Motors buys 38.6 percent of Isuzu Motors or 50 percent of Daewoo Motors of Korea, it is not engaging in automobile manufacturing. It is investing surplus cash—cash it has earned elsewhere but can't think how to invest or spend elsewhere. Its earnings from Isuzu and Daewoo will show up on its profit-and-loss statement, but not in the top or manufacturing half. By these investments General Motors makes money by helping foreign industry to compete with American industry—even to compete with General Motors itself.

This is not so strange as it may seem. It's only a short step from the Sloan management system whereby Chevrolet competes with Buick and Pontiac as fiercely as it competes with Ford and Chrysler. The theory is that Buick and Chevrolet and Pontiac will meet competition from somewhere anyhow, and that if some of the competition can be internalized, General Motors will win, regardless of the outcome for the subsidiaries. As might be expected, the system acquires a life of its own. The corporation needs a whole new layer or two of staff to supervise the subsidiaries, set their goals, approve their budgets, and pass judgment on their achievements. Looking at what is complacently called the larger picture, the top layers find fulfillment in expanding or contracting manufacturing divisions and often in buying or selling them. In short, the tendency is toward finance, not industry.

Management neither produces nor sells; its triumphs are financial and legal, especially so its triumphs overseas. Americans are constantly being asked to take pride in this company or that as the largest of its sort in the world, or to be alarmed that, because of some regulation or other, American companies are said to be losing out to foreign competition. If these jingoistic problems are more substantial than totting up Olympic medals as a measure of the success of our society, it is because the gold medals are relatively harmless, while the overseas operations of American multinationals are generally adverse to domestic employment and prosperity.

Then, the banks. Their self-advertised achievement has been the recycling of the tremendous profits of OPEC's early years into nonperforming loans of American money to the Third World. Had the banks not been available to take this money out of immediate circulation, the OPEC countries would have had to spend it. God knows what they would have bought, but the countries that sold it to them would have become more prosperous and their economies would surely have become more active.

Led by Citicorp, the American banks did not hesitate. If they had, they would have lost out to British and French and German and Italian competitors, thus injuring our national pride. (Orientals are concerned about face; we have our pride.) In competition with foreigners and with each other, the major American banks scrambled for their share of the gold mine. The obvious way of attracting the Arabs' attention was to offer high interest rates, a procedure to which bankers are not constitutionally averse. At home they were restrained by Regulation Q from offering prospective depositors more than a toaster or, rarely, a TV.

This was nickel-and-dime stuff. Overseas the blue sky was the limit.

Having attracted their share of OPEC's money, the banks now had to complete the cycle. Again they did not hesitate. What with one thing and another, Third World debt went from $7.6 billion in 1960 to over $1,300 billion—that is, a trillion and a third dollars—thirty years later. The disastrous effects of this indebtedness (not all of which is owing to banks) on the debtors is much commented on.

The effect on the lenders is also disastrous. For to the extent that the borrowings were not squandered on the spot or thriftily sequestered in Swiss numbered accounts belonging to Third World leaders, they were largely spent on enterprises intended to compete with existing enterprises of the banks' home countries. Thus Brazil was lent money to build a steel industry that contributed to the decline of Pittsburgh and Youngstown.

In order to pay off the loans, Brazil has to export more than she imports, thus lowering her standard of living. In order to export, she must underprice American mills, which she can do by cutting pay, thus further lowering her standard of living. This is known, in International Monetary Fund circles, as austerity, and is much admired from a distance.

The IMF is also a doctrinaire enthusiast for economic "reform," by which is meant radical deregulation and privatization. The announced purpose generally is to reduce payrolls, especially government payrolls. It is seldom or never suggested that debtor countries impose equitable taxes on their rich or even make a serious attempt to collect the taxes already on the books, as a condition for international assistance. And no one would dream of attempting to stop the flight of capital to numbered accounts in Switzerland. Austerity is for the poor and, if unavoidable, for the middle class.

As Brazil is successful in her austerity, she ruins American mills. Not only does the failure of American mills enforce the austerity of unemployment on American workers, it reduces American exports, thus aggravating the American trade deficit. In order to pay off the deficits Americans must emulate Brazilians and lower their standard of living in the same austere ways.

This, unfortunately, is not all. No one really believes that Brazil and the rest will, in spite of the best austerity in the world, pay off their trillion and a third dollars of indebtedness. There will be defaults.

These, too, will impose austerity, for American banks will surely wangle subsidies from a government afraid to let them fail, and the subsidies will require higher taxes from those of us who are not bankers. At the same time the banks' American taxes will fall because of the nonperforming loans, even though, since the loans were made abroad, no American taxes were paid on the profits when the loans were performing.

The great recycling was surely as wondrous as the wheels Ezekiel saw, 'way up there in the middle of the air. It has been our sad fate that the recycling occurred on earth.

IV

Important though the skills of the entrepreneurs were, improbably feckless though the bankers, the changes foreseen by Professor Leontief could not have come about except through exploitation of Third World workers. It would be more accurate to say that the First World workers are the ones being exploited.

Third World workers rush to take jobs at 35 cents an hour, 50 cents, a dollar, or a lordly dollar and a half. These jobs would not be available if First World workers did not perversely resist reducing their wages below the subsistence level, though in recent years they have been relentlessly forced downward. American weekly nonagricultural, nonsupervisory wages fell (in "constant" dollars) from $189.00 in 1977 to $169.28 in 1987. For a 52-week year (by no means the standard for hourly workers), the 1977 figure was slightly above the poverty level, the 1987 level considerably below it. Both figures are of course above the minimum wage that was so rigidly resisted by conventional economists.

At present deals are arranged in China for relatively simple steps in electronics manufacture. The procedures must be simple because skilled workers and sophisticated machines are either reserved for domestic industry or lacking altogether. As a result, quality control may cost as much as 20 percent of the total. But consider the wages: 70 U.S. dollars a month for six eight-hour days a week. That's about 35 cents an hour—and no overtime, no paid vacation, no Social Security, no workers compensation, no health insurance. Also, no rent (the work often being done by housewives in the basements of housing developments), and not much in the way of safety regulations (whence Chinese surgeons' vaunted expertise in reattaching severed fingers). This is not to say that the workers have no fringe benefits, but that the welfare and overhead costs, whatever they may be, are met by the commune and not by the entrepreneur.

The entrepreneur's wage costs of 35 cents an hour (without benefits) are in competition with American minimums ten or twelve times higher (with benefits). Even if we accept Professor Leontief's estimate that American workers are three times as efficient as those elsewhere (and it is fashionable now to doubt this), that's not good enough to overcome the wage differential. We see the results at every hand. There is practically nothing that cannot be made more cheaply abroad than in the United States. Even Japan has seen its shipbuilding industry follow its garment trades to Korea, while it imports electronic components from Hong Kong entrepreneurs, just as does the United States.

The fundamentally irresponsible multinational corporation knows no boundaries other than the bottom line. Today capital is perfectly fluid. Aside from a few temporarily secret processes, technology anywhere is quickly available to literate people everywhere. Domestic availability of raw materials has not dictated a country's industry since the Industrial Revolution and certainly does not do so now (nineteenth century England grew no cotton; twentieth century Japan pumps no oil). Today the costs of all but one of the factors of production are nearly homogeneous throughout the world.

But the cost of labor is not internationally homogeneous. And since labor is usually the single most costly factor, as well as always the original and necessary factor, the heterogeneity of wage scales and working conditions overrides all other considerations. Labor, moreover, is not impersonal. Labor is people, fellow citizens.

V

Today, as in the eighteenth and nineteenth centuries, the more-developed countries need the less-developed countries as sources of raw materials, some of which are not available elsewhere. The multi-national corporations also use the LDCs, or some of them, as sources of cheap labor and cheap working conditions. The banks of the First World found the feeble nations of the Third World eager borrowers of money at high interest rates. What was, before independence, impe-rialism became neo-imperialism.

There has long been a lively debate about whether gunboat imperial-ism was good for the mother countries. Adam Smith, as we have seen, thought not. Bismarck concurred. "All the advantages claimed for the mother country," he said, "are for the most part illusions." People as various as Cecil Rhodes and Hjalmar Schacht were among those who disagreed.

The Marxian position, scarcely developed by Marx and Engels, was given shape by J. A. Hobson, by Lenin, by Rudolf Hilferding, by Rosa Luxemburg, and finally by Stalin. In the end, the emphasis was on the imperialist wars that were expected to be the last stage of capitalism; but initially and fundamentally it was argued that mature capitalism needed overseas outlets for investments discouraged at home by the alleged law of diminishing returns and overseas markets for goods that couldn't be sold at home because labor wasn't paid enough.

All sides acknowledged that the colonies were more or less mis-treated, perhaps in the course of the white man's civilizing mission, perhaps because of white men's inherent viciousness. Cultivated Brah-mans were insulted by half-educated British majors. Belgium kept the subject peoples of the Congo in ignorance. And so on. All this was bad, but it should have ended—and largely did end—with the political liberation of the colonies. Yet neo-imperialism took the place of imperi-alism.

The vice of gunboat imperialism was not so much the social and political domination as the economic extraction. What was extracted was paid for at going world prices, which somehow were almost always low. Farmers everywhere are seldom able to demand good prices be-cause they are too dispersed for easy organization, their industry is relatively inexpensive to enter, and their products have many substitutes and are perishable and at the mercy of the weather. What is true of farming is also largely true of mining. The farming and mining industries struggle under these difficulties even in the United States, but here they have been able to organize political power to obtain some relief. Nothing like this has proved possible internationally, with the exceptions of OPEC and the diamond cartel.

What is new about neo-imperialism is the influx of the multinational corporations, especially in the Orient. There have of course been international business organizations for hundreds of years. The old-line companies were in agriculture, like the United Fruit Company, or mining, like Cerro Chemicals. The new multinationals are engaged in manufacturing, and they are first and foremost international marketing organizations having close connections with retail chains and ready access to big finance. It is no secret why the multinationals have moved into the Third World. They are seldom interested in natural resources. They certainly are not in search of capital or of technology. As everyone knows, the factor of production that attracts them is labor—labor that is cheap, unorganized, and undemanding, willing to work long hours for low wages in substandard conditions.

Thus the distinguishing mark of neo-imperialism is the extraction of labor power. This comes about because the things the multinationals manufacture in the Third World are sold in the First World. The plastic-frame irons General Electric manufactures in Singapore are sold in American discount houses. The steel produced by new Brazilian mills is bought in markets formerly served by Pittsburgh. The textbooks printed in Hong Kong are studied in British classrooms. The California sports shirts run up in Korea are sold in Florida. In short, the Marxian theory of imperialism doesn't fit what is going on now. The multinationals are not looking for markets in the Third World; they are looking for labor. The markets—most of the time—are still in the First World.

As a result of all this activity, the Third World has things to export, though it seems never enough. The reason why there is never enough is that the exports to the First World are paid for with imports from the First World. It is at this point that the extraction of labor power shows itself, for many times as much labor goes into the exports as into the imports.

The wage differential varies from country to country and from industry to industry, but a very rough idea of comparative wage rates can be gathered from the figures the World Bank publishes on GNP per capita. In 1985–87, for a few examples, the figures were $310 in the People's Republic of China, $800 in Nigeria, $2,150 in the Republic of Korea, $1,640 in Brazil, and $2,070 in Yugoslavia. In the United States, the figure was $18,403. On the basis of these figures, we'll not be overstating the case if we say that a dollar commands five times as much labor in the Third World as it does in the First World. This means that when the two worlds exchange goods, the Third World is the net loser of four-fifths of the labor involved. This four-fifths is extracted and gone forever.

It is this extraction of labor power that is the vice of neo-imperialism. It is very likely true that the multinationals, or some of them, are not above diddling their books so that they can declare their profits where taxes are lowest. It is certainly true that the international banks, or some of them, are capable of persuading—or bribing—naive or corrupt Third World officials to borrow money at ultra-usurious rates to build power lines to nowhere and skyscrapers among mud huts. It is also true that the International Monetary Fund then counsels austerity (meaning a widening of the wage differential) for the hapless citizens of the countries accepting the loans. There is little in these activities of which the participants can be proud, but their effects are small in comparison with the effect of the extraction of labor power.

VI

Those advocating the industrialization of the Third World have had before them a working model of how it can be done. The development of the fledgling United States was financed by loans from England and, to a lesser extent, from the Continent. For a century and a quarter, until World War I, the United States was a debtor nation. American canals and railroads, American steel mills and thread factories, American shipyards and coal mines, all relied on foreign capital. Sometimes the foreigners were swindled, as in the Crédit Mobilier, but usually they got their money back with interest. The United States was a good investment for foreigners, and the investments were good for the United States.

But the nineteenth century United States model does not fit today's Third World. The difference is simple. The industry financed by today's multinationals manufactures goods for export. In contrast, the infrastructure built in the United States with foreign capital was necessarily used in the United States; it could not be exported. Moreover, almost all the goods produced in foreign-financed factories were sold and used in the United States. Britain imported food and raw materials from America, but very little in the way of manufactures.

Ironically, the United States after the Civil War was almost a copybook example of the Marxian theory of imperialism, but it had a diametrically opposite result. Raw materials were extracted; finance charges were exacted; an outlet for excess capital was found and so, too, was a large and eager market. According to the Marxian theory, the United States should have been a disaster, exploited and despoiled by Europe. But it was a success, while the Third World, which does not fit the Marxian theory for failure, is failing.

The United States was able to withstand the pressures of imperialism, and indeed to profit from them, for a reason that may seem surprising: its wage scales were the highest in the world. This used to be a proud and proper boast. Consequently, if there was an extraction of labor power, it was from Europe, not from the United States.

It would be making an irrelevant claim to suggest that the relatively high American wages were, except in a few idiosyncratic cases like that of Henry Ford, the result of deliberate policy. High wages were resisted by the entrepreneurs of the time, but they were in fact inevitable, given the small population in relation to the large country, and given the strong egalitarian tradition of the new nation. Today's Third World nations are not so fortunately situated. In general, their territories are small and their populations overflowing. There is no way in the foreseeable future for their wage scales to approach the highest in the world. They cannot offer the industrialized world much of a market. They present financiers with opportunities to practice usury and skulduggery, rather than investment.

VII

Neo-imperialism is as grave a threat to the industrialized world as to the less-developed countries. Before World War II, shelves of American five-and-dime stores were plentifully stocked with imported goods—novelties and notions, mostly: figurines from China or Bavaria, costume jewelry from Mexico or India, Christmas-tree ornaments from Czechoslovakia or Japan. Carriage-trade shops made a snobbish point of offering foreign luxuries of all kinds. American industry necessarily imported certain raw materials and specialties such as German optics and Swiss watch movements.

Taken all together, these imports did not amount to much. Even as late as 1950, imports totaled less than $10 billion, or 4.6 percent of GNP ex services. Furthermore, the imports generally did not displace existing American industry. In most cases the foreign novelties and specialties were long established, and American competition was hardly contemplated.

The situation today is quite different. By 1986, imports were running at a rate of 17.4 percent of GNP ex services, and competition with existing American industry was widespread and intensifying, although exports were beginning an uncertain recovery with the decline of the dollar. Certain industries were particularly hard hit. Electronics and optics were decimated; textiles were cut in half; steel and automobiles were savaged. There was scarcely an industry that did not feel the effects of foreign competition.

Explanations for what was happening were of two sorts. The one most popular with the Chamber of Commerce, the Business Roundtable, and the National Association of Manufacturers was that American wages were too high and American workingmen too concerned about working conditions to be properly productive. Classical economists also shared this view, since they are disposed to prescribe a drop in wages as the cure for most economic ills.

The other explanation was advanced mainly by investment bankers and a few technologically oriented neoclassical economists. According to this view, there is a natural history of business enterprise. When a corporation or—especially—an industry is launched, it grows very rapidly, partly because its initial base is narrow, but mainly because it is vigorous and innovative. As the industry matures, it becomes increasingly preoccupied with consolidating its gains. Too much has been invested in existing factories for newer and more efficient processes to be adopted. As Professor Schumpeter foresaw, the more creative but disorderly entrepreneurial type is replaced by the more reliable but overly cautious manager. Near-term goals are set; attention is directed to the next quarter's bottom line rather than toward a glorious future. The path to the executive suite, which had lain open to production and marketing geniuses, now is trod mostly by accountants and lawyers. The enterprise, or the whole industry, stagnates. In the currently popular phrase, it has become a sunset industry and should be written off in favor of some industry whose sun is rising.

Of the two explanations, the wage-scale theory is the more widely accepted. It can even co-opt some liberal arguments in its support, for Galbraith called attention to the willingness (not so common now as formerly) of big business to raise prices in tacit collaboration with big labor, while Sidney Weintraub studied the effect of the unit wage/ productivity ratio on inflation.

The wage theory has relied on extensive comparisons of foreign, especially Japanese, industry with American industry. Many of these studies are no doubt casually or deliberately misleading, but there is no need to examine them closely because they are, in any case, inconclusive. There are always two ways of looking at a comparison. In the present instance, it may be accepted that American wages are higher than Japanese (though lower than Scandinavian, West German, and Swiss). From this fact it may be deduced either that American workers are overpaid—or that Japanese are underpaid. One conclusion is precisely as logical as the other. In view of the history of labor relations, it would seem probable that the latter conclusion is nearer the truth.

This conclusion is the more certain as one moves from the automobile to the garment industry. The latter is far from a high-wage industry in the United States, but it is being overwhelmed by Oriental competition. In 1980 in the People's Republic of China, workers in this industry were paid 16 cents an hour; in the Federal Republic of China, the rate was 57 cents an hour; in Hong Kong, it was about a dollar. The rates in Korea and the Philippines were within that range. As a result, imports now account for over half of the United States sales of ladies' and children's apparel, up from only 5 percent thirty years ago. The sweatshop has reappeared in America, with illegal immigrants held to virtual peonage in conditions approaching those of the Triangle Shirt-waist fire of 1911.

In short, the argument over wages is irrelevant as it is stated. The question is not whether American workers are better paid than foreign workers, but whether American workers are paid a just wage. Not even the most doctrinaire economist can seriously propose that American workers be paid only 16 cents an hour; yet if free trade made sense, that is the wage that would be arrived at.

Classical economists are not, of course, primarily concerned about wages or the people who earn them. They contend that cheap imports save consumers so much money that the economy gains enormously from them. This argument is plausible enough as long as each industry is considered separately. If a particular American industry cannot meet Oriental competition, the thing to do might be to scrap it (as Ricardo suggested the Portuguese should give up weaving) and concentrate on something to be sold in the Orient. Displaced workers could be relocated or pensioned off. No one can claim a perpetual right to a special job merely because he or she likes it or is experienced in it.

It is, however, an example of the familiar fallacy of composition to transfer this possibly valid argument about a single industry to the economy as a whole.

And the economy as a whole must be considered, because today there is nothing whatever that cannot be manufactured more cheaply in the Third World than in the developed world. On the basis of the Law of Comparative Advantage, all American industry—hi-tech as well as smokestack—should be shipped abroad, and the United States, the industrial giant of the middle half of the twentieth century, should return to cultivating its gardens. There is, to be sure, some brave talk about a role in information processing, but with only agriculture and the service industries (including information processing itself) to be informed about, the role at best is not likely to be a large one and at worst would seem to be contemplating one's navel. Since agriculture now employs 2.6 percent of our labor force (and pays its workers poorly), most Americans would have nothing to do and consequently no earnings with which to buy the cheap imports.

Obviously such a scenario is absurd, but there is nothing in standard economics that contradicts it. Just as Keynes showed that a domestic economy does not automatically operate at full employment, it can be said that the world economy does not automatically employ all the available factors of production.

The absurd conclusion of the scenario is duplicated by the sunset-sunrise explanation of international trade. Indeed, the two views differ mainly in their choice of metaphor. The sunset theorists see that once-proud American industries have faltered and been weakened by foreign competition, mainly Oriental. Following their metaphor, they think the phenomenon natural, inevitable, and irreversible. They therefore recommend abandoning such doomed industries to their fate and mobilizing a massive R & D effort to locate and nurture sunrise industries to take their place. These theorists seem no more impressed than was Ricardo by the waste and suffering consequent on the death of an industry. And it seems not to have occurred to them that what happened once may happen again. There is no reason on earth why our new sunrise industries, whatever they may be, cannot be quickly copied in the Third World and subjected to the same low-wage competition as our sunset industries. Nor is there any reason why our multinationals, having participated in the national R & D program, should not at once open sunrise factories in the Third World, causing our sun to set before it rises. Investment bankers stand ready to finance them, using our money for the purpose, and relying on our government to bail them out if anything goes wrong.

VIII

The Third World nations will escape from neo-imperialism only as they are able to reduce manufacturing things for the First World and to increase manufacturing things for trading with each other. For many and obvious reasons, this will not be easy, though they will be helped if we help ourselves. That is to say, they may be nudged into trading among themselves if we cut down our labor-extracting trade with them. It is in our interest to protect ourselves from such trade because it hurts our fellow citizens and disrupts our economy.

The way to protect is to protect. First we decide that a few of our important industries are threatened in our home market by severe competition from foreign industries. Second, we determine whether that threat is made possible by wages or conditions that we would consider exploitative. Third, we refuse entry to goods produced in grossly exploitative conditions.

The proposal is not complicated. It does not cover all industry but only a few industries we declare to be important and threatened in our home market. It does not require elaborate cost accounting (as do the GATT provisions against "dumping") but simple, straightforward questions of fact: What are the wage scales? What are the working conditions? Is child labor employed? The proposal does not interfere with foreigners' or multinationals' trade anywhere else in the world. In every respect the proposal is analogous to our present laws refusing entry to contaminated foods or dangerous drugs or unsafe automobiles. Those laws protect Americans as consumers; the proposed law would protect us as workers and, incidentally, as entrepreneurs.

It will be objected that the proposal can't work because it is impossible to compare foreign wage scales and working conditions with ours. How, if the comparisons can't be made, do the critics of American workers know they are overpaid? What is proposed is merely the reverse of the critics' coin.

Of course the comparisons can be made, and they will be invidious. The real question is, as the lawyers say, who should have the burden of proof? In the present case, we could reasonably ask those who want access to our markets to prove that their workers are fairly paid and fairly treated by our standards. American unions and American companies would have the right to challenge the proof. No need to make a big fuss about it, any more than a big fuss is now made about determining that certain foreign automobiles don't meet our emissions standards or that certain drugs are inadmissible.

No doubt many will argue against protecting the American standard of living. Two arguments stand out. The first purports to be consumer oriented. Cheap imports, it says, benefit everybody. But they don't benefit those millions whose jobs are taken by the imports, and those other millions who are being forced back to the poverty level.

The second argument purports to be producer oriented. Restrictions on international trade, it says, invite retaliation and threaten all our industries, because exports now represent our margin of profit. To this argument there are two answers: (1) Our really threatened industries—automobiles, steel, textiles—have already lost their export markets; and (2) we have at home an unexplored market larger than any we might lose.

Our millions of unemployed, plus the millions of working poor, plus their dependents, comprise a "nation" of up to 50 million people—bigger than any but a handful of the 157 members of the UN. In spite of our failures—and theirs—these people are better educated than most of the rest of the world, are more familiar with the American work ethic, and are closer to the rest of us in needs and wants. If our national industrial policies were directed to helping these our fellow citizens so that their undeniable wants became effective economic demands, there would be plenty of domestic business to keep U.S. industry fully occupied and highly profitable.

IX

The skeleton in the protective closet is the Smoot-Hawley Tariff (technically the Hawley-Smoot Tariff, but it's easier to make fun of this way) sponsored by reactionary Republicans in 1930 and ever after blamed by junior-high-school civics textbooks for the Great Depression, the rise of fascism, World War II, the Cold War, and innumerable minor irritations. The analysis doesn't rise even to the level of *post hoc, ergo propter hoc,* for the Great Depression was already well under way when Smoot-Hawley was passed, while fascism had been in power in Italy for eight years and was rapidly growing in Germany and the military was firmly in charge in Japan.

At the time of Smoot-Hawley, international trade, especially American international trade, was relatively unimportant. In the boom year of 1929, United States exports totaled $5 billion and imports $4.1 billion. GNP was $103.1 billion. Exports are a positive component of GNP and imports a negative component; so the net export-import effect in that year was $0.9 billion. By the depression year 1932, exports had fallen to $1.6 billion, imports to $1.3 billion, and GNP to $58.0 billion. Although the net export-import effect had fallen to $0.3 billion, it was still positive, a situation that scarcely obtains today. From 1929 to 1932, GNP fell $45.1 billion and net foreign trade fell $0.6 billion. It is preposterous to claim that the fall in foreign trade caused the Great Depression; whatever causation there was surely ran the other way.

Professor Frank Taussig, author of the leading economics textbook of that day and an organizer of a statement signed by 1,028 economists opposing Smoot-Hawley, later published *The Tariff History of the United States*, in which he wrote: "Regarded as whole, the act of 1930 must be characterized as futile. The new duties on manufactured goods were mostly of a petty sort; most noticeably in such schedules as the cotton, silk, chinaware schedules. This or that article was more heavily taxed, and doubtless some domestic producers got an advantage. On the important branches of these industries the protective system had already been carried so far that no considerable further displacement of imports could be expected."[9]

What was the fuss all about? No one needs to pretend that Smoot-Hawley was a wise law in every respect, or in any respect; at the same time, it is contrary to fact to claim that it made a decisive difference.

A very high percentage of foreign trade merely distorts economies everywhere, to the principal benefit of bankers. There are, naturally, many things we want or need to import—oil (because we are too witless to cope with our energy requirements), tungsten, chrome, bauxite, coffee—and there are many things we can, without special government assistance, export to pay for them. But the necessity, or even the desirability, of foreign trade has been grossly oversold.

Trade is one of the modes of civilization. Trade also adds to wealth—the wealth of individuals, of nations, of the world. It does this by increasing and rationalizing employment, for wealth is the product of work. When trade expands employment for both partners, the prosperity of both is advanced. Conversely, when trade brings about unemployment for one of the partners, its advantage disappears. Trade will usually result in some unemployment in a competitive situation, and the unemployment will be compounded where the competition is based on gross wage differentials. If Japanese citizens were to buy up the output of Korea's nascent automobile industry in preference to Subarus and Toyotas, Japanese wealth would be decreased; we may be sure that the Japanese government has imposed effective restrictions.

Microeconomically—that is, company by company—foreign trade

can be attractive. Once a company is successful in its home market—factories built and paid for, experience gained—it takes little extra effort to open an export business, and economies of scale will make that business extraordinarily profitable, especially when stimulated by tax incentives.

When we shift from microeconomics to macroeconomics—from firm to nation—we find the fallacy of composition again. What is good for each firm individually is not necessarily good for the nation. In the circumstances we have been discussing, some (not all) American exports are being paid for by us in the shape of high interest rates that inordinately benefit a few, and we will doubtless bear the further cost of rescuing banks in danger of failing. On the other side, some (not all) American imports are being paid for by individual citizens in the shape of their shattered prospects and hopeless poverty.

These outcomes are not divinely ordained. They are the result of policies deliberately, albeit perhaps blindly, adopted. Rational policies would be in the direction of that millennial day when the world standard of living is uniformly high and trade can be uniformly free.

In the meantime, one would not select extractive or agricultural industries for protection because in general our commonwealth will be the stronger the more of our natural resources remain for future use. For similar reasons, it would be prudent to be especially attentive to strategic industries; it would be foolish to allow the steel industry to collapse, regardless of how much cheaper imports might be. We are sensible enough not to import our battle tanks from the Soviet Union, regardless of how efficient they are; our howitzers from Czechoslovakia, regardless of the expertise of the Skoda works and the liberation of its workers; or Silkworm missiles from China, regardless of their cost-effectiveness. How preposterous then, to imagine that we should rely on foreign suppliers for the steel to make these weapons. Whatever the market may be, it is not a proper judge of national interest.

17

CONCLUSION
The Prospect of Slow Deterioration

I

There is a fatality about economics that in the end chokes any society that makes too great a distinction between the rewards of the favored and of the disfavored. It is a commonplace of legal theory that a law must not only be just but must also be seen to be just. It is the other way around with economics, where it is more important for a policy to be fair than to be accepted as fair. This is particularly true when it comes to policies determining the distribution of society's rewards.

We now stand at the intersection of four historical movements, one of them very ancient, one originating in the Industrial Revolution, one becoming manifest in the latter half of the nineteenth century, and one arising in the Great Depression and World War II. These events or factors are, respectively, gross inequality of economic rewards, mass production, liquid finance, and big government. Taken separately, they are world-historical; taken together, they may prove world shattering.

Gross inequality of economic rewards is certainly nothing new. It has been with us from the beginning of time. It may actually be less now than in previous centuries. Slavery has been largely abolished, and some sort of egalitarianism is at least a widely endorsed ideal. Nevertheless, the gap between the rich and the poor is enormous, unconscionable,

221

and probably growing again, not only in the United States but in the rest of the world, especially in the Third World.

What has changed, and continues to change at an accelerating rate, is what the rich do with their money. Before the middle of the nineteenth century there was little question what they did with it. They invested in land and in improvements thereon: chateaus and stately homes and protoscientific agriculture. Of course, there were always commissions and sinecures to buy, and colonial adventures for younger sons, and gambles to take a flyer on; but land was everlasting. Money that was made by craft methods on the land was invested in craft improvements on the land.

In the eighteenth century, maldistribution showed its effects at the top as well as at the bottom of the income scale. Prospective lenders on the Continent were frequently unable to find willing borrowers at 4 percent or less. The situation was somewhat different in Britain, partly because she was notoriously a nation of shopkeepers. Even so, Braudel tells us, England "did not summon up all her reserves to finance her industrial revolution."[1] The South Sea Bubble in Britain and the Mississippi Bubble in France, both of which burst in 1720, were only the most dramatic instances of the speculation that developed in place of productive investment.

The economics of the rational greedy economic man sees no connection between such "bubbles" and the wastes and the horrors and the griefs of early industrialization. But the money that blew away as bubble after bubble burst had been accumulated at the expense of appalling labor and suffering of underpaid men, women, and children in mines and in milltowns, on ships and on industrialized farms—at the expense, too, of wanton destruction of the natural environment.

II

Changes that had started in the Commercial Revolution came very rapidly in the Industrial Revolution. Immense fortunes could be made in the new factories, which quickly overwhelmed their craft-based predecessors, first in textiles, and then in all sorts of industry, especially iron and steel. Two conditions impeded industrialization: illiquidity and exposure, both of which made it imperative for prudent gentlemen to become actively concerned in the enterprises they invested in. This was something that few gentlemen were inclined or qualified to do. Fortuitously, the development of efficient stock markets took care of one impediment, and the invention of the limited liability company took care of the other. And then, as we have seen in Chapter 9, another momentous change took place; property—the bundle of rights the law would protect—was enlarged from use-value to exchange-value.

The opportunities for what came to be called the functionless investor seemed almost limitless. Industrial capacity was now theoretically very great. The practical problem was to find a market worthy of it. Technological advances in agriculture had released a large population desperate for factory work at low wages. The low wages made low prices possible but at the same time restricted the size of the effective market.

At this point the inequities of economic rewards became a decisive restraint on production. Since the Great Depression, the restraint has been appreciably relaxed by the expenditures of big government; but we still have 7 million people we cannot think how to employ at all and 37 million more people we count as employed but cannot think how to employ full time. This costs us, and may finally destroy us; yet it would seem that substantial majorities of American voters have been satisfied with current policies. The policies are seen to be fair, but their actual unfairness may be our undoing.

Industry today is built on mass production. Giant corporations serve giant markets. Karl Polyani's "great transformation" to a market economy has become a giant transformation to a mass economy. Giant markets are crucial; without them, the giant corporations cannot exist. Giant markets are masses of people willing and able to buy. Such masses are impossible unless they include the employees of the giant corporations, and the employees are able to buy only to the extent that they are well paid. Henry Ford talked as if he understood this, but even his "high" wages were not enough to raise his employees out of the ranks of the working poor. In any case, this has remained a minority view among American business people. The majority view, in recent years embraced by the electorate at large, is that consumption should be curtailed and that government should not be big enough to maintain an effective demand for the goods the economy could produce.

We have no right to sit in judgment of our forebears, but we do have an obligation to understand what they did and a duty to judge ourselves. We have our burgeoning "institutions,"—and we have the devastated lives lived in our inner cities and decaying towns. We have our international financial empires—and we have the *favelas* of Rio and the slums of Cairo and Lagos and Bombay and—yes—Tokyo. We could afford to throw away a trillion dollars in 1987 and another large sum in 1989,—yet we do not summon up the will to afford fair jobs and decent living conditions for millions of our fellow citizens.

The bull market that started in 1982 took five years to absorb a trillion dollars. The bull market that started in 1988 has absorbed a trillion dollars in less than two years. The words "two trillion dollars" can be spoken trippingly on the tongue, but the devastation, disorder, and despair resulting from the extraction of $2,000,000,000,000 from the producing economy in less than seven years challenge our capacity to understand. "Challenge our capacity to understand" likewise can be spoken trippingly on the tongue. I do not know how to be emphatic enough. We are talking of tragedies compounded.

The economics of the rational greedy economic man failed our forebears. It is failing us. We fail ourselves if we refuse to understand that failure.

III

Economic polarization has malign consequences all across the distribution scale. The poor are unable to buy the products that giant industry could produce; industry consequently has fewer opportunities for further expansion; the rich consequently have fewer opportunities for investment; workers consequently have fewer job opportunities. If the rich are then frustrated in their attempts to consume their incomes, they turn to speculation. The amount of money that flows into speculative markets—preeminently the securities markets—is increased; so prices in these markets escalate. Escalating security prices mean escalating opportunity costs; corporations of the producing economy must increase their normal profit in order to attract the capital necessary just to continue in business. Normal profit—not, it will be remembered, actual profit—is in conflict with wages; so wages must be further restrained or employment reduced or "rationalized," thus increasing polarization and reducing the market for industry's products—a consequence Professor Robert Averitt calls the Paradox of Cost Reduction.

An essentially unrelated factor has a vast and unexpected effect in the same direction. Prudent individuals save for their old age and insure against risks of various kinds, particularly torts, accidents, illness, and unemployment. What is here prudent in an individual, however, is foolish in a society, where its pursuit is a fallacy of composition. A society cannot insure itself, because insurance merely spreads the risk through the society. In an economy as large as the United States, the actuarial problem is easily managed. The risks are as level as can be. The number of people to reach old age in any given period can be accurately foretold, and the number to suffer injury or illness can be foretold within reasonably narrow limits. Catastrophes, like Hurricane Hugo and the San Francisco earthquake of 1989, must be specially met anyhow. This being the case, it would be sensible to treat the costs of all these risks as a current expense. Instead, we are funding them.

It happens that all public and many if not most private funds are set up as costs of employment, as burdens on jobs. Social Security taxes are paid only by people who work and people who employ them. Corporate fringe benefits are paid for in roughly the same way. Medical malpractice insurance is an expense of doctoring. In these cases, the cost always inhibits and sometimes prohibits work.

Even if these bad designs were corrected, the funds are now so enormous that they will continue to have such consequences on Wall Street as we have recently observed. For by far the largest part of the trading now being done on the securities exchanges is being done by "institutions," that is, by pension plans and insurance companies, by colleges and churches and foundations of all sorts, and also by mutual funds.

Most of the institutions, it will be seen, are owned by or are for the primary benefit of the middle class. There is surely little harm in that, for in a certain sense the middle class is the society, the superrich feeling themselves exclusive and the infrapoor feeling excluded. Yet these institutions, by their means of existence, soak up purchasing power and weaken aggregate demand. By their speculating, they deprive the producing economy of efficient financing. The consequent constriction of the producing economy increases unemployment, exacerbates the polarization of society, advances the erosion of the middle class the institutions were created to shelter, and intensifies speculation itself.

Thus the distortion of the economy is compounded. Not so long ago, it was thought that an interest rate of 4 or 5 percent, an inflation rate of 2 or 3 percent, and an unemployment rate of 3 or 4 percent was an achievable ideal. It was, in all conscience, a shabby ideal, but it was certainly superior to what we hear now: 10 or 12 percent interest, 5 or 6 percent inflation, and 6 or 7 percent unemployment (counting as unemployed those too discouraged to seek work).

IV

In Chapter 10 we noted that the stock market crash of 1987 had little impact on the state of business because the speculating economy had become partially separated from the producing economy. This separation was largely the result of a series of lender-of-last-resort operations by the Federal Reserve Board and by the government generally. Such operations, one of the original missions of the Federal Reserve, can have the effect of validating questionable financial practices, unless the rescues are accompanied by appropriate regulations.[2] In this way the rescue of Continental Illinois effectively guaranteed all deposits in all major banks regardless of FDIC insurance.

The Reserve's 1987 offer of support to bankers and brokers, even though it was evidently not widely taken up, was certainly a factor in the bull market that started in the following year. There was much talk of regulating program trading and so on, but in the end practically nothing was done, thus giving speculators a green light to do it all again, but with more abandon.

It is not likely that the producing economy will continue to be so insulated from the speculating economy. The leveraged-buyout movement may already have effectively breached the barrier. In good times, shrewd businesspeople borrow as much as they can in order to expand as much as they can. If they don't, they're liable to be overwhelmed by their more active competitors. If times turn bad, they're liable to be overwhelmed by their debts.

V

Regardless of what a society considers good, there is, at least in theory, some point above which an individual's income can provide more of that good than a person has civilized use for—and also some point below which an individual's income provides little or none of the good. Those with the high incomes then have excess funds that they cannot invest in productive enterprise because those with the low incomes cannot afford to buy. Such a situation cannot correct itself. On the contrary, the amplitude of the difference between the rich and the poor tends to increase, and the numbers of the rich and the poor tend to increase, too.

The rich can turn to hoarding or speculation, but the poor can turn only to the state, which may fail them. It will certainly fail them if all it offers is some form of the dole, and that is all it will offer unless we can somehow be aroused from our long bemusement with the self-interested economic man. I dare not predict when this will occur or if it will occur. Massive and sudden shifts are surely possible. The Great Society was derailed by the Vietnam War. The "me generation" of quintessential economic men and women may yet become appalled at its own greediness.

In 1929, on the eve of the Great Depression, income distribution in the United States was so skewed that the total incomes of the top one-tenth of 1 percent of American families equaled the total incomes of the bottom 42 percent, and some 60 percent of all families were living below the poverty level (then about $2,000).[3] These figures are for what is still thought of as a time of unexampled prosperity; four years later, with almost a quarter of the civilian population unemployed (not counting most women as even prospective workers), things were exponentially worse.

It took four harrowing years to shock the nation into making a start on reform, and it took the industrial mobilization of World War II to show how reform was possible. By 1973 the family poverty rate had been brought down to 8.8 percent—nothing to be proud of, except in contrast with the 1920s. It has subsequently moved sluggishly, reaching 12.3 percent in the recession of 1982-83, and drifting to 10.4 percent in 1988.

It is an open question whether our morale is so corrupt, our power of empathy so feeble, and our interest in economics so meager that it would take another depression to make resumed reform possible. If so, the prospect is dark—ironically dark, because big government has made a full-fledged depression unlikely.[4]

The gravamen of the charge is unjust treatment of our fellow human beings. In the light of that charge, it is barely worth considering that gross maldistribution of income and wealth, although evidently effective in the rise of our civilization, is now leading us to its decline. The maldistribution may, as many argue, be the consequence of cyclical swings in the economy. It may, as others say, be the result of technological change. For centuries, it was thought necessary to goad economic man to work. The explanation of the maldistribution will influence the corrective measures we take; it does not affect the necessity for correction.

In the meantime, as long as we refuse to make fundamental reforms,[5*] we can expect further difficulties, which may come about as a result of Third World debt, or consumer debt, or a crisis in the insurance business, or bankruptcy of the FDIC, or collapse of the Pension Benefit Guaranty Corporation, or resurgence of OPEC, or another market crash, or (ironically) the end of the arms race, or something quite unforeseen; and each time unemployment and inflation will inch upward. We may nevertheless avoid an old-fashioned depression—unless doctrinaire bias simultaneously prevents big government from taking up the slack.

Big government can bolster aggregate demand sufficiently to forestall panic selling of assets and panic cutting of prices. Sophisticated businesspeople will avoid price cutting anyhow, to the extent of their ability. Modern doctrine teaches that the most profitable (or least damaging) response to bad business is to maintain price but cut production. Cutting production of course cuts employment. Consequently each pallid recovery tends to start with higher prices and higher unemployment than the one before it, and the successive stagflations tend to become slowly more severe.

The slow deterioration of a society can go on for a very long time. The Pharaonic World, the Roman World, the Medieval World, the Mandarin World, all stagnated for centuries. The Modern World (it will be our successors who name it) can do the same.[6]☆ And it will do the same as long as we the people continue to believe that the economy and government and society and we ourselves are merely natural phenomena determined as are the phenomena of classical mechanics. Keynes was right about the power of ideas; but he may have underestimated the staying power of old ideas.[7] As long as we think intuitively in mechanistic metaphors we shall pursue policies suitable for the operation of machines, not for the guidance of free men and women.

If there is a dead hand lying upon contemporary economic thought, it is the invisible hand discovered by Adam Smith. Two hundred years ago, this was, as we saw in the first chapter, a liberating hand, which participated in freeing us from arbitrary rulers. But it did so at the cost of conceiving of us as greedy servomechanisms.

Since it is not in our stars that we are underlings; since we are the captains of our souls; since, as we have said more prosaically, we are autonomous, then we all, severally and collectively, have the opportunity—the right and the duty—to participate in shaping an open and confident and generous economy that allows and even challenges all its members to be fully human. This is the task of any future economics.

APPENDIX A
On Perfect Competition

For a century after Adam Smith, one might have rested fairly comfortably in the belief that perfect competition was not only possible but actually existent in the real world; that it was in fact the normal state of affairs; and that exceptions, when they appeared, were always, or almost always, the result of the sovereign's interference with the market. The articulated, elaborate, and imposing structure of classical economics was erected on this belief, and so was the mathematically elegant supporting theory of marginal analysis.

It took the Great Depression to shock experts into seeing what the naive (and the ruthless) had always seen—that perfect competition did not exist. Yet no sooner were the economic crisis and World War II ended than the old belief reasserted itself.

It was claimed, first, that the real world operated *as if* there were perfect competition, and that predictions made on the assumption of perfect competition were generally correct, while predictions made on the assumption of imperfect or monopolistic competition were indeterminate.

Second, it was claimed that the assumption of perfect competition was an axiom, like the axioms of Euclid, which were said to assume points without dimension, and so on, that everyone knew did not exist in the real world.

Third, it was claimed that physics made similar assumptions, for example, the assumption of a perfect vacuum, without which the formula $S = 1/2gt^2$ wouldn't work.[1]

On the first claim, we may consider the analogous case of the Brownian movements in a Wilson cloud chamber, where the tracks of droplets look as if whatever caused them were alive. If these movements were actually living, the distinction between biology and physics would ultimately collapse. Either all things would be living, or all things would be inanimate. Similarly, if the economy were actually ruled by perfect competition, oligopoly and monopoly could not exist, and the *Fortune* 500 would be a mirage. In both cases, the *as if* argument is the ancient fallacy of affirming the consequent. If the earth is flat, then we won't fall off. The consequent (we won't fall off) is true, but that doesn't prove that the earth is flat, nor would the fact (if it is a fact) that people act as if there were perfect competition prove that there actually is perfect competition. More important, it would not prove (what libertarians go on to assert) that there should be untrammeled competition, and that all government regulation should therefore be repealed.

The second claim betrays misunderstanding of what Euclid is about. A straight line, says Euclid, is the shortest distance between two points. Yet if you try to draw a straight line, your result will have breadth and height as well as extension and will, moreover, display various irregularities, especially under a magnifying glass. Euclid's line is claimed to be an abstraction from the real world, and the notion of perfect competition is said also to be an abstraction from the real world.

But Euclid is not an abstraction. Euclidean diagrams are a convenience but are no part of the proofs. Euclid is not describing forms he finds in the world, he is defining space. In order to do this, he must, for one thing, be able to say that one object is farther away than another; and to say that, he must be able to say that the distance to one is greater than to the other. He must, in short, establish rules for comparing distances; hence the straight-line axiom.

Geometry has practical uses and these expand our world. A little elementary trigonometry was used by Thales in the 6th century B.C. to make a fortune by determining which grain ship was likely to reach Miletus first, and he could not have done this if distance were indeterminate.

The 3, 4, 5 triangle was early used to lay out fields with square corners (and I have done the same with the lines of a tennis court). The Pythagorean theorem is not an abstraction; it is a consequence of the definitions of triangle and right angle. The Pythagorean Brotherhood did not make a collection of real-world objects and abstract from them the idea of a right triangle. Without the definition they could not have known which real-world objects to collect.

Euclid is about space. Space is not an abstraction; it is a necessity. Perfect competition may be an abstraction, but it obviously is not a necessity.

The formula $S = 1/2gt^2$ is different because it clearly has an inductive origin. Galileo may not have disproved Aristotle by dropping stones of different weights from the Leaning Tower (a similar experiment had anyway been performed by Simon Stevin in Holland a half century earlier). But Galileo did make "a brazen ball, very hard, round, and smooth"; he did roll it down an inclined plane; he did time its fall with a jury-rigged water clock "with such exactness that the trials being many and many times repeated, they never differed any considerable matter."[2] And on the basis of the statistics so compiled he did develop his version of what became this formula.

Here we have a true case of abstraction. Galileo considered only distance and clock time. He disregarded the color, taste, sound, and odor of his brass ball. He disregarded especially its weight. And he came up with a formula that applied to all falling objects. The slow and erratic fall of a feather was not an exception, because he also disregarded the atmosphere.

Libertarians claim that Galileo thereby assumed a perfect vacuum, and that a perfect vacuum is no more possible in the real world than is perfect competition. But physics does not assume a vacuum, and the feather is not an exception. The brass ball, too, was affected in its fall by the atmosphere. Science proceeds by isolating and studying such effects, not by assuming them away. In contrast, advocates of perfect competition assume its existence, fallaciously affirm its validity by assuming its alleged consequences, and proceed to lobby for policies supposed to be in harmony with their original assumption.

APPENDIX B
On Games

The idea of competition is embedded in current ideology and folklore. There is scarcely an aspect of private or public life that is not touched by it. We expect males to compete for the favors of females, and vice versa; and we expect the resulting pairs to compete within themselves for dominance. Consequently we are not surprised to hear that siblings compete with each other for their parents' attention, and that the Oedipus complex is a form of competition. We expect very young children to compete to get on the fast track at school, and we expect all children to compete in sports, which are said to be character builders and essential preparation for the great game of life.

The first theory of competition was advanced by Thomas Hobbes in the seventeenth century. Inspired by the example of Galileo to look for a motive force common to all men, Hobbes concluded that the fear of death leads to "a perpetual and restless desire of power after power. And the cause of this is not always that a man hopes for a more intensive delight than he has already attained to, but because he cannot assure the power and means to live well . . . without the acquisition of more."[1]

The Hobbesian war of all against all is explicitly brutalized by the not-uncommon assumption that social life recapitulates Malthusian

234

demography and Darwinian evolution. Let competition be unre-
strained, it is enthusiastically urged, and the best will survive and the
incompetent be eliminated.

The foil to competition is cooperation. It, too, is embedded in our
ideology and folklore. In kindergarten we learned how two donkeys
could both have their fill of hay if they shared the piles instead of each
trying to get a pile all for itself. Later we understood why the colonies
had to hang together if they did not want to hang separately and why
the Constitution formed a more perfect Union than the Articles of
Confederation. We mourned the failure of the League of Nations and
greeted the United Nations with resurgent hope. On the playing field,
we celebrated the team effort, cheered the team player, emphasized the
teamwork in sports from tennis doubles to soccer.

With this background, we are predisposed to take game theory
seriously and to look to it for solutions to social problems. There is even
a game that is thought to reveal the origins and relative merits of
competition and cooperation. It is called Prisoner's Dilemma. Two
prisoners are separately questioned by their captors, who promise each
one freedom if he implicates the other in an alleged crime. What are
the poor prisoners to do? If both steadfastly refuse the offer, they will
be punished, but probably not harshly. If only one gives evidence, he
will be freed and the other severely punished. But if they implicate each
other, they will both be in for it.

There are thus four possible outcomes: both lightly punished, the
first freed and the second heavily punished, the second freed and the
first punished, and both condemned. Game theorists assign scores to
these outcomes (say 3–3 for the first, 5–1 for the second, 1–5 for the
third, and 1–1 for the last). They then use the game as a model for
social or economic competition, with refusal to implicate representing
cooperation and mutual incrimination representing destructive competition.

The game is played many times (it lends itself to computerization),
each player trying to achieve the higher total score, no matter what the
other player does. Many patterns of play are possible, and it is said that
this particular game is almost always won by a player who initially
makes a cooperative move and thereafter mimics what the other player
does. This is called, in capital letters, TIT-FOR-TAT.[2]

It will be quickly seen, however, that TIT-FOR-TAT is, appropriately enough, a case of GIGO, or garbage in, garbage out. If instead of 5, 3, 1, scores of 100, 95, −10 were assigned to the moves (and why not?), the outcome of the game would be quite different. The outcome would be altogether unpredictable if different scores were assigned each time the game went into the computer (which would surely be more "realistic"). Since there is nothing immutable or even plausible about the scoring, there is nothing enlightening about the outcome. Prisoner's Dilemma is a game, like contract bridge or field hockey; its scoring system dictates the way the game is played; and the winners win merely a game.

Of the many differences between games and the real world, perhaps the most important is that the progress of a game does not affect the rules of an ongoing or subsequent game. But, as Richard Levins observes, "In nature, unlike game theory, the plays of the game are not permanently distinct from a change in the rules."[3] That is to say, the rules of a game are imposed, while in nature they are organic and are continually changing. A mutation may produce a biological form more successful in a given ecological niche than the previous form. Not only is the previous form pushed aside, but also the new form changes the niche.

Something like this happens in business. The mass-market paperback book business was created in the 1930s by the invention of a new set of publishing "rules," which included certain manufacturing processes, a new method of distribution, new (and very low) royalty rates, and a new low price. After the Second World War, increased printing and shipping costs forced paperback publishers to raise their cover prices. The increased cover prices yielded higher dollar royalties even at the existing royalty rates, whereupon it was seen that a further increase in cover prices would so increase gross profits that the royalty rates could be increased, thus exponentially increasing dollar royalties, and stimulating increased demands from authors. Step by step, prices and royalty rates were increased until it became possible for publishers to bid in the millions for expected best-sellers, and it became necessary to make such bids to maintain their place in the market. In this way, the plays in the paperback "game" changed the rules and, of course, the game, which continues to change. In "real life," the rules are always changing. Our universe is not absolute but historical.

APPENDIX C
On Utility

I

Thirteen years after the invisible hand had its epiphany in *The Wealth of Nations,* another world-historical idea was launched—Jeremy Bentham's utilitarianism. It sought some impersonal factor of personality, and it aimed from the start at being mathematical. Bentham developed what he called the "felicific calculus," which assigned utility values to commodities in accordance with their contribution to pleasure or to the avoidance of pain. Bentham thought his calculus objective in the same way Newton's laws of motion were objective.

What is astonishing is that the idea has hung on for so long. Even today, power company lawyers talk solemnly about the "utils" of satisfaction their services afford their customers. Bentham himself pointed to a fatal weakness. "Quantity of pleasure being the same," he said aphoristically, "pushpin is as good as poetry."[1] In other words, one man's pleasure is another man's pain, and both are private. What is useful is what provides pleasure or enables the avoidance of pain, but pleasure and pain are exquisitely subjective. As the old wheeze has it, a sadist is one who enjoys giving pleasure to masochists. It would be arbitrary for you to insist that I really derive pleasure from something I say pains me. How could you know? Pierre Dumont, who translated Bentham into French, put it baldly: "Everyone will constitute himself judge of his own utility."[2]

In spite of its inescapable subjectivism, utilitarianism tantalized the nineteenth-century mind. Independently and almost simultaneously, three writers—Léon Walras in Switzerland, Carl Menger in Austria, and W. Stanley Jevons in England—hit upon the idea of marginal utility, which seemed to them and still seems to most economists today to purge the theory of its subjective taint. It was done by means of the differential calculus.

Walras defined the role of the calculus as follows: "We may say in ordinary language, 'The desire that we have of things, or the utility that things have for us, diminishes in proportion to the consumption. The more a man eats, the less hungry he is; the more he drinks, the less thirsty, at least in general and saving certain regrettable exceptions. . . .' But in mathematical terms we say: 'The intensity of the last desire satisfied is a decreasing function of the quantity of commodity consumed'. . . . It is not an appreciable quantity, but it is only necessary to conceive it in order to found upon the fact of its diminution the demonstration of the great laws of pure political economy."[3]

Because of this conceivable but nonappreciable quantity, it is possible for each of us to rank our utilities and to make mathematically reasonable choices. Economists tend to talk of equally (or "indifferently") desirable commodities, but if trade is to occur at all, some commodity seems to someone at the moment of trading more desirable than all other possibilities.

In the same way, infinitesimal differences will recommend one investment over another and over all others. In each industry one firm will become strongest in resources and most successful in trading. The outcome is described by Walras: "If, in short, at a given point a certain quantity of manufactured products corresponds to the absence of gain and loss [that is, if price equals cost], the parties in the transaction who manufactured less take the losses, restrain their production, and finish by liquidating; those who manufactured more take the gains, develop their production, and attract to themselves the business of others; thus . . . production in free competition, after being engaged in a great number of small enterprises, tends to distribute itself among a number less great of medium enterprises, then among a small number of great enterprises, to end finally, first in a *monopoly at cost price,* then in a *monopoly at price of maximum gain.* "[4] Walras comments, "This statement is corroborated by the facts."

From this unexceptionable analysis, we must infer that on the assumptions of marginal utility, free competition is impossible except perhaps as a transient initial point. Since free competition is itself an assumption of marginal utility, we might expect the theory to have been abandoned at this point. Instead, the contradiction was swept under the rug, just as Adam Smith blithely continued to rely on competition and the invisible hand even though fully aware that "To widen the market and to narrow the competition, is always to the interest of the dealers . . . an order of men, whose interest is never exactly the same with that of the public, and who accordingly have, on many occasions, both deceived and oppressed it."[5]

It may also be observed that Walras did not pursue the calculus as far as it will go. Infinitesimal differences will enforce preference of one industry over all others, just as one firm is preferred within each industry. The really final end will be one firm making one product; and complete analysis might well determine that the single firm had a single owner, a single employee, and a single customer for its single product, whose sale is a single apocalyptic event.

Such a conclusion is obviously absurd, but this outcome is perfectly congruent with the traditional theory of free competition, which contemplates the reduction of price to cost, the survival of the fittest enterprise, the cost-minimizing settling of each industry on its "best" product, and the flocking of investors to the most profitable industry. In the world we live and move in, it is a historical fact that this absurd conclusion has so far been avoided. The bright radiance of pure political economy is necessarily stained by the willful actions of us poor mortals, whose last desires satisfied are not imaginary utils but historical or biographical facts—which is fortunate, since whatever the ultimate single product proved to be, the final single consumer would either starve to death or choke to death on it, provided that he (or she) didn't sooner die of boredom.

II

Walras's notion of a decreasing function has suggested a somewhat different attempt, made by economists as various as Abba Lerner and Milton Friedman, to establish an "objective" basis for motivation.[6] A rich man, it is said, suffers less pain from the loss of a dollar than a poor man gains in pleasure from the acquisition of a dollar. This is certainly not universally true, for there are misers among us and also blithe spirits aware that the best things in life are free. Bob Cratchit was a happier man than Ebenezer Scrooge. Experienced money raisers know that in general the rich are less likely to tithe than the poor. And experienced politicians know that it is harder to increase the top income tax brackets than to boost a sales tax, regardless of the relative numbers of people involved and the relative worth to each of them of a dollar more or less. To be sure, a case can be made that progressive taxation is more just than regressive taxation; but once justice is admitted to economic discourse it becomes the dominant consideration. I insist that it is dominant, but I point out that marginalism is an attempt to escape what it thinks of as the subjectivism of moral judgments, and that with the admission of justice, marginalism has failed.

Marginalism fails, anyhow, it should be noted, when comparisons turn on questions of money, for the purpose of marginalism is to establish a base for value, and its need follows from the feeling that price needs explanation. Price, of course, does not exist without money, and vice versa. Thus arguments about the psychology of rich men and poor men seek to find objective values to explain prices—but they must use prices to do so. It cannot even be said who is rich and who is poor without appeal to the prices of the goods the rich and the poor possess as wealth or income. An appeal to satisfaction rather than to price makes Cratchit a richer man than Scrooge; the theory would then have to explain why the loss of a sentimental satisfaction would be less important to Bob than a sentimental gain would be to his employer. But no such game is played; and if it were, it would make a shambles of the allegedly predictable or "rational" behavior of economic man.

III

Even when not reduced to absurdity, the calculus of marginal utility did not claim to do more than rank utilities for a given individual, and that at a given moment. Your pleasures and mine cannot be compared, nor can the utilities we exchange be explained mathematically. It turns out that on the assumptions of profit maximization and free competition, nothing happens. No exchange takes place, and so no exchange value appears.

Authority for this judgment is Léon Walras himself, who writes, "What reason is there to exchange net income against net income, to sell, for example, a house yielding 2,500 francs in rentals for 100,000 francs, only to buy a piece of land for 100,000 francs yielding 2,500 francs in rent? Such an exchange of one capital good for another makes no more sense than the exchange of a commodity for itself." Then he adds, "To understand why purchases and sales take place in the market for capital goods we have to fall back upon certain crucial facts of experience in the world of reality."[7] Quite so. As Pogo might say, we have met these crucial facts, and they are us.

Walras talks only of production goods, but Carl Menger, the second of the independent developers of marginal utility, made a more general observation: "Commodities that can be exchanged against each other in certain definite quantities (a sum of money and a quantity of some other economic good, for example), that can be exchanged for each other at will by a *sale* or a *purchase,* in short, commodities that are *equivalents in the objective sense of the term,* do not exist—even on given markets and at a given point in time. And what is more important, deeper understanding of the causes that lead to the exchange of goods and to human trade in general teaches us that equivalents of this sort are utterly impossible in the very nature of the case and cannot exist in reality at all."[8]

If every good had, as Bentham imagined, a determinate objective value, there would be no point in trading (unless one cheated). For trade to proceed, traders must put personal valuations on the goods to be bought or sold. I may want to sell my cow because I'm tired of feeding her, or because her milk makes me sick, or because I lust after more gold to fondle, or because I want to do you a favor. You may want to buy her for reasons equally subjective and idiosyncratic. All this is indeterminate. Our subjective valuations are made objective and determinate in the money that changes hands in the act of buying or selling, and only thus.

Or put the issue this way: If every good has a determinate objective value, how do we know what it is? If utility explains price, the question then becomes, How do we know what has utility, what affords pleasure or suppresses pain? W. Stanley Jevons, the third of our triumvirate (though actually the first in time) has the answer. In his classic exposition of marginal utility, he calls for increased efforts to collect economic statistics. "The price of a commodity," he writes, "is the only test we have of the utility of the commodity to the purchaser. . . ."[9] And, he might have added, to the seller, too. The theory says that price is explained by utility, but unhappily all we know of utility is price. The theory of utility tells us nothing we did not already know. We are back where we started.

The same point had, indeed, been made sixty-eight years earlier by Jean-Baptiste Say. He wrote, ". . . Price is the measure of the value of things, and their value is the measure of their utility. . . ."[10] Although Say's observation destroyed the foundations of marginal utility almost before Bentham finished pouring the footings, and although Jevons destroyed the framing even as he erected it, this dizzily circular argument is today the leading doctrine taught in American universities.

No matter how we try to explain price, all we know is price. The impulse behind an offer to buy or sell may be physiological or psychological or sociological—or chemical or physical. It doesn't matter. The "cry" in the market is certainly physical; so how many ergs of energy result in a dollar bid for wheat? Or if, as has been assumed since Bentham, the impulse is merely psychological, how many "utils" of satisfaction, depending on how severe a course of toilet training, result in a dollar bid? All that is nonsense. Everyone knows it is nonsense. There is no way of starting with ergs or utils or the Oedipus complex and getting to dollars. A connection might be shown in a particular case after the event, but it has to be after, and it has to be shown. It cannot be assumed to be regular, nor can it be assumed to have been proved. As there is no way of starting with ergs and getting to utils, so there is no way of starting with utils and getting to price.

APPENDIX D
On the Margin

The idea of a margin was proposed as an answer to the indeterminateness of the satisfactions encountered in utility analysis. The margin is the point at which utility changes to disutility or the point at which profit changes to loss. On one side of the point or line, values are positive; on the other, they are negative. Marginal analysis studies the last item consumed or the last item produced before the line is crossed, and that last item seems clear and determinate.

From the point of view of the producer, wherever supply and income curves cross, business stops because each additional sale would represent a loss. This can occur in short periods or long periods—or never. In the typical business enterprise, the curves do not cross because short periods are irrelevant. Just as a year's supply of butter is not sold in a day, so a year's supply is not churned in a day. The supply cost may be subject to seasonal variations, but sales and production plans (and consumer purchasing) include at least a cycle of seasons.

In an ongoing enterprise there is, strictly speaking, no margin.[1] There are various pseudo-margins. The most commonly used are the end of a production run and the point at which sunk costs are recovered, and these may serve to direct management's attention to questions that should be answered before an enterprise is undertaken or expanded. They do not provide the answers.

The costs of each production run are given, and prices are what the market will bear. Obviously the enterprise will be more profitable if costs can be shaved and prices raised; you don't need an economist to tell you that. Obviously, too, in the typical enterprise, the first production run will be a loser. What you have to decide is whether you'll be able to sell enough product at a high enough price to get a satisfactory return on your investment in a reasonable time. All of these points call for judgment, and for what I've elsewhere called will, and marginal analysis has nothing definitive to say on any of them.

It is ordinarily useful to separate overhead costs and start-up costs from run-on costs, and in such a classification run-on costs seem something like marginal costs. But you'd be a fool, and soon bankrupt, to start a project with only run-on costs in mind.

Pricing is a different problem altogether. A price may be perfectly "justified" by costs; but if it is too high for the market, the result is misery. If, on the other hand, you can bring your product in well under the market, you are well advised to have a good ulterior reason (like establishing a reputation for bargains) before you pass the difference on to the customers.

Something like marginal analysis is also done in respect to elective costs. The advertising manager, for example, may produce charts showing that an extra $100,000 for space will pull in at least an extra $100,001 in business. He may persuade you. But then the sales manager may have charts showing that putting a couple of extra reps on the road will also bring in $100,001. You'd better not believe them both unless you also believe your market is infinitely expandable, for there will be plenty of other claimants with plausible proposals; the production manager may advocate a state-of-the-art plant, and the art director may advocate a more attractive design. It may even occur to you to wonder whether you'd not work a lot harder if your own pay were bumped up another $100,000. Somebody has to think of these things.

Every business cost is more or less elective. Unimaginative types may doubt the relevance of a modernistic sculpture garden to the soft-drink business, but Pepsi Cola management evidently feels that their headquarters in Purchase, New York, helps attract good staff and helps impress customers and licensees.

Professor Fritz Machlup brushed aside studies purporting to show that most businesspeople do not consciously use marginal analysis in their work. He argued that they use it intuitively in the same way an automobile driver intuitively gauges the chances of passing a trailer truck before a bend in the road.[2] He was no doubt right, but the whole point of marginal analysis is precision. Professor Machlup's answer merely says that successful businesspeople are successful, and that successful automobile drivers live to pass another truck. That's not very much to say.

In allocating costs to the various factors (especially labor) it is claimed that the costs at the margin are the "real" ones, which should be guidelines for future costs, if not reasons for renegotiating previous contracts. If, however, the factors producing the marginal item are proportional to those producing the total output, there is no change. On the other hand, if the factors are not proportional, the change is uninformative unless total output can be produced with the new mix of inputs; it is a technological, not an economic, question. In either case, the pseudo-margin (or genuine one) is a function of costs already incurred and prices already charged. The factors of the marginal item are functions of the original factors, whatever they may have been, for if the original factors had been different, the margin would have been different. The marginal factors are therefore no more authoritative or "objective" than the original factors.

Vilfredo Pareto proposed to use marginal analysis to determine the proper "scientific" wage for labor. What he actually proved, as Wicksell said, was "simply that under free competition the worker received the greatest possible wage *compatible with the state of rents and interest.*"[3] Pareto assumed the price system, as everyone must. Since the wage scale is part of the price system, he assumed what he pretended to discover.

In short, marginal analysis is irrelevant in practical affairs and theoretically indeterminate.

APPENDIX E
On General Equilibrium

I

A fundamental doctrine of both classical and neoclassical economics is that the economy tends toward an equilibrium, which is described in various ways. Adam Smith's "natural price" is an equilibrium because whenever a quoted price is too high, competing producers will rush to increase the supply and thus force the price down, while whenever the price is too low, suppliers will leave the business, whereupon competing consumers will bid the price up. Similar equilibriums are said to control the interest rate, unemployment, international trade, and indeed every aspect of the economy. A corollary of these propositions is that it is a mistake to interfere with "natural" economic processes.

A somewhat different theory describes equilibrium as an optimum growth path for the economy, which steadily moves upward because saving, investment, and consumption are in proper balance. Another, advanced by Professor Frank Hahn of Cambridge and Professor Edmund S. Phelps of Columbia, makes equilibrium an at least partially psychological state in which the expectations of economic agents are generally satisfied, so that they continue doing what they have been doing.[1]

The century-long effort to reduce economics to mathematics has understandably reinforced the interest in equilibriums. Since a mathematical equation is itself in equilibrium and achieves its powerful results by continuing in equilibrium, its conclusion will necessarily be in equilibrium.

Mathematical analysis is not fitted to reach any other result. In addition, as Professor Philip Mirowski argues, the historical choice of a metaphor for economics has predisposed the neoclassicals to equilibrium. "In pre-entropic physics," Mirowski writes, "all physical phenomena are variegated manifestations of a protean energy which is fully and reversibly transformed from one state to another. When this idea was transported into the context of economic theory, it dictated that all economic goods were fully and reversibly transformed into utility, and thus into all other goods through the intermediacy of the act of trade."[2]☆

A convenient statement of general equilibrium analysis is *Theory of Value: An Axiomatic Analysis of Economic Equilibrium* by Professor Gerard Debreu, a winner of the Nobel Memorial Prize in Economics.[3] This little book is now thirty years old, and a vast amount of work has been done since it was first published.[4] Nevertheless, it remains a canonical book in the field, and its assumptions or axioms are still largely those of its successors, as they were of its predecessors, and it is these assumptions that cry out to be questioned. What is at stake is not their "realism" (or lack thereof) but their logical consequence.

II

Debreu begins with the definition of "commodity." He writes, "Summing up, a commodity is a good or service completely specified physically, temporally, and spatially."[5]

To avoid a possible misunderstanding, let it be emphasized that physical, temporal, and spatial specifications will enable us to distinguish one commodity from another. No matter how complete, they do not define "commodity," nor, I think, does Debreu intend them to.

Any thing whatever can be physically described and exists, has existed, or will exist at a time and place. So far, a thing is merely that—a thing. A rainy low-pressure area such as now exists in our part of the country is not a commodity, nor is the chipmunk that used to be in our back yard, nor the trash in our cellar, nor the second joint of the third finger on my left hand; yet all these objects may be physically described and exist or existed at a time and place. As objects so specified, they are in the domain of physics, and the laws that govern them are physical laws, not economic laws, whatever they may be.

The specifications, in short, are no part of a definition. For that, Debreu leaves us with a synonym: "a commodity is a good or service." He does not attempt to define either "good" or "service." Instead, he gives us many examples of each, ranging from No. 2 Red Winter Wheat available in Chicago a year from now to oil fields, and from the labor of a coal miner to transportation facilities. The examples are introduced to show how the goods and services fit into the price system.

Debreu makes the point that "wheat available now and wheat available in a week play entirely different economic roles for a flour mill which is to use them."[6] On similar reasoning, the farmer planting wheat today is economically different from the farmer selling wheat some months later, the mill buying wheat today is economically different from the same mill next week, and the consumer eating bread today is economically different from the same fellow tomorrow. Such fragmentation is easy; but unless commodities, mills, and people can be put back together again, it is impossible to reason about such entirely isolated things and people. How can we call them the same on different dates?

We call them the same because they say they are. Agents hold themselves together by acts of will, that is, by doing something. Every doing has consequences and requires further action. The farmers declare that they will grow this kind of wheat instead of something else; the mill proprietors declare that they are in the business of milling certain flour; and the consumers declare that they live, at least to a degree, by bread. It is because of these declarations that No. 2 Red Winter Wheat is defined as it is. Of all the myriad possible physical specifications, only certain ones are relevant, and the relevance is determined by the growers', users', and consumers' acts of will. Without such acts, No. 2 Red Winter Wheat could not be distinguished from other types of wheat, from other vegetables, or even from other things, and it certainly could not be classified as a commodity.

It is of course impossible to define all the words that one uses. Schoolchildren learn, from their first introduction to a dictionary, that one word leads to another. Fundamental terms (and, actually, all terms) are defined as they are used, as they function. They have meaning because they have previously been used and understood, and that meaning is progressively clarified (or confused) as they are used.

Nevertheless, it would have been possible to be clearer at the beginning than Debreu has been, for "good" and "service" have been around for a long time and have disclosed some of the difficulties of some of their uses. Thus many schools of economics start with Robinson Crusoe and his old nanny goat; he is said to weigh opportunity costs as he ponders whether to make a coat out of her. If poor Robinson is an economic agent (for my part, I'd deny that he is), the possible goods he has to choose among are, for all practical purposes, infinite. The difficulty is not merely that he has to decide whether to lie in the sun or to stroll to the other end of his island in search of a succulent berry. It is not merely that he faces decisions and decisions, that his indifference curves seem beyond number. The difficulty is not that he can't, as a practical matter, complete the counting of possible goods and services, but that he doesn't know where to begin—what to count and especially what not to, and how to avoid overlooking something or counting the same thing several times.[7]

Let me emphasize the point, for it is crucial. For example, how many *things* is the typewriter I'm pecking away at? Well, it is one *typewriter*; it is also several hundred *parts* named or numbered in the manufacturer's parts list; it is several dozens of chemical *elements*, millions of *molecules*, multibillions of *electrons*; it is several *old* things, several *new* things (because it was repaired last week), several *blue* things, several *truly square* things, and it is a thing that stands in certain *relations* to other things in its environs. These classifications obviously overlap; each part appears both in its own right and as a part of many wholes. The same electron may turn out to be counted almost as many times as we have classifications. More important, in order to count electrons or molecules or elements or typewriters at all, we must specify that these specially classified and defined things are to be counted. Pointing to the things to be counted—ostensive definition—will not do, because it's not clear whether one is pointing to a part or to an electron. We might reasonably decide to exclude electrons from our tally. Or we might not. Whatever we decide, we can no longer pretend to be counting *things* as such. We are counting the *sorts* of things we have decided to count; and unless we make some decision, we can't count at all.

III

At this point, Debreu's explicit assumption, stated immediately after his definition of commodity and reiterated several times throughout his book, looms large: "It is assumed that there is only a finite number l of distinguishable commodities." Robinson Crusoe would have found the assumption false. The situation is no different in our teeming cities if goods and services are merely what give utility or pleasure. Even on a city street, one may amuse oneself by taking a soccer kick at a loose stone, as Robinson might have derived pleasure from the most unlikely and nondescript stone if, when he idly kicked it, he recalled some game played in his youth.

The issue obviously must be shifted out of the domain of psychology, and this Debreu does. He writes, "What is made available *to* an economic agent is called an *input* for him; what is made available *by* an economic agent is an *output* for him."[8] Although he is not explicit on this point, I think we may understand that all commodities are inputs or outputs. Thus only goods and services that are available are subject to his equations.

We may, however, wonder precisely what Debreu means by "available." In ordinary usage, all the goods in the Sears, Roebuck catalog are available to me. If I ask Sears, the reply will be, yes, they are available. And not only to me, but to virtually everyone in the United States or Canada or (Sears would like to boast) the whole world. Each item is thus an input to each one of the five or more billion of us, *whether we buy or not.* Even if Sears were the only entity that makes things available, the number of inputs and outputs becomes an absurd and meaningless figure. The meaning of input and output must be limited in some way; otherwise we shall be in the quandary of not knowing what is *not* an input or output and consequently of not being able to determine what *are* inputs or outputs.

A limitation that suggests itself defines inputs and outputs as exchanges that are actually made or contracted for. J. R. Hicks puts it this way: "An input is merely something which is bought for the enterprise; an output something which is sold."[9] At whatever point in time we choose to count them, actual exchanges are clearly finite in number, and so commodities are finite in number. Every actual exchange is a balance of inputs and outputs. Whatever the number of exchanges at a given time, the inputs and outputs are in balance, severally and collectively. They could not be otherwise. What is an input to me must be an output for someone else. Such a balance cannot even be disturbed, because every modification of one side entails an exactly coequal and coincident modification of the other side.

Some say that this balance of inputs and outputs is merely an accounting identity. It is at least that. It leaves no economic factor out of account, nor does it introduce a balancing item, as in a corporate balance sheet or in monetarism's treatment of the velocity of money. Whatever it is, it exists by definition, and it is finite.

A similar conclusion is reached when we follow Debreu and direct our attention to producers (who produce outputs) and consumers (who consume inputs). He writes that given "the production possibilities of the whole economy"[10] and the price system, a producer "chooses his production . . . so as to maximize his profit. The resulting action is called an equilibrium production of the . . . producer relative to [the price system]."[11] We may call Debreu's equilibrium production a micro-equilibrium. Every producer achieves it by definition. This is what producers do. They maximize profits, which means that they can't do any better than they actually do, which means that they have no reason to do anything different from what they do, which means that they are in an equilibrium state, and an optimum equilibrium at that.

This micro-equilibrium is finite. It depends on the producer's selling his products (or his company), because otherwise there are no profits. Like any action, selling is finite. It is done here, not there; now, not then; at this price, not at some other; in this quantity, not more or less. Thus it is the actual selling that achieves equilibrium production, deals in a finite number of commodities, and at least partially satisfies Debreu's assumption.

It is not surprising that the actions of the consumer are a mirror image of those of the producer. Given the price system, the consumer seeks "utility maximization," subject to the constraint imposed by his wealth. "The resulting action is called an equilibrium consumption of the . . . consumer relative to [the price system and wealth distribution]."[12] Regardless of whether his wealth is great or small, a consumer will maximize no utility unless he actually buys something with his wealth. Again we have a micro-equilibrium that is dependent upon finite activity in the market place.

IV

As a matter of common introspection, everyone—or almost everyone—is aware of occasions, when, as Browning said of spiritual aspirations, a man's reach exceeds his grasp. Adam Smith spoke of a distinction between absolute demand and effectual demand. A similar idea appears in Debreu as excess demand, which "describes the excess of the net demand of all agents over the total resources."[13]

It will be easily seen that the problem of defining total resources is merely an extension of the problem of defining commodity. As Debreu says, "The *total resources* of an economy are the *a priori given* quantities of commodities that are made available to (or by) its agents."[14] As we have seen, a finite number of commodities is defined only in the moment of being actually exchanged; and only in the same moment (whatever it is) can the total of resources be calculated.

But if commodities and resources are finite, it is not clear what Debreu means by net demand. Cases of market failure are all too common. Not enough bread was available on the eve of the French Revolution, nor enough gasoline when OPEC had its early success. Here we had what might be called excess microdemand. Excess microsupply is familiar, too. A publisher prints more copies of a novel than it can sell, and it is sadly true that many writers scribble more manuscripts than ever are published. Excess microsupply is the same as deficient microdemand.

We seem now in a position to calculate "the excess of net demand of all agents." We simply add all the excess microdemands and subtract from their total the deficient microdemands; the result should be net excess (or, possibly, deficient) macrodemand. But what do we have when we subtract deficient demand for a novel from excess demand for gasoline? Plainly, the exercise is nonsense. Excess microdemand and deficient microdemand are incommensurable; they do not net out, nor can even various excess (or deficient) demands be added together. Net macrodemand cannot be determined unless it is understood to be the same as the demand actually satisfied by the exchanges actually made—in which case the modifier "net" is irrelevant.

V

There is a much more serious consequence. Debreu's equation for what he calls market equilibrium is as follows: "[T]he net demand must equal the total resources."[15] But this always happens if both net demand and total resources are defined by the exchanges actually made. They are identical by definition. Since Debreu's proof of the possibility of general equilibrium depends on the equation for market equilibrium,[16] the possibility becomes an inevitability. Since equilibrium is inevitable, there is no way of using equilibrium as a standard by which to judge an economy's efficiency. All economies are perfectly efficient, and there is nothing to be done about them.

Debreu says several times, "It is assumed that there is only a finite number l of distinguishable commodities." He discusses his assumption only briefly in a note, where he says that it "has the great mathematical convenience of enabling one to stay within a finite-dimensional commodity space." He recognizes that unnamed "conceptual difficulties" ensue, and he adds that "many of the results of the following chapters can be extended to infinite-dimensional commodity spaces."[17]

Let us test the contrary assumption: that there is an infinite number of commodities. Intuitively this is just as plausible as Debreu's assumption, for everyone knows that the world is wondrous and various, including (but, as the lawyers say, not limited to) industrial waste that in

Debreu's example is unexpectedly made valuable by technological inno-vation.[18] If commodities are infinite in number, resources are infinite also; and no matter how great demand becomes, there are resources left over. Debreu's market equilibrium dissolves into a dew. Furthermore, regardless of how many resources are demanded and utilized, those not demanded are still infinite in number; so there is not even a way of saying that one state of an economy is more nearly in balance than another.

Here we have the dilemma of general equilibrium analysis: If there is an infinite number of commodities, general equilibrium cannot even be described. But if there is a finite number of commodities, general equilibrium has at most the sterile consequence that it reasserts itself in some indeterminate way after an upset caused by some exogenous and hence unpredictable force or factor.

When applied to policy, it generally is claimed that equilibrium requires wage rates to be perfectly flexible (ordinarily downward). There is obviously no point to this claim unless commodity prices are rigid (or falling) and interest rates are rigid (or rising). None of these claims or conditions is a necessary consequence of general equilibrium analysis, which is, as aforesaid, sterile. Only a prejudice against labor would prompt one to demand flexibility of wage rates rather than of prices and interest rates.

VI

General equilibrium analysis is presented by Professor De-breu as axiomatic but is actually empirical. There is no curve or equa-tion that fits every demand schedule or every aggregation of demand schedules.

There are, in fact, few if any determinate demand schedules anyhow. As we have previously noted, the textbooks are full of them, but they are almost all "illustrative." The figures are assumed, made up, to show how figures can be plotted on a graph. If no wheat was in fact sold at $x a bushel, who knows how many bushels would be demanded at that price? No one knows. Market research may make a guess, but it is only a guess, as the Edsel is our witness. More important, basing the theory on market research would beg the question, because the research necessarily assumes some theory, very likely the theory in question.

No less an authority than Walras wrote, "Both the curve and the equation ['of the demand schedule in the mind of holder (1) of commodity (B)'] are empirical."[19] The curve being empirical, Walras grants that we must expect it to be discontinuous. There is no law that says it is not. But, says Walras, "[t]he aggregate demand curve . . . can, for all practical purposes, be considered as continuous by virtue of the so-called *law of large numbers.*"[20] This is a fair-enough solution—provided we do have large numbers. There are certainly large numbers out there, but do we have them? Actually we do not. We have, as noted, large numbers of prices, but we do not have large numbers—or any number—of demands quantified in any other way.

The prices we have are of course empirical. Walras conceived of the market place as a series of auctions in which, through groping (*"tâtonnement"*), economic agents arrive at definite prices. The groping cannot be assumed; it has to be actually performed, and there is no way of telling how it will come out. Nor is it certain that it will come out at all. There is no axiom that says that the series of bids and the series of asks must converge, or that they must exhibit any regularity at all. In fact, they are pretty erratic in the securities and commodities exchanges, the real-life auctions that most resemble the one imagined by Walras.

Equilibrium appears only in the actual sale. There need be no groping from sale to sale, nor must the next offer, leading to the next sale, be the same; it may be higher or lower. The prices actually agreed to are therefore the only determinate values in Walras's equations. Walras himself made the same point on another occasion: *"Rareté* is *personal* or *subjective*; value in exchange is *real* or *objective.*"[21] Again we come back to Jevons: "The price of a commodity is the only test we have of the utility of the commodity to the purchaser. . . ."

APPENDIX F
On Economies of Scale

In a note Professor Debreu writes that among the phenomena his analysis does not cover are "increasing returns to scale."[1] This is grave weakness, as is shown by the argument of Piero Sraffa's 1926 article, "The Laws of Returns under Competitive Conditions."[2]

In brief, Sraffa observed that self-regulating competition depends on the "law" of diminishing returns, which prevents any firm from expanding beyond a certain point. Consequently no firm can monopolize the market; and, whenever disturbed, the equilibrium of perfect competition reestablishes itself. But modern mass production is founded on the rock of economies of scale. Expanding production generally makes possible the utilization of more—not less—efficient machines and processes; and large enterprises, by exploiting opportunities for the division of labor, are able to employ more specialized and more productive laborers. Progressive division of labor makes possible progressive expansion of the market; and as Allyn A. Young showed, the two leapfrog each other.[3]

When this happens, there is no longer an automatic limit to the expansion of the firm. More precisely, there is nothing to prevent any given firm from expanding so vigorously and cutting costs and prices so aggressively that all other firms are driven from the market. There may be a moment of cutthroat competition as a few oligopolists battle for survival. Bankruptcies may proliferate, and even the ultimate winner may be grievously wounded. Not only is this struggle wasteful and inefficient, but in the end, instead of an equilibrium of interchangeable competitors who take the market price, it subjects us to a monopolist able thereafter to set the price.

It is difficult to overstate how devastating Sraffa's argument is. A strength of traditional economics, like that of its successor, general equilibrium analysis, lies in the claim that it is automatic. Adam Smith's metaphor of the invisible hand was a world-historical idea of profound and pervasive implications. It appealed to the practical world of the Industrial Revolution, because its acceptance ended the state's control of or even interference in business affairs. It appealed to the intellectual world of the scientific revolution, because it offered an impersonal, quasi-mechanical explanation of one aspect of human behavior. It even appealed to some of the religious world, because the invisible hand, which could be thought of as the hand of God, was an inexorable force for good. All of this depended upon the economic world as a self-regulating equilibrium that, no matter how disturbed, always returned to the best possible position in this best of all possible worlds. And the equilibrium depended on the law of diminishing returns—which failed.

As was noted in Appendix C,[4] Léon Walras, the acknowledged progenitor of general equilibrium analysis, recorded scenes not unlike Sraffa's scenario, although he made no special point of the law of diminishing returns. But Vilfredo Pareto, his successor at the University of Lausanne, while discussing the "equilibrium of the producer," wrote, "[T]here are certain goods such that the quantity of B obtained per unit of A increases when the total quantity of A transformed increases. . . ." In these cases, "equilibrium takes place at terminal points." No further movement occurs, because competition is then "complete."[5] In short, enterprises exhibiting economies of scale are in equilibrium only in the moment of their extinction, or when they no longer achieve such economies.

The reason for this outcome was given by Knut Wicksell: "[I]f, in an enterprise which becomes more productive the larger the scale of operations, the labour and the land employed were both paid in accordance with the law of marginal productivity, then the sum of their shares would *exceed* the whole product, so that the entrepreneur would suffer a loss. . . . Under such conditions, equilibrium is impossible."[6]

Thus for Pareto and Wicksell, as for Walras before them and Debreu after them, the ideal or characteristic mode of modern enterprise is beyond the scope of equilibrium analysis.

APPENDIX G

On the Money Supply

One of the most publicized equations in economics is what is called the transactions form of the quantity of money equation. It was put into its present form some eighty years ago by Professor Irving Fisher of Yale, and is regarded by some authorities (though not by others) as the essense of monetarism.[1]

The equation, written all in capitals, looks formidable $(MV = PQ)$. It merely means that the quantity of money, multiplied by the velocity of its circulation, is equal to the general price level, multiplied by the goods and services produced.

Difficulties occur with each term, starting of course with M, for there is no agreement on the definition of the money supply, and hence none on its size. Next, it turns out that velocity (V) cannot be determined except by means of this equation. Fanciers of the quantity theory contend that over the past several years, the velocity of M2 has been fairly constant; so M2 is the now-favored quantity, and MV becomes a simple term, meaning the total money spent for goods and services.

The right-hand side of the equation presents different problems. Q represents the total of the goods and services produced, that is, the real (stated in things), as opposed to the nominal (stated in money), gross national product. I've expressed doubts about the GNP, whether real or nominal, but for the moment we may accept it at its face value. We are immediately struck by the fact that its face value is expressed in money, that is, nominally. Moreover, it cannot be expressed in any other way, for money is the only unit of economic measurement applicable to apples and pears and tons of steel and all the rest. The paradoxical fact is that the real GNP can only be quantified nominally.

What, then, is the price level (P)? It is an index, such as we have discussed, derived by combining the prices of a great variety of goods and services, each one weighted to allow it its proper importance in the economy. But of course the actual prices of the goods and services are already and necessarily included in the GNP, which cannot otherwise be added up, while the price level is necessarily derived from those prices. So the only way that multiplying the price level by the GNP could make any sense would be for the GNP to be expressed somehow other than in money. And that we have seen to be impossible. For this reason, PQ becomes a simple term, meaning the total money charged for goods and services. Translating this equation back into English, we learn that the total money spent for goods and services equals the total prices of those goods and services, which is a tautology and sterile as a guide to policy.[2]

The only way to tease policy recommendations out of the equation is to restore it to its original form and forget about the ambiguities and imprecisions and contradictions. Then one can solve it for P, like this: $P = MV/Q$. From this equation, it would appear that the way to keep the price level down is either to restrict the money supply or to increase real output. Since the Federal Reserve Board's direct powers run to the money supply, that's what the Reserve worries about, regardless of the effects on every other aspect of the economy.

But still taking the equation in its original form $(MV = PQ)$, reducing the money supply must reduce either the price level or real output, and there is nothing in the equation to tell us which will be the result. Monetarists hope it will be the price level that falls; but if prices are at all sticky (and there are enough contracts of various sorts in force to ensure that at least a great many are sticky), then output must be the factor to fall. And if output falls, the money supply must be further reduced to compensate—and so on and on, until total collapse.

APPENDIX H
On the Reform of Corporations

I

Although it is impossible to imagine the easy success of any movement to reform the modern corporation, it is not difficult to suggest points that such reform might encompass. Starting with the understanding that the corporation is the entrepreneur and so entitled to the profits and the capital gains, one would ask, Who are the *people* of the corporation? And the answer would be that they are first and foremost those who do the work of the corporation, namely, the management and the other workers, and secondarily the stockholders, under the present system, and that they should all be able to share in both rewards and control.

As a first approximation of how these shares should be allocated, one might assume that there is some rationality behind the present distribution. At present, management and other workers get wages and bonuses and fringe benefits, and stockholders get dividends, and these are the more or less satisfactory result of explicit or implicit negotiations. Each individual's proper share might then be determined by taking the individual's income from the corporation, whether wages or dividends or both, and dividing it by the total of all such incomes from the corporation (not counting interest, which is a cost of doing business). Cash dividends would be paid in accordance with such shares, which would be recalculated annually. In addition to cash dividends—and it is a crucial addition—new stock equal in value to the corporation's increase in net worth would be issued in the same proportions as cash dividends (or stock would be canceled if net worth fell). This stock—and sooner or later all stock in the corporation—would be inalienable. It could not be sold or bequeathed or pledged as security for a loan or given away; but it could at any time be exchanged with the corporation for a negotiable note or bond, or, at the corporation's option, cash. And such an exchange would *have* to be made when the owner of the stock left the corporation, retired, was fired, or died. Over the years—within a generation at the outside—most of the present stockholders would be converted into bondholders. They would have their reward. The remaining stockholders would all be active in the business. They could, of course, like their predecessors, run it well or ill; could sell it or merge it or abandon it; but whatever happened, it would be their doing, and they would be the ones to benefit or suffer from it.

Let me state most emphatically that what I call the Labor Theory of Right leads to employee ownership, not to profit sharing. Profit is, as we have repeatedly noted, a residual. It is systematically unpredictable. It is, nevertheless, affected by decisions regarding everything from product development to marketing. The interests of laborers and owners in such decisions are rarely identical; sometimes they are diametrically opposed. In profit sharing, conflicts are resolved in favor of owners. When laborers and owners are the same people, decisions can turn on the interests of the enterprise rather than on class advantage. Decisions may still turn out to be right or wrong, but they will be so for everyone. There will be neither scapegoats nor windfall profiteers.

It is very likely that reform of corporate internal structure would have to be complemented by reform of external structure. Certainly all corporations, regardless of internal reform, should be nationally chartered and subject only to national taxation and regulation. Only in this way can one hope to overcome the states' temptations to play beggar my neighbor by luring companies away from each other with tax breaks and permissive regulation.

Friedrich Hayek makes a more important point: "Once we extend the power to make contracts from natural persons to corporations and the like, it no longer can be the contract but it must be the law which decides who is liable and how the property is to be determined and safeguarded which limits the liability of the corporation."[1]

Sooner or later, too, it will probably become apparent that antitrust laws should turn on size, not on "competition"—partly because the courts have proved incapable of defining competition without interminable and inconclusive litigation, partly because competition is by no means always efficient, and partly because small is beautiful.[2]

II

In an essay entitled "The Ethics of Competition," Professor Frank H. Knight examined in careful detail what we know in our hearts, namely, that the competitive race is seldom fair, and that the effort it stimulates is as likely to result in chicanery as in beneficial innovation.[3] On the other side, Milovan Djilas and a great many others are witness that cooperative societies, with the best will in the world, tend to degenerate into stultifying dictatorships.[4]

Having experienced the courts' inability to define competition, much less enforce it, Fred I. Raymond put forward what he called a limitist law.[5] The speed limit is such a law. If you go over fifty-five miles an hour, you are in violation, no matter what arguments you can make about safety or efficiency or the similar behavior of others. Observing the way business works, Raymond concluded that seeming economies of scale are often (if not generally) fruit not of technology but of the favored access great size can command to financing and to special markets. Raymond therefore proposed that a business organization could be as large and as spread out, horizontally and vertically, as it wished, provided that it had only one place of shipment to its customers. If a business had more than one point of delivery, like a chain of stores, it would be limited to a certain number of employees. Raymond suggested one thousand as the maximum.

The beauty of Raymond's scheme is that it does not interfere with the advertised virtues of the free enterprise system, nor with the necessity for large-scale planning in major industries. Any limitation based on profits or sales would interfere, for once a business reached those limits, it would have no incentive to improve its performance. Raymond's proposal, however, leaves every honorable incentive in place.

The sad fact is that we once had, in banking, a limitist law in the shape of Regulation Q, which limited the interest certain banks could pay. Regulation Q was not altogether effective because it could not (given the patchwork control of our financial system) cover all it should have covered.

APPENDIX I
On Comparative Advantage

I

The figures Ricardo used in his example of comparative advantage were of course merely illustrative suppositions. No one has ever claimed anything more for them, nor, so far as I know, has anyone made even a casual study of the outcomes to be expected from different suppositions. John Stuart Mill credits his father, James, with noticing as early as 1821 that what I shall call Cases 3 and 4 are not to the advantage of both countries, although he seems not to have seen that they are to the definite disadvantage of one;[1] and many have been aware that Ricardo's theory will not work at all if Portugal is supposed to specialize in cloth instead of wine; but these observations somehow have not aroused curiosity about other possibilities.

In fact, there are eight different possible cases, which are set forth in Table 1. Within each country it may be supposed that productivities are homogeneous, that is, that it takes as many man-years to produce a unit of cloth as to produce a unit of wine, or the productivities may be supposed to be heterogeneous. Between the countries, the productivity of each industry may be homogeneous or heterogeneous. Moreover, when productivities are heterogeneous within each country, they may be parallel between the countries, that is, the productivity of the English cloth industry may be to the productivity of the English wine

265

TABLE 1

POSSIBLE CASES OF COMPARATIVE ADVANTAGE

Country	Men per Unit Cloth	Wine	Specialty	Product per Man	Total Men	National Product		Total Product	
Case 1 (Ricardo's)									
England	100	120	C	1/100	220	2.2	units		
Portugal	90	80	W	1/80	170	2.125	units	4.325	units
Case 2 (Ricardo Reversed)									
England	100	120	W	1/120	220	1.833	units		
Portugal	90	80	C	1/90	170	1.889	units	3.722	units
Case 3 (Parallel Productivities)									
England	100	120	C	1/100	220	2.2	units		
Portugal	90	108	W	1/108	198	1.833	units	4.033	units
Case 4 (Case 3 Reversed)									
England	100	120	W	1/120	220	1.833	units		
Portugal	90	108	C	1/90	198	2.2	units	4.033	units
Case 5 (Countries Separately Homogeneous)									
England	100	100	C–W	1/100	200	2	units		
Portugal	90	90	W–C	1/90	180	2	units	4.0	units
Case 6 (Both Homogeneous and Identical)									
England	100	100	C–W	1/100	200	2	units		
Portugal	100	100	W–C	1/100	200	2	units	4.0	units
Case 7 (One Homogeneous, One Not)									
England	100	100	C	1/100	200	2	units		
Portugal	90	80	W	1/80	170	2.125	units	4.125	units
Case 8 (Case 7 Reversed)									
England	100	100	W	1/100	200	2	units		
Portugal	90	80	C	1/90	170	1.889	units	3.889	units

industry the same as the productivity of the Portuguese cloth industry is to the productivity of the Portuguese wine industry. We have had occasion to doubt the meaning of productivity, but for the moment we can be satisfied that the table will stand, whatever definition (if any) we adopt, and whatever the actual figures may be. Actual figures that fit Case 1 will always be advantageous for both countries and for the world, just as Ricardo said, although of course the degrees of the advantages may be larger or smaller. Likewise, figures that fit Case 2 will always be disadvantageous for both countries and for the world, and the degree of disadvantage may be very large or infinitesimally small.

There is one other case—autarky—which is not included in the table because it is the case of no international trade at all. It may nevertheless serve as the control with which the results of the other cases may be compared. Under autarky, both England and Portugal will produce one unit of cloth and one of wine, or (since the units are of equal value) two units of goods, for an international total of four. Thus, any case that yields a total output greater than four units is advantageous for world output. In the same way, any case that yields an output greater than two units for either country is advantageous for that country.

It should be emphasized that all the cases are Ricardian in shape. Neither economies of scale, nor diminishing returns, nor transportation costs, nor tariffs, nor subsidies, nor the wastefulness of abandoning going concerns, nor the expenses and uncertainties of the passage of time, nor the consequences for individuals will be considered. All are cheerfully assumed away. Furthermore, the table requires none of the more fundamental assumptions of the various schools of theory, such as whether economic agents maximize profits, or money is an illusion, or goods are grossly substitutable, or commodities are or are not finite in number. What we have may be called the pure theory of comparative advantage.

The results of Table 1 are summarized in Table 2 and Table 3. Ricardo's "law" turns out to consist mostly of exceptions. Of the eight possibilities, only one is as advertised (advantageous for both trading partners), and only four result in a net gain for world output. Perhaps more significant: Only half of the cases are in any respect better than autarky for even one of the partners. Regardless of what we have repeatedly been told, it simply is not true that international trade is invariably desirable for all concerned. It would, in all conscience, be

TABLE 2

CASES CLASSIFIED ACCORDING TO
CONTRIBUTION TO WORLD OUTPUT

---

4 cases advantageous for total (1, 3, 4, 6)
2 cases indifferent for total (5, 6)
2 cases disadvantageous for total (2, 8)

TABLE 3

CASES CLASSIFIED ACCORDING TO CONTRIBUTION TO
NATIONAL OUTPUT

---

1 case advantageous for both nations (1)
1 case advantageous for one, indifferent for other (7)
2 cases advantageous for one, disadvantageous for other (3, 4)
2 cases indifferent for both (5, 6)
1 case indifferent for one, disadvantageous for other (8)
1 case disadvantageous for both (2)

---

astonishing if it were. After all, intranational trade isn't invariably
desirable for all concerned. Why should international trade be exempt
from the heartache and the thousand natural shocks that domestic
business is heir to?

II

What makes Ricardo so important here is that he offered an
economic law that seemed to prove it against a nation's interest to
interfere with foreign trade. This law (as proposed or as amended) has
seemed to Professor Paul Samuelson an example, perhaps the only
example, of "a proposition in all the social sciences which is both true
and nontrivial."[2]

If this is so, we must be struck by the profession's lack of interest in testing Ricardo's ability to explain empirical data. He published his book in 1817, but it was not until 1951 that a serious attempt was made to find confirmation of his law. The attempt was made by Professor G. D. A. MacDougal of Oxford, who published his results in two issues of *Economic Journal.*

In point of fact, regardless of his intentions, MacDougal did not address the Ricardian theory at all. He set out to study British trade with the United States, but the two countries are not substantial trading partners in the products of the industries MacDougal studied. He therefore decided to compare the trade of these countries with the rest of the world instead of their trade with each other. Consequently what is presented as an empirical test of Ricardo is rather an answer to the question of whether the rest of the world prefers American to British goods when American goods are cheaper.

Not surprisingly, the answer to this question was found to be generally affirmative. MacDougal wrote, "Before the war, American weekly wages in manufacturing were roughly double the British, and we find that, where American output per worker was more than twice the British, the United States had in general the bulk of the export market, while for products where it was less than twice as high, the bulk of the market was held by the British."[3]

This finding is surely plausible, but it is not Ricardian.

Though understood by the profession to be a scientific proposition, Ricardo's law had to wait one hundred thirty-four years for an extensive test. This test was, in fact, a test of a quite different proposition, and in the forty years since MacDougal, no one seems to have bothered to redo the test or undertake another as ambitious. This is odd behavior for a discipline that claims to be a science. One can scarcely imagine a proposition in physics being taught as a law for 134 years before anyone seriously tried to test it. Nor can one imagine it still taught as a law when the test was of an only superficially similar proposition. Nor in one's wildest nightmare can one imagine this still untested proposition used to design a structure on which the livelihoods of literally billions of people may depend. An engineer who proposed to build on such a basis would be treated as a madman and locked up as a threat to humanity.

III

What the textbooks call the Heckscher-Ohlin Theorem is usually described as another modification of Ricardo. The Swedish economist Eli F. Heckscher presented it in a journal article in 1919 as follows: "The prerequisites for initiating international trade may thus be summarized as *different relative scarcity, i. e., different relative prices of the factors of production in the exchanging countries* as well as *different proportions between the factors of production in different commodities.*"[4]

In 1933 Heckscher's student Bertil Ohlin developed the theory in a book entitled *Interregional and International Trade.* As his title suggests, he saw the factor-proportion theory as an elaboration of location theory. He wrote, "It is important to note that our interregional analysis applies to domestic as well as to international trade."[5] This being so, their theory is no more an overriding argument for foreign trade than is the law of supply and demand.

And even if it were, it is evidently unreliable, if not false. Heckscher-Ohlin didn't have to wait so long as Ricardo for a test; but when it came, it was devastating. After his painstaking analysis (to which I have referred on page 206), of America's 1947 foreign trade Professor Leontief concluded, "The widely held opinion that—as compared with the rest of the world—the United States' economy is characterized by a relative surplus of capital and a relative shortage of labor proves to be wrong. As a matter of fact, the opposite is true."[6] From this he made a surprising inference: "In other words, a more rapid rise in our average productive investment per worker would diminish rather than increase the advantage derived by the United States from its foreign trade. . . . This signifies, of course, a reduced incentive to the continued exchange of commodities and services between the United States and the rest of the world."[7]

Supporters of Heckscher-Ohlin suggested that Leontief had chosen an unrepresentative year for the test; so he took another year, and the theorem still failed, though not quite so badly. In the revised edition of his book, Dr. Ohlin protested (without rancor) that Leontief had considered only two factors (capital and labor), while the number of factors was practically unlimited. But the two factors Leontief considered are hardly insignificant.

Psychologists say that the first step in mastering a fear is being able to name it. This the economics profession now did. The inconvenient results of Professor Leontief's work were dubbed Leontief's Paradox—in capital letters. The choice of name was a stroke of genius. Had a more accurate name, such as Leontief's Refutation, been chosen, what has developed into an entire new subprofession would have been stopped ere it began.

IV

One may speculate that acceptance of Ricardo's theory among scholars has been stimulated by delighted surprise. When one first hears of it, it certainly seems improbable that, in Professor Samuelson's words, "trade is mutually profitable even when one country is absolutely more or less productive in terms of every commodity."[8] How charming to find the implausible made plausible by Ricardo's fortuitous example of Case 1! How congenial to a scholar's passion for hidden truths!

More cynically, one may speculate that men and women of affairs have been attracted to the scheme by the pseudoscientific excuse it provides for a jolly round of labor-bashing.

International trade has its uses. Mill put it as well as anyone: "It is hardly possible to overrate the value, in the present low state of human improvement, of placing human beings in contact with persons dissimilar to themselves, and with modes of thought and action unlike those with which they are familiar."[9] One may accept Mill's judgment here and still consider, on their separate and proper merits, proposals to restrict or reorganize international trade.

It is ironical that conventional economics, based as it is on the notion of self-interest, should be so vehement in its insistence that self-protection is invariably reprehensible.

NOTES

1. INTRODUCTION

1. Adam Smith, *The Wealth of Nations* (New York: Modern Library, n.d.), p. 5.

2. Karl Marx, *The Holy Family,* in Robert C. Tucker, ed., *The Marx-Engels Reader* (2d ed.; New York: W. W. Norton, 1978), p. 159.

3. Smith, *Wealth,* p. 13.

4. Ibid., p. 423.

5. Ibid., p. 651.

6. Alexander Hamilton wrote in *Report on Manufactures* (1791): "[T]he power to raise money is plenary and indefinite, and the objects to which it may be appropriated are no less comprehensive than the payment of the public debt, and the providing for the common defense and general welfare."

2. PSYCHOLOGY

1. Adam Smith, *The Theory of Moral Sentiments* (Oxford: Oxford University Press, 1976), p. 9.

2. John Maynard Keynes, *The General Theory of Employment, Interest and Money* (New York: Harcourt, Brace, 1936), p. 96.

3.   Wesley Clair Mitchell, "Quantitative Analysis in Economic Theory," *American Economic Review* (March 1925).

4.   For another example of the "as if" argument, see Appendix A: On Perfect Competition, p. 231.

5.   Amartya Sen, *On Ethics and Economics* (Oxford: Blackwell, 1987), p. 19.

6.   St. Augustine, *Confessions.* Book I.

7.   James Steuart, "An Inquiry into the Principles of Political Economy," in Philip C. Newman, Arthur D. Gayer, and Milton H. Spencer, eds., *Source Readings in Economic Thought* (New York: W. W. Norton, 1954), p. 49.

8.   Frank Hahn, *Equilibrium and Macroeconomics* (Cambridge, Mass.: MIT Press, 1984), p. 68.

9.   Karl Marx, *The German Ideology,* in Robert C. Tucker, ed., *The Marx-Engels Reader,* (2d ed.; New York: W. W. Norton, 1978), p. 160.

10.   Karl Marx, *Critique of the Gotha Program,* in Tucker, ed., *Reader,* p. 531.

11.   Keynes, *General Theory,* p. 195.

3. MATHEMATICS

1.   William Petty, *Economic Writings* (New York: Kelley, 1962), vol. 1.

2.   Smith, *Wealth,* p. 500.

3.   Robert L. Heilbroner, *The Worldly Philosophers* (5th ed.; New York: Simon & Schuster, 1980), p. 49.

4.   Smith, *Wealth,* p. 500.

5.   W. Stanley Jevons, *Theory of Political Economy* (New York: Kelley, 1965), p. 3.

6.   Ibid., p. 7.

7.   Mitchell, op. cit.

8.   Jevons, *Theory,* p. 6.

9.   Max Planck, *The Philosophy of Physics* (New York: W. W. Norton, 1936), chap. 4.

10.   Keynes, *General Theory,* p. 305.

11.   Alfred Marshall, *Principles of Economics* (8th ed.; London: Macmillan, 1969), p. ix.

4. PEOPLE

1. Pierre Simon de Laplace, *A Philosophical Essay on Probabilities* (Gloucester, Mass.: Smith, 1965), p. 4.

2. Werner Heisenberg, *The Physicist's Conception of Nature* (London: Hutchinson, 1958), pp. 39–40.

3. John William Miller, "History and Case History," *American Scholar* 49:2 (Spring 1980), pp. 241–243.

4. José Ortega y Gasset, *History as a System* (New York: W. W. Norton, 1961), p. 217.

5. MONEY

1. Karl Marx, *Capital* (New York: Modern Library, n.d.), vol. 1, p. 107.

2. Hans von Raumer, quoted in Stewart B. Clough et al., eds., *Economic History of Europe: Twentieth Century* (New York: Harper & Row, 1968), p. 126.

3☆. Understanding trade as barter, St. Thomas wrote, "Now money, according to the Philosopher [Aristotle], . . . was invented chiefly for the purpose of exchange [*Nichomachean Ethics*, 1133a]: and consequently the proper and principal use of money is in its consumption or alienation whereby it is sunk in exchange." ("Whether It Is a Sin To Take Usury for Money Lent," *Summa Theologica.*) The picture seems to be that I sell you so much beef for a dollar and you sell me so much bread for a dollar; I eat my roll and you eat your hamburger and you have your dollar back. The dollar was merely a convenience or, as Say put it much later, a veil; hence St. Thomas could argue the money was not necessary and did not deserve to earn interest.

4. Bertrand Russell, *Our Knowledge of the External World* (New York: New American Library, 1956), p. 147.

5. For a comprehensive analysis of the fateful consequences of this commonplace observation, see Paul Davidson, *Money and the Real World* (2d ed.; London: Macmillan, 1978).

6. David Hume, "Of Money," in *Political Discourses*.

7. Paul Volcker, the new chairman of the Federal Reserve Board, announced that thereafter the Reserve would "be placing greater emphasis on day-to-day operations of the supply of bank reserves, and less emphasis on confining short-term fluctuations in the federal rate."

8. Milton Friedman, "A Response to Burns," in Marin N. Baily and Arthur M. Okun, eds., *The Battle against Unemployment and Inflation* (3d ed.; New York: W. W. Norton, 1982), p. 111.

9.   For a critique, see James Tobin, *Essays in Economics*, vol. 1, *Macroeconomics* (Cambridge, Mass.: MIT Press, 1981), pp. 272–282.

10.   Thomas Mayer, *The Structure of Monetarism* (New York: W. W. Norton, 1978), p. 10.

11.   Karl Brunner, *"Money Supply,"* in John Eatwell, Murray Milgate, and Peter Newman, eds., *The New Palgrave: Money* (New York: W. W. Norton, 1989), p. 267.

12.   Raymond de Roover, *The Rise and Fall of the Medici Bank, 1397–1494* (New York: W. W. Norton, 1966), p. 32.

6. PRICE

1.   Aristotle, *Nichomachean Ethics*, 1133a.

2.   Plato, *The Republic*, II, 370–376.

3.   St. Thomas Aquinas, "Of Cheating, Which Is Committed in Buying and Selling," *Summa Theologica*.

4.   Smith, *Wealth*, pp. 55–56.

5.   David Ricardo, *The Principles of Political Economy and Taxation* (New York: Everyman's, 1973), p. 52.

6.   Léon Walras, *Elements of Pure Economics* (Philadelphia: Orion Editions, 1984), p. 64; John Neville Keynes, *The Scope and Method of Political Philosophy* (4th ed.; New York: Kelley, 1965), pp. 32–33; Milton Friedman, *Essays in Positive Economics*, (Chicago: University of Chicago Press, 1953), p. 3.

7.   Joseph A. Schumpeter, *History of Economic Analysis* (New York: Oxford University Press, 1954), p. 827.

8.   Walras, *Elements*, p. 83.

9.   William James, *Psychology*, chap. 10.

10.   Gerard Debreu, *Theory of Value* (New Haven, Conn.: Yale University Press, 1959), p. 33. (Debreu's emphases and ellipsis.)

7. LABOR

1.   Smith, *Wealth*, p. 33.

2.   Ricardo, *Principles*, p. 52; Keynes, *General Theory*, p. 214; Marx, *Capital*, p. 48.

3.   Marx, *Capital*, p. 46.

4.   Ibid., p. 48.

5. Ibid., p. 221.

6. Ibid., pp. 218–219.

7. Ibid., p. 189.

8. R. H. Tawney, *The Acquisitive Society* (London: Collins, 1961), p. 56 ff.; A. A. Berle and Gardiner C. Means, *The Modern Corporation and Private Property* (New York: Macmillan, 1933), passim; John Kenneth Galbraith, *Economics and the Public Purpose* (Boston: Houghton, Mifflin, 1973), chap. 10.

9. Joseph A. Schumpeter, *Capitalism, Socialism and Democracy* (New York: Harper & Row, 1950), p. 133.

10. Keynes, *General Theory*, p. 151.

11. Schumpeter, *Capitalism, Socialism and Democracy*, p. 132.

12. Keynes, *General Theory*, p. 150.

13. John Kenneth Galbraith, *American Capitalism* (Armonk, N.Y.: Sharpe, 1980), chap. 9.

14. John Locke, *Second Treatise of Government*, chap. 5, secs. 32 and 50.

15. Aristotle, *Politics*, 1258a.

8. GOODS

1. See Eric D. Larson, Marc H. Ross, and Robert H. Williams, "Beyond the Age of Materials," *Scientific American* 254:6 (June 1986) p. 34 ff.

2. Marx, *The German Ideology*, in Tucker, *The Marx-Engels Reader*, p. 159.

3. J. S. Mill, *Principles of Political Economy*, Book I, chap. 5, sec. 7.

4. Smith, *Wealth*, p. 625.

5. Marx, *Critique of the Gotha Program*, in Tucker, ed., *The Marx-Engels Reader*, p. 531.

6. R. H. Tawney, *Religion and the Rise of Capitalism*. (New York: Harcourt, Brace, 1952), pp. 35–36.

7. Thorstein Veblen, *The Theory of the Leisure Class*. (New York: Modern Library), p. 121.

8. Mary Douglas and Baron Isherwood, *The World of Goods* (New York: W. W. Norton, 1979), p. 4.

9. Ibid., p. 61.

10. Charles Darwin, *The Origin of Species*, chap. 14.

9. CAPITAL

1. John Maynard Keynes, *Essays in Persuasion* (New York: W. W. Norton, 1963), p. 373.

2. Lester Thurow, *New York Times*, August 23, 1981, op-ed page.

3. Keynes, *General Theory*, p. 63.

4.✩ Keynes, *General Theory*, p. 65. Compare Jevons and the determination of demand, infra., p 246.

5. Keynes, *General Theory*, pp. 74–75.

6.✩ At this point Keynes was more interested in the macroeconomic equivalence of saving and investment than in his rather offhand definition of investment. In his Preface to the French edition of *The General Theory*, he writes: "[T]his relationship between saving and investment, which necessarily holds good for the system as a whole, does not hold good at all for a particular individual. There is no reason whatever why the new investment for which I am responsible should bear any relation whatever to the amount of my own savings." (John Maynard Keynes, *Collected Writings*, vol. 7 [London: Macmillan, 1973], p. xxxii.)

My point is the quite different one that while some of Keynes's "investments" yield only personal satisfactions, others generate income and thus are macroeconomically as well as microeconomically effective. Keynes wrote, "Any reasonable definition of the line between consumer-purchases and investor-purchases will serve us equally well, provided that it is consistently applied" (*General Theory*, p. 61). For some purposes this dictum is perhaps acceptable, but it leaves us without a way of explaining, say, the relative success of England and the relative failure of Spain.

7. Keynes, *General Theory*, p. 210.

8. Joseph A. Pechman, *Federal Tax Policy* (rev. ed.; New York: W. W. Norton, 1971), p. 256.

10. SPECULATION

1. *The New Leader* 64:17 (September 7, 1981), pp. 9–10.

2.✩ A slightly different picture is given by the fact that "the weekly reporting banks in New York City expanded their loans to brokers and to individuals to purchase or carry securities from $16.7 billion in the week ending October 7 to $24.4 billion in the week ending October 21." (Andrew F. Brimmer, "Distinguished Lecture on Economics in Government: Central Banking and Systemic Risks in Capital Markets," *Journal of Economic Perspectives* 3 (2)

[Spring 1989], p. 15.) It will be noticed that $7.7 billion in new loans amounts to less than 1 percent of the money said to have been lost in the crash.

3.✩ Ibid., p. 11.

I should not be surprised if professional opinion finally accepted a much lower figure for the amount lost. Either way, apologists for the stock market are faced with a dilemma. If the amount lost was large, the exchanges must be brought under tighter control; but if the amount lost was small, no harm will be done to the economy by bringing them under tighter control.

4.   The distinction between the producing economy and the speculating economy is essentially the same as that made by Keynes and others between the "industrial circulation" and the "financial circulation." I have chosen to use different terms because speculation today plays a much greater role than it ever has before, with the possible exception of the first quarter of the eighteenth century.

5.   Marilyn G. Fedack, "Volatility in the Equity Market," *Investing* (Fall 1989), p. 10.

6.   To be sure, the German interest rate has tended to range between the American and the Japanese—and so has German investment in long-term projects.

7.   Thomas Mayer, James S. Duesenberry, and Robert Z. Aliber, *Money, Banking, and the Economy* (2d ed.; New York: W. W. Norton, 1984), p. 466.

8.   *New York Times*, May 20, 1990, p. D13.

9.✩ There is no doubt that many people plan to make a speculative profit when they buy artifacts ranging from Old Masters to a match-folder collection like the one G. Gordon Liddy sorrowfully shredded to destroy possible Watergate evidence. Such dealing concerns actual commodities, whose sale and purchase function like those of more ordinary commodities in the producing economy. An Old Master may be hung on the livingroom wall and so be "consumed" as the other furnishings of the room are consumed, and as the room itself is consumed. Or the painting may be held for sale and stored like any other item in the inventory of a profit-making enterprise. It may be consumers' goods one day and producers' the next. In contrast, and regardless of the jargon of brokers, securities are not products and are never either consumers' goods or producers' goods. The principle of opportunity cost puts the prices paid for works of art and "collectibles" on a track parallel to that of the securities markets.

11. PROPERTY

1.☆   Normal profit is, in Myrdal's terminology, *ex ante*, and actual profit is
ex post. (See Gunnar Myrdal, *Monetary Equilibrium* [London: William
Hodge, 1939], pp. 45–47.) The present analysis, however, is primarily concerned with pricing policies of the firm, while Myrdal was concerned, as
Keynes was after him, with the interest rate as a macroeconomic problem.
What is here called normal profit is similar to what Keynes called "marginal
efficiency of capital." (Keynes, *General Theory* pp. 135–146.) There are,
however, differences: (1) Normal profit moves correspondingly with its opportunity cost (the interest rate), while the marginal efficiency of capital moves
inversely to the interest rate; (2) Keynes insisted that the marginal efficiency
of capital was a *schedule,* while normal profit is idiosyncratic for each firm and
even for each project within a firm; (3) even if a schedule were possible to
compile it would be no more determinate than, say, the traditional indifference curve; and (4) marginal analysis is questionable anyhow (see Appendix
D: On the Margin, p. 243).

2.   Smith, *Wealth,* pp. 97–98.

3.   John R. Commons, *Legal Foundations of Capitalism* (New York: Kelley,
1974), p. 14. See also Robert L. Heilbroner, *The Nature and Logic of Capitalism* (New York: W. W. Norton, 1985), esp. pp. 34–37.

4.   Joan Robinson, *An Essay on Marxian Economics* (2d ed.; London:
Macmillan Press, 1966), p. 18.

5.   Josiah Royce, *The Philosophy of Loyalty.* (New York: Macmillan, 1908),
p. 139.

6.   See Appendix H: On the Reform of Corporations, p. 261.

7.   Friedrich Hayek, *The Road to Serfdom* (Chicago: University of Chicago
Press, 1944), p. 38. On the other hand, in *Individualism and Economic Order*
(London: Routledge & Kegan Paul, 1949), p. 96, Hayek wrote, "Perfect
competition means the absence of all competitive activities," because advertising, undercutting, improving, or otherwise differentiating the goods and services produced are all excluded by definition.

8.   Antitrust cases are, as Professor George L. Stigler has said, "an almost
impudent exercise in economic gerrymandering. The plaintiff sets the market,
at a maximum, as one state in area and including only aperture-priority SRL
cameras selling between $200 and $250. . . . The defendant will in turn insist
that the market is worldwide, and includes not only cameras, but also portrait
artists and possibly transportation media because a visit is a substitute for a
picture." George L. Stigler, *The Economist as Preacher* (Chicago: University
of Chicago Press, 1982), p. 51.

9. John Kenneth Galbraith, *Economics and the Public Purpose* (Boston: Houghton, Mifflin, 1973), chap. 9.

10. A. C. Pigou, *The Economics of Welfare* (4th ed.; London: Macmillan, 1982), p. 200.

12. PRODUCTIVITY

1. Joseph A. Schumpeter, *Capitalism, Socialism and Democracy.* (New York: Harper & Row, 1950), chap. 7.

2. See supra, p. 75.

3. Keynes, *General Theory*, p. 41.

13. INTEREST

1. Nassau Senior, *Industrial Efficiency and Social Economy* (New York: Arno, 1972), vol. 1, pp. 197–202; Marshall, *Principles*, p. 193; Keynes, *General Theory*, p. 174; Irving Fisher, *The Theory of Interest* (Philadelphia: Porcupine Press, 1977), p. 66 ff.

2. Richard Lombardi, *Debt Trap* (New York: Praeger, 1985), chap. 10.

3. Alice M. Rivlin, ed., *Economic Choices, 1984* (Washington: The Brookings Institution, 1984), p. 31.

4. Keynes, *General Theory*, p. 131.

5. See Jeff Faux, "Reducing the Deficits: Send the Bill to Those Who Went to the Party," *Briefing Paper* (Washington, D.C.: Economic Policy Institute, November 1987).

6. *Federal Reserve Bulletin* (September 1979), pp. 739, 740.

7. See William Greider, *Secrets of the Temple* (New York: Simon & Schuster, 1987), esp. p. 752.

14. INFLATION I

1. Keynes, *General Theory*, p. 322.

2.✶ Commons, in *Legal Foundations of Capitalism*, dates a transformation of the American economy from the Minnesota Rate Case decision of 1890. The growth of the holding company followed, despite the Sherman Antitrust Act of the same year. The prime example was United States Steel, which in 1901 completed the amalgamation of some 228 mills (see Louis D. Brandeis, *Other People's Money* [Washington: National Home Library,

1933], p. 104). I suggest topics for research: (1) To what extent was this transformation paralleled abroad? (2) To what extent was this transformation responsible for the roughly coincident upward turn of the general trend of prices?

3.✯   The debts almost certainly will not be fully paid. Whether or not they could be paid is a moot point. Schuker argues convincingly that Germany had the economic capability of paying World War I reparations, and that Latin America is similarly able to pay its debts today (See Stephen A. Schuker, *American "Reparations" to Germany, 1919–33: Implications for the Third World Debt Crisis*, Princeton Studies in International Finance, no. 61 (July 1988). Germany would not pay because the reparations were considered unjust, and Latin America will not pay because the interest rates are considered usurious.

4.✯   Debasement surely has a bad name. Keynes, for example, cited a remark attributed to Lenin to the effect that "the best way to destroy the Capitalist System was to debauch the currency." (John Maynard Keynes, *Economic Consequences of the Peace* [New York: Harcourt, Brace, 1920], p. 235.) Later in his career, Keynes might have been less dogmatic on the subject of debasement, which is an obvious defense available to government if a "liquidity trap" should actually occur, or when, for whatever reason, the wealthy hoard their money instead of investing it in productive enterprise or spending it in consumption. Carlo Cipolla observed that "during the Middle Ages the countries which experienced the greatest economic development were also those which experienced the greatest debasement." (Carlo Cipolla, *Before the Industrial Revolution* [2d ed.; New York: W. W. Norton, 1980], p. 201.) In post–World War II Germany, selective debasement was effective in eliminating "liquidity overhang." (Thomas Mayer and Gunther Thumann, "Radical Currency Reform: Germany, 1948," *Finance & Development* [March 1990], pp. 6–8.)

5.   Keynes, *The Collected Writings of John Maynard Keynes* (Cambridge: Cambridge University Press, 1979), vol. 29, p. 237.

6.   W. A. Phillips, "The Relationship between the Rate of Change of Money-Wage Rates and Unemployment in the United Kingdom, 1861–1957," *Economica* (November 1958). Phillips concluded that a 2 percent annual increase in productivity and a 2 1/2 percent level of unemployment would generally result in stable prices (p. 299). An unmentioned factor in his calculations is the interest rate, which in the nineteenth century and the first half of the twentieth century was only a fraction of what it is today, and which may well account for the 4–7 percent unemployment now advocated.

7.☆   Hyman P. Minsky, *Stabilizing an Unstable Economy* (New Haven: Yale University Press, 1986), p. 263. On the graphs reproduced below, the rate of unemployment is plotted on the horizontal axis, and the annual change in the Consumer Price Index is plotted on the vertical axis.

UNEMPLOYMENT AND INFLATION, 1952–84
1961–69   1952–60 and 1970–84

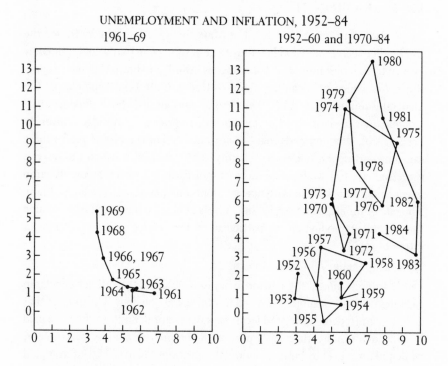

8.   Say, *Treatise,* pp. 134–35. Say's law is related to the "real bills" doctrine of finance (see supra, p. 55), the use-value theory of property (see supra, p. 124), and the wage-fund theory of enterprise (see infra, p. 182). In all these cases, commodities are assumed to be "real" and finite in number. For a discussion of some of the consequences of these assumptions, see Appendix E: On General Equilibrium, p. 246.

9.   Say, *Treatise*, p. 139.

10.   Keynes, *General Theory,* chap. 2.

11.   Paul Davidson, *Money and the Real World* (2d ed.; London: Macmillan, 1978), chap. 6. Frank H. Knight, *Risk, Uncertainty and Profit* (Boston: Houghton Mifflin, 1921), chaps. 7 and 9. G. L. S. Shackle, *Business, Time and Thought* (New York: New York University Press, 1988), chap. 7.

12.   The readily available payroll statistics cover only the private sector; therefore only the private sector's contribution to the GNP is included in this calculation.

15. INFLATION II

1.☆   Ricardo, *Principles*, p. 21. For Marx the wage-fund theory turned the conflict between capital and labor into a zero-sum game that would ultimately be won by the most numerous team. It can, I think, be shown that such a game is a consequence of regarding commodities as finite (see Appendix E: On General Equilibrium, p. 246). Piero Sraffa's curious little book, *Production of Commodities by Means of Commodities* (Cambridge: Cambridge University Press, 1960), thus contends that "to any one level of the rate of profits there can only correspond one wage, whatever the standard in which the wage is expressed" (p. 62). Sraffa, who was editor of Ricardo's works, follows Ricardo in confusing actual profits with normal profits and hence with the interest rate. The rate of profits, he writes, is "susceptible of being determined from outside the system of production, in particular by the level of the money rate of interest" (p.33).

2.   Schumpeter, *History* p. 655, n. 22.

3.☆   Interest affects the cost of living in several ways. Its direct effects, in the rates paid on consumer loans and mortgages, are obvious. The interest that government (federal, state, and local) pays is a factor in taxes; so the taxes paid by individuals indirectly cover a portion of the interest paid by government, while the taxes paid by business indirectly cover the balance. The interest paid directly and indirectly by business is a cost of doing business and thus is a factor in prices charged by business (and paid by consumers). These various direct and indirect payments, when summed, may be divided by the total of personal incomes (less savings) to determine the portion of personal expenditures that goes to pay interest charges. These personal expenditures, it should be emphasized, are attempts to estimate the actual cost of living of the population as a whole and are not to be confused with the Consumer Price Index, which of course is a statistical construct in every respect.

We here consider only the interest paid by the nonfinancial sectors of the economy. The interest paid by the financial sectors (the federal funds rate, the discount rate, the money-market rate, the brokers' call rate, the rate paid on deposits, and so forth) is obviously a cost of finance and so must be covered by the financial institutions in the rates they charge nonfinancial institutions and individuals. But to include the interest paid by the financial sectors in the interest costs of the economy would be comparable to including the costs of components of finished goods, along with the finished goods themselves, in the GNP.

On the other hand, speculation in the securities markets is an activity within the financial sector. The level of the markets is affected by the quantity and cost of money available to them, and the profits of speculating are an opportunity cost of investment in productive enterprise. Interest paid by financial corporations consequently has an important long-term effect on the economy as a whole, but its immediate effect on prices is negligible.

4. *Employment and Earnings*, (November 1988), p. 32; (January 1989), p. 7. About half of the part-timers say they like it that way, but at least some of these are moonlighters who could not handle two full-time jobs.

5. Fernand Braudel, *Civilization and Capitalism* (New York: Harper & Row, 1985), vol. 2, p. 205.

6. Ibid., p. 218.

7. John E. Schwartz, *America's Hidden Success* (New York: W. W. Norton, 1983), chap. 2.

16. INTERNATIONAL TRADE

1. Smith, *Wealth*, p. 581.

2. Ricardo, *Principles*, p. 82.

3. Ibid., p. 82–83.

4. Ibid., p. 83.

5. Carlo Cipolla, *Before the Industrial Revolution* (2d ed.; New York: W. W. Norton, 1980), p. 251.

6. Wassily Leontief, "Domestic Production and Foreign Trade: the American Capital Position Re-examined." In Richard E. Caves and Harvey G. Johnson, eds., *Readings in International Economics* (Homewood, Ill.: Richard D. Irwin, 1968), pp. 522–523.

7. Ibid., p. 523.

8. Ibid., p. 527. See also infra, p. 270.

9. Frank Taussig, *The Tariff History of the United States* (8th ed.; New York: Johnson Reprint, 1966), p. 519.

17. CONCLUSION

1.   Braudel, *Civilization and Capitalism*, vol. 2, pp. 395–400.

2.   Hyman P. Minsky, *Stabilizing an Unstable Economy* (New Haven, Conn.: Yale University Press, 1986), part 2.

3.   Maurice Leven, Harold C. Moulton, and Clark Warburton, *America's Capacity to Consume* (New York: McGraw-Hill, 1934), pp. 55–56.

4.   Hyman P. Minsky, *Can "It" Happen Again?* (Armonk, N.Y.: Sharpe, 1982), pp. xxiii–xxiv, 3–13.

5.☆   The most equitable and effective measure to correct the current maldistribution of wealth would be a confiscatory or near-confiscatory death duty. It would not deny achievers the enjoyment of their achievement and so would not, as the saying goes, sap their incentive. Nor would it deny the offspring of achievers the satisfaction of earning their own living. And it would have the incidental consequence of reducing the national debt. Economists as far apart otherwise as Hayek and Keynes are in favor of it. I leave to the reader the listing of reasons why it's not an immediate possibility.

A progressive income tax would still be necessary. See Joseph A. Pechman's posthumous presidential address to the American Economic Association: "The Future of the Income Tax," *The American Economic Review* 80: 1 (March 1990), pp. 1–20.

For suggestions for corporate reform, see Appendix H: On the Reform of Corporations, p. 261.

6.☆   It is perhaps worth distinguishing this dismal prognosis from two that are superficially similar. Marx expected the polarization of society to lead to revolution rather than to stagnation. And in the 1940s Professor Alvin Hansen expected stagnation to be the consequence of four factors then apparent: (1) the growth of personal and corporate saving, (2) the declining rate of population growth, (3) the disappearance of geographic frontiers, and (4) the tendency for inventions to be capital saving rather than capital absorbing. (See Benjamin Higgins in *Income, Employment and Public Policy: Essays in Honor of Alvin H. Hansen* [New York: W. W. Norton, 1948], p. 90.) In contrast, the present analysis turns on polarization and on speculative profits as the opportunity cost of productive investment.

7.   Keynes, *General Theory*, pp. 383–384.

APPENDIX A: *On Perfect Competition*

1.   These claims are paraphrased from Friedman, *Positive Economics*, pp. 3–46. $S = 1/2gt^2$ is the formula for the distance (in feet) a freely falling body will fall in a given time (in seconds).

2.   Galileo Galilei, *Dialogues Concerning Two New Sciences* (New York: McGraw-Hill, 1963).

APPENDIX B: *On Games*

1.   Thomas Hobbes, *The Leviathan* (Harmondsworth: Penguin, 1968), p. 161.

2.   Robert Axelrod, *The Evolution of Cooperation* (New York: Basic Books, 1984), pp. 22-73.

3.   Richard Levins, *Evolution in Changing Environments* (Princeton: Princeton University Press, 1965), p. 99. The same point is made from the other direction by Erik Erikson: "The sunlight playing on the waves qualifies for the attribute 'playful' because it faithfully remains within the rules of the game." Erik H. Erikson, *Childhood and Society* (35th anniversary ed.; New York: W. W. Norton, 1985), p. 212.

APPENDIX C: *On Utility*

1.   *The Encyclopedia of Philosophy.* (New York: Macmillan and Free Press, 1967, vol. I), p. 283.

2.   Pierre Dumont, quoted in Philip Newman et al., eds., *Source Readings in Economic Thought* (New York, W. W. Norton, 1954), p. 169.

3.   Léon Walras, "Geometrical Theory of the Determination of Prices," *Annals of the American Academy of Political and Social Science*, (July 1892), pp. 47-48.

4.   Ibid., p. 57. (Walras's emphases.)

5.   Smith, *Wealth*, p. 250.

6.   Milton Friedman, "Lerner on the Economics of Control," in *Essays in Positive Economics*, pp. 310-319.

7.   Léon Walras, *Elements of Pure Economics* (Philadelphia: Orion Editions, 1984), p. 310.

8.   Carl Menger, *Principles of Economics* (New York: New York University Press, 1976), p. 193. (Menger's emphases.)

9.   W. Stanley Jevons, *The Theory of Political Economy* (5th ed.; New York: Kelley, 1965), p. 146.

10.   Jean-Baptiste Say, *A Treatise on Political Economy* (New York: Kelley, 1971), p. 32.

APPENDIX D: *On The Margin*

1. Philip H. Wicksteed, *The Alphabet of Economic Science* (New York: Kelley, 1970), p. 102.

2. Fritz Machlup, "Marginal Analysis and Empirical Research," *American Economic Review* 36 (September 1946), p. 535.

3. Knut Wicksell, *Selected Papers on Economic Theory* (New York: Kelley, 1969), p. 144. (Wicksell's emphasis.)

APPENDIX E: *On General Equilibrium*

1. Frank Hahn, *Equilibrium and Macroeconomics.* Cambridge, Mass: MIT Press, 1984), p. 24 ff. Edmund S. Phelps, *Political Economy* (New York: W. W. Norton, 1985), p. 60 ff.

2.☆ Philip Mirowski, *The Reconstruction of Economic Theory* (Boston: Kluwer-Nijhoff, 1986), p. 189. See also Mirowski, *Against Mechanism* (Totowa, NJ: Rowan & Littlefield, 1988), esp. chaps. 1 and 6, and Greg Davidson and Paul Davidson, *Economics for a Civilized Society* (New York: W. W. Norton, 1988), pp. 56–59.

Ecology also has struggled to model itself on classical mechanics. Nature has been assumed to be "naturally" in a state of equilibrium, to which it eventually returns whenever disturbed. A symposium at the 1990 annual meeting of the Ecological Society of America raised doubts about the assumption. Dr. S. T. A. Pickett of the New York Botanical Garden said it "makes nice poetry," but it's not such great science" (*New York Times*, July 31, 1990, p. C1).

3. All references to this work are to the paperback reprint. (New Haven: Yale University Press, 1959).

4. See E. Roy Weintraub, *General Equilibrium Analysis* (Cambridge: Cambridge University Press, 1985).

5. Debreu, *Theory of Value*, p. 32.

6. Ibid., p. 29.

7. John William Miller, *The Midworld of Symbols and Functioning Objects* (New York: W. W. Norton, 1982), pp. 173–175.

8. Debreu, *Theory of Value*, p. 30. (Debreu's emphases.)

9. J. R. Hicks, *Value and Capital* (2d ed.; Oxford: Oxford University Press, 1946), p. 193.

10. Debreu, *Theory of Value*, p. 38.

11. Ibid., p. 43.

12. Ibid., p. 62.

13. Ibid., p. 75.

14. Ibid., p. 74. (Debreu's emphases.)

15. Ibid., p. 76.

16. Ibid., p. 76 ff.

17. Ibid., p. 35, n. 2.

18. Ibid., p. 33.

19. Walras, *Elements,* p. 94.

20. Ibid., p. 95.

21. Ibid., p. 146. (Walras's emphasis.)

APPENDIX F: *On Economies of Scale*

1. Debreu, p. 49, n. 2.

2. Piero Sraffa, "The Laws of Returns under Competitive Conditions," *Economic Journal* 36 (December 1926), pp. 535–550.

3. Allyn A. Young, "Increasing Returns and Economic Progress," *Economic Journal* 38 (December 1928), pp. 527–542.

4. Supra, p. 238.

5. Vilfredo Pareto, *Manual of Political Economy* (New York: Kelley, 1971), pp. 124–135.

6. Knut Wicksell, *Lectures on Political Economy* (New York: Kelley, 1977), vol. 1, p. 128. (Wicksell's emphasis.)

APPENDIX G: *On the Quantity of Money*

1. Professor Fisher wrote that "under the conditions assumed [by the equation of exchange], the price level varies . . . directly as the quantity of money in circulation. . . . [This relation] constitutes the 'quantity theory of money.'" (Irving Fisher, *The Purchasing Power of Money* [2d ed.; Fairfield, N.J.: Kelley, 1985], p. 29.) Professor Friedman, however, disagrees. See Milton Friedman, "Quantity Theory of Money," in John Eatwell, Murray Milgate, and Peter Newman, eds. *The New Palgrave: Money* (New York: W. W. Norton, 1989), p. 3.

2. Professor Schumpeter held that "this equation is *not* an identity but an equilibrium condition. . . . [G]iven values of M, V, T tend to *bring about* a determined value of P, but they do not simply *spell* a certain P" (Schumpeter, *History,* p. 1096). This seems a meaningless distinction, since the value of V is determined only by the equation. See also supra, Appendix E: On General Equilibrium, esp. p. 251.

APPENDIX H: *On the Reform of Corporations*

1.   Friedrich A. Hayek, *Individualism and Economic Order* (London: Routledge & Kegan Paul, 1949), p. 115.

2.   Friedrich von Wieser, *Social Economics* (New York: Kelley, 1967), pp. 209–210.

3.   Frank H. Knight, *The Ethics of Competition and Other Essays*, Milton Friedman, Homer Jones, George Stigler, and Allen Wallis, eds. (New York: Harper & Bros., 1935), pp. 41–75.

4.   Milovan Djilas, *The New Class* (New York: Praeger, 1957), passim.

5.   Fred I. Raymond, *The Limitist* (New York: W. W. Norton, 1947), passim.

APPENDIX I: *On Comparative Advantage*

1.   Mill, *Principles,* Book III, chap. 17, sec. 2.

2.   See Thomas Balogh, *The Irrelevance of Conventional Economics* (New York: Liveright, 1982), p. 244.

3.   G. D. A. MacDougal, "British and American Exports: A Study Suggested by the Theory of Comparative Costs," *Economic Journal* 61 (December 1951), pp. 697–698.

4.   Eli Hecksher, "Foreign Trade and Distribution of Income," in Howard S. Ellis and Lloyd A. Metzler, eds., *Readings in the Theory of International Trade* (Philadelphia: Blakiston, 1949), p. 278.

5.   Bertil Ohlin, *Interregional and International Trade* (rev. ed.; Cambridge, Mass.: Harvard, 1967), p. 159.

6.   Leontief, "Domestic Production and Foreign Trade," p. 523.

7.   Ibid., pp. 526, 527.

8.   Balogh, *The Irrelevance of Conventional Economics*, p. 244.

9.   Mill, *Principles*, Book III, chap. 17, sec. 2.

INDEX

abstinence, 126–127
Acquisitive Society, The (Tawney), 277
Affluent Society, The (Galbraith), 85
Against Mechanism (Mirowski), 288
agriculture, 158, 176, 192, 202, 209–210,
    215, 220, 223
Aliber, Robert Z., 279
Alphabet of Economic Science, The
    (Wicksteed), 288
altruism, 14, 15, 16
American Capitalism (Galbraith), 277
*American "Reparations" to Germany,
    1919–33: Implications for the Third
    World Debt Crisis* (Schuker), 282
America's Capacity to Consume (Leven,
    Moulton, and Warburton), 286
America's Hidden Success (Schwartz), 285
anthropology, 9, 95
antitrust laws, 76, 134, 263, 280
appearance vs. reality, 10, 166–167
Argentina, 171–172, 202
Aristotle, 2, 22, 61–62, 85–86, 101, 154,
    233, 275, 276, 277
astronomy, 24, 26, 42
astrophysics, 25
auctions, 125
    stock market compared with, 109
Augustine, Saint, 5, 13, 15, 274
automobile industry, 218
    competition in, 204–205, 213
    wage increase in, 187
autonomy, 17, 31–37, 229

Averitt, Robert, 225
Axelrod, Robert, 287

Baily, Marin N., 275
Balogh, Thomas, 290
bankruptcies, 151, 158, 174
banks, banking, 5, 47, 100, 164, 167, 169
    COLAs of, 187–190
    competition of, 156–159
    concentration of, 159
    deregulation of, 156, 157
    disintermediation crises of, 155–156
    international, 158–159, 205–207
    investment, 108, 129, 188, 213, 216
    lending by, 53–54, 55, 58, 90, 158, 159,
        165–166, 186, 188, 205–207
    Regulation Q and, 58, 156, 205, 264
    reserve requirements of, 54, 168
barter, 1, 51, 275
Battle Against Unemployment and Inflation
    (Baily and Okun, eds.), 275
Beauty Looks After Herself (Gill), 132
Before the Industrial Revolution (Cipolla),
    282, 285
behaviorism, 4, 9, 25
Bentham, Jeremy, 154, 237, 241, 242
Berle, A. A., 77, 277
"Beyond the Age of Materials" (Larson,
    Ross, and Williams), 277
big government, 221, 223, 228
Bismarck, Otto von, 209
blacks, in labor force, 145, 163

Blanc, Louis, 77
Bondage of the Will, The (Luther), 190
bonds, 49, 106, 110
    government, 54, 160–161, 162, 188
borrowing, borrowers, 50, 58, 143, 156,
    205–206
    creation of money and, 55
    see also debt
Brandeis, Louis D., 281
Braudel, Fernand, 191, 222, 285, 286
Brazil, 141, 171–172, 202, 211
Brimmer, Andrew F., 278
"British and American Exports: A Study
    Suggested by the Theory of
    Comparative Costs" (MacDougal), 290
Browne, Sir Thomas, 27
Brownian movements, 232
Brown v. *Board of Education,* 152
Brunner, Karl, 276
budget deficit, U.S., 160–164, 185
bull market, 110, 114, 224, 226
Bureau of Labor Statistics, 45
business, 44–45
    changes in, 163–164
    costs of, 54, 56, 57, 147, 148, 149, 165,
        182–183, 185–187, 244–245
    credit relationship in, 47–48
    ethics and, x, 68–70
    management of, 77, 78, 80, 82, 115,
        125–126, 129, 143, 147, 261
    natural history theory of, 213–214
    organization of, 125
    price increases and, 18, 25, 54, 56
    relationships in, 125
    in Renaissance, 5
    sale of, 122
    speculation compared with, 107
    speculation's triumph over, 77–78, 116,
        118, 185
    time factor in, 144, 178
    uncertainty of, 55, 56
    see also corporations; trade
Business, Time and Thought (Shackle), 283
business cycle, 171

calculus:
    differential, 238–239, 241
    "felicific," 237
Calvinism, 91–92
Campeau fiasco, 108
Can "It" Happen Again? (Minsky), 286
capital, 97–105
    durability of, 98–99
    fixed, 102, 106
    home as, 98–100
    labor vs., 130
    liquid, 102, 103, 105
    profits and, 122
    rights of, 126–127
    U.S. comparative advantage and, 201–202
    wealth vs., 90
    working, 102, 106
Capital (Marx), 75, 275, 276, 277

capital gains, 118
capitalism, capitalists, 77–79, 122
    Marx on, 75, 76, 79
    transition from mercantilism to, 51, 70
Capitalism, Socialism and Democracy
    (Schumpeter), 277, 281
Carlyle, Thomas, x, 133
Carnegie, Andrew, 91
Caves, Richard E., 285
certificates of deposit, 156
chaos, lawlessness and, 32–33
checking accounts, 49, 51, 156, 164
checks, personal, 137, 163, 164
chemistry, uniformity and, 44
Childhood and Society (Erikson), 287
Chile, 202
China, People's Republic of, 89, 211, 214
    Cultural Revolution in, 17
    wages in, 207–208
Churchill, Winston, 150
Cipolla, Carlo, 282, 285
Citicorp, 205
Civilization and Capitalism (Braudel), 285,
    286
classical economics, 96, 145, 178, 191–192,
    213, 215, 246
    comparative advantage in, 198–199
    perfect competition in, 231–233
Clayton Antitrust Act, 76, 134
Clough, Stewart B., 275
COLA (cost-of-living adjustment), 166,
    187–190, 193
*Collected Writings of John Maynard Keynes,
    The* (Keynes), 278, 282
commerce, *see* trade
Commercial Revolution, 222
commitment, 70
commodities, 51, 53, 57, 73
    Debreu's definition of, 247–248
    general equilibrium analysis and, 247–254
    labor compared with, 76, 84
    money as, 47, 70, 155
commodities markets, 108, 110
Commons, John R., 124, 125, 280, 281
communism, capital and, 122
comparative advantage, 201–202, 265–271
    Law of, 198–199, 215
competition, 15, 63–64, 65, 68, 82–83, 280
    antitrust law and, 134, 263
    of banks, 156–159
    foreign, 145, 201–207, 213–217
    free, 238–239, 241
    game theory and, 234–236
    imperfect, 231
    law of diminishing returns and, 256–257
    limitist law and, 263–264
    perfect, 133, 231–233
    prices and, 134–136
    property and, 133–136
compulsion, for self-maintenance, 34, 37
Confessions (St. Augustine), 274
conflict, exchange and, 69, 70
Congress, U.S., 168

Congressional Budget Office, 160
conservation, 141–142
conservatives, 141, 150, 166, 177
consistency, 35, 36, 37, 42
conspiracy, 134
Consumer Price Index (CPI), 45, 46–47,
    183–185, 193, 194, 284
consumers' goods, 279
    producers' goods vs., 97–99, 104
    as property, 123
consumption, consumers, 28, 55, 91–97,
    110, 112
    anthropology of, 95
    conspicuous, 91, 94
    increase of, 8
    of money, 48
    propensity to consume and, 18–19
    sovereignty of, 96
    utility maximization and, 10–13
    Veblen's views on, 91, 94
Continental Illinois, 159, 226
continuity, existence and, 33–34
contracts:
    interest and, 153–154
    labor, 187–188
Coolidge, Calvin, 108, 149
cooperation, 133, 134, 235–236, 263
Copernicus, Nicolaus, 5, 20, 36
corporations:
    cash flow of, 155
    directors of, 122, 126
    as entrepreneurs, 122–123
    multinational, 198, 199, 204–205,
        207–211
    production priority and, 100–101
    public board members of, 131–132
    reform of, 261–264
    stockholders of, 122–123, 128–132, 138,
        261–262
    theory of, 77
cost of living, 284
cost-of-living adjustment (COLA), 187–190,
    193
cost ratios, 147
Cost Reduction, Paradox of, 225
costs:
    business, 54, 56, 57, 147, 148, 149, 165,
        182–183, 185–187, 244–245
    investment, 186–187
    labor, 180–183, 202–203, 207–208, 245
    marginal analysis of, 244–245
    production, 244
    wage goods, 66
counterfeiting, combating of, 59
Crash of 1987, 110–114, 278–279
creativity, 17, 121
credit, 47–50, 100, 137, 163, 164, 186, 189
criminal law, 137–138
Critique of the Gotha Program (Marx), 17,
    77, 274, 277

Darwin, Charles, 95, 277
Davidson, Greg, 288

Davidson, Paul, 146, 275, 283, 288
debasement of currency, 172, 282
Debreu, Gerard, 70, 247–254, 256, 258,
    276, 288, 289
debt, 50, 54, 55, 70, 100–101, 143
    consumer, 164
    domestic, 188–189
    national, 113, 168, 172
    Third World, 168, 172, 205–207
Debt Trap (Lombardi), 281
decision making, 80–81, 103–104
deflation, 171
demand, 26, 56, 84, 192
    aggregate, 55, 160, 161, 255
    effective, 63–64, 90, 113, 224, 252
    excess, 252
    for money, 54, 162
    net, 252–253
    utility maximization and, 10–12
    see also supply and demand, law of
demand curve, 65, 71, 255
democracy, 7, 77
depression, 2, 130, 149, 228
    see also Great Depression
de Roover, Raymond, 276
destruction, 37, 87–88, 129
    "creative," 143–144
deterioration, prospect of, 221–229
Dialogues Concerning Two New Sciences
    (Galileo), 287
diminishing returns, law of, 176, 209,
    256–257
dissolution, threat of, 34
"Distinguished Lecture on Economics in
    Government: Central Banking and
    Systemic Risks in Capital Markets"
    (Brimmer), 278
Djilas, Milovan, 263, 290
dollar, U.S., 145–146
    constant, 46, 150, 194, 207
    strength of, 161–162, 165
    value of, 45
"Domestic Production and Foreign Trade:
    the American Capital Position
    Re-examined" (Leontief), 285
Douglas, Mary, 94–95, 277
Drake, Sir Francis, 97–98
Dumont, Pierre, 237, 287
Duesenberry, James S., 279

earth, radius of, 22, 40
Eatwell, John, 276, 289
Ecological Society of America, 288
Economic Choices (Rivlin), 281
Economic Consequences of the Peace
    (Keynes), 282
Economic History of Europe: Twentieth
    Century (Clough), 275
economic man, 4, 10–16, 70, 87–88, 222,
    224, 227
    defined, ix
    as organizing principle, ix–x

economic man *(cont.)*
 profit vs. utility maximization and, 10–13
 as servomechanism, 4
Economic Report of the President, 22, 283
economics:
 defined, 1–2, 87
 history of, 2–3
 human relations and, 37–38
 need for, 1–7
 pure, as impossibility, 68–69
 as science, 6, 22–29, 68
Economics (Brockway), x
Economics and the Public Purpose
 (Galbraith), 277, 281
economics fallacy (fallacy of composition),
 142–143, 145, 149, 215, 225
Economics for a Civilized Society (Davidson
 and Davidson), 288
Economics of Welfare, The (Pigou), 281
economic vs. political problems, 3, 92
Economic Writings (Petty), 274
economies of scale, 56, 176, 256–258, 263
 banking and, 158–159
Economist as Preacher (Stigler), 280
efficiency, 58, 65, 138, 139
 productivity as measure of, 149
 of U.S. labor, 202, 208
Egypt, ancient, 41, 172–173
Einstein, Albert, 26, 35, 36
Eisenhower, Dwight D., 183
electrons, 28, 33
Elements of Pure Economics (Walras), 276,
 287, 289
Eliot, T. S., 10
Ellis, Howard S., 290
Emerson, Ralph Waldo, 79
employee ownership, 138–139, 262
employment, 96
 full, 2, 105, 169, 173–180
 see also unemployment
Employment and Earnings, 285
Encyclopedia of Philosophy, The, 287
Engels, Friedrich, 209
entrepreneurs, 50, 77–84, 119, 133, 261
 and changes in international trade,
 202–204
 corporations as, 122–123
equilibrium, 50, 96, 256
 economies of scale and, 256–258
 general, 176, 246–255
 market, 253
 price, 64, 246
Equilibrium and Macroeconomics (Hahn),
 274, 288
Eratosthenes, 40, 42
Erikson, Erik H., 287
error:
 mathematical, 24
 truth and, 35–36
Essay on Marxian Economics, An
 (Robinson), 280
Essays in Economics (Tobin), 275
Essays in Persuasion (Keynes), 278

Essays in Positive Economics (Friedman),
 276
ethics, 18, 24, 29, 86
 business, x, 68–70
 destruction and, 37
 medieval, 5
 mores, morals, morale, x, 86
 price and, 68–72
 productivity and, 151–152
 "Ethics of Competition, The" (Knight), 263
*Ethics of Competition and Other Essays,
 The* (Knight), 290
Euclid, 231–233
Evolution in Changing Environments
 (Levins), 287
Evolution of Cooperation, The (Axelrod),
 287
exchange, *see* trade
exchange rates, 146, 161, 162
exchange-value, 74, 124–125, 223
executives, 77, 80–84, 86
existence, requirements of, 33–34, 37
experts, social values and, 86
exports, U.S., 162, 165, 202, 206, 213,
 217–218

factory system, 3
faith, money and, 45, 59–60
fallacy of composition (economics fallacy),
 142–143, 145, 149, 215, 225
Faux, Jeff, 281
Fedack, Marilyn G., 279
Federal Reserve Board, 45, 51–57, 161–165,
 189, 193, 226, 275
 interest rates and, 53–58, 116, 155, 156,
 157, 161, 162, 183, 185–186, 194
 money supply and, 51–57, 110, 111,
 115–116, 117, 155, 168, 184, 260
 "real bills" theory and, 55–56
Federal Reserve Bulletin, 281
Federal Reserve notes, 50
Federal Reserve System, weaknesses of,
 167–169
Federal Tax Policy (Pechman), 278
"felicific calculus," 237
Feminine Mystique, The (Friedan), 163
Filene, Edward A., 138
fiscal policy, *see* taxes
Fisher, Irving, 154, 259, 281, 289
Five Discourses on Political Arithmetick
 (Petty), 21
Florence, 59
Forbes, 56
Ford, Henry, 32, 135, 212, 223
"Foreign Trade and Distribution of
 Income" (Hecksher), 290
Fourteenth Amendment, 124
France, 93, 165, 172
free competition, 238–239, 241
freedom, ix, 6–7, 17, 104
 Marxism and, 4
 responsibility and, 16
free market, 6–7, 66, 84, 185–186

French Revolution, 40, 46
Freud, Sigmund, 84
Friedan, Betty, 163
Friedman, Milton, 68, 240, 275, 276, 286, 287, 289, 290
Fuller, Margaret, 28
future, 32, 50, 120, 151
    exchange-value and, 124–125
"Future of the Income Tax, The" (Pechman), 286
futures exchanges, 108, 115

Galbraith, John Kenneth, 77, 80, 82, 85, 134, 214, 277, 281
Galileo Galilei, 9, 20, 35, 36, 42, 233, 234, 287
gambling, 106–107
games, theory of, 41, 69, 234–236
garment industry, competition in, 214–215
Gayer, Arthur D., 274
General Equilibrium Analysis (Weintraub), 288
general equilibrium theory, 176, 246–255
General Motors, 142, 145, 204, 205
General Theory of Employment, Interest and Money, The (Keynes), 8, 17, 192, 273, 274, 276, 277, 278, 280, 281, 282, 286
general welfare, 7
genetics, 34–35, 81
"Geometrical Theory of the Determination of Prices" (Walras), 287
geometry, 24–25, 40
    Euclidean, 231–233
German Ideology, The (Marx), 17, 274, 277
Germany, 91, 161, 282
    hyperinflation in, 47, 171–172, 175
Gill, Eric, 132
gold, 47, 51, 59–60, 191–192
goods, 87–97
    consumers' vs. producers', 97–99, 104
    consumption of, 91–97
    loss of marketability of, 89–90
    natural objects as, 87
    services as, 88–90
    substitute, 64
    wage, 66
goods and services, 28, 55, 56, 113
    exchange of, *see* trade
    money compared with, 48
    transactions form of the quantity of money equation and, 259–260
good will, 121, 125
government:
    big, 221, 223, 228
    economic dependence of, 7
    as employer of last resort, 179–180
    regulation by, 58, 136–138, 156, 165, 232
government bonds, 54, 160–161, 162, 188
Graunt, John, 20, 21
Great Britain, 97–98, 99, 130, 176, 208, 212, 222
    comparative advantage and, 265–267, 269

free trade and, 197–200
    mercantilism of, 191–192
Great Depression, 54, 156, 171, 221, 223, 227
    foreign trade and, 218–219
    perfect competition and, 231
greed, 13–17, 71, 121, 154–155
    partial analysis and, 14–15
    Three Antinomies of, 16, 70
Greeks, ancient, 61–62, 79, 85–86
    oikonomia of, 2–3
    trade of, 101
Greenspan, Alan, 111
Greider, William, 281
gross national product (GNP), 1, 54, 110, 145–151, 169, 184, 213
    export-import effect and, 218–219
    in foreign countries, 211
    limited usefulness of, 140–141
    real and nominal, 260

Hahn, Frank, 16, 246, 274, 288
Hamilton, Alexander, 273
Hansen, Alvin H., 286
Hayek, Friedrich, 133, 262–263, 280, 286, 290
Heckscher, Eli F., 270, 290
Heckscher-Ohlin Theorem, 270
hedging, speculation and, 117
Heilbroner, Robert L., 21, 274, 280
Heisenberg, Werner, 26, 33, 275
Hesiod, 2, 79
Hicks, J. R., 251, 288
Higgins, Benjamin, 286
Hilferding, Rudolf, 209
history, 31–32, 36, 46, 151–152
    Marx's view of, 4
History as a System (Ortega y Gasset), 275
History of Economic Analysis (Schumpeter), 170–171, 276, 284, 289
Hobbes, Thomas, 133, 234, 287
Hobson, J. A., 209
holding company, 281
Holy Family, The (Marx), 273
home ownership, 98–100, 104
Honda, 202
Hong Kong, 203–204, 208, 214
household management, economics and, 2–3, 7, 37
humanism, ix, 24
human nature, 8–9, 36, 78–79
Hume, David, 39, 52–53, 275
hyperinflation, 47, 170–172, 175

identity, 33–34
imperialism, 209–216
imports, U.S., 162, 165, 202, 213, 214, 218–220
income, 8, 49
    of CEOs, 80–84
    distribution of, 113–114, 227, 228

income *(cont.)*
  fixed, 193–195
  see also wages
*Income, Employment and Public Policy:
  Essays in Honor of Alvin H. Hansen,*
  286
income curve, 243
income tax, saving and, 105
"Increasing Returns and Economic
  Progress" (Young), 289
indexes, indexing, 45–47, 93
  productivity, 149
  stock, 110
  see also Consumer Price Index
India, 90, 92
individual, society and, 95, 151
Individualism and Economic Order (Hayek),
  280, 290
Industrial Efficiency and Social Economy
  (Senior), 281
industrialization, of Third World, 211–212
Industrial Production Index, 45
Industrial Revolution, 3, 130, 171, 202, 208,
  221, 222–223, 257
inequality, economic, 221–224
inflation, 47, 99, 170–195, 226
  budget deficit and, 160
  COLAs and, 187–190, 193
  full employment and, 173–177
  hyper-, 47, 170–172, 175
  theories of, 52–53, 55, 161–162, 173–177,
    186
inflation control, 169
  interest rates and, 116, 155, 173, 183–187
  unemployment and, 2, 113, 116, 174–176
inputs, 250–251
"Inquiry into the Principles of Political
  Economy" (Steuart), 274
"institutions," 128–129, 224–226
insurance, 225
intentions, 18–19
interest, interest rates, 53–57, 153–169, 226,
    282, 284–285
  Americans, Japanese, 115
  COLAs and, 187–190
  compound, 97–98, 121
  defined, 119
  determination of, 154
  discount, 53
  federal-funds, 53
  Federal Reserve and, 53–58, 116, 155,
    156, 157, 161, 162, 183, 185–186, 194
  increase of, 18, 53–54, 56–57, 113,
    116–117, 155–156, 157, 162, 164,
    185–186
  inflation control and, 116, 155, 173,
    183–187
  prime, 56–57, 116, 155, 183–184, 187,
    188, 189
  profit and, 119–120, 121
  real, 166–167, 188, 189, 190
  Regulation Q and, 58, 156, 205, 264

speculation and, 113–117, 184–185, 186
  wages and, 154
International Monetary Fund (IMF), 206
international trade, 196–220
  comparative advantage in, 198–199,
    201–202, 265–271
  entrepreneurial-related changes in,
    202–204
  financial-related changes in, 202, 204–207
  limits to discussion of, 197
  multinationals and, 198, 199, 204–205,
    207–211
  neo-imperialism and, 209–216
  protection and, 216–219
  requirements of, 196
  Ricardo's views on, 198–199
  Smith's views on, 197–198
  sunset-sunrise explanation of, 213–214,
    216
  wage-related changes in, 202, 207–211,
    213, 214–215
Interregional and International Trade
  (Ohlin), 270, 290
inverse-square law, 22, 27
investment, 78, 96–105, 110, 112, 113, 123,
    192
  cost of, 186–187
  foreign, 161, 162
  long-term, 116
  short-term, 115
  in stock, 104–105
  taxes and, 105, 113
investment banking, 108, 129, 188, 213, 216
invisible hand, 5–6, 11, 63, 134, 136, 229,
    239, 257
Iron Law of Wages, 133
Irrelevance of Conventional Economics, The
  (Balogh), 290
irresponsibility, 34, 35
Isherwood, Baron, 94–95, 277
Italy, 202

James, William, 69, 276
Japan, 90, 105, 115, 161, 176, 200, 208, 219
  competition of, 145–146, 202–203, 208,
    214
  productivity of, 145–146
Jefferson, Thomas, 127
Jevons, William Stanley, 23–27, 238, 242,
    255, 274, 278, 287
Johns Manville asbestos products, GNP and,
    140–141
Johnson, Harvey G., 285
Johnson, Lyndon B., 163, 183
Jones, Homer, 290
justice, 139, 221, 240
  price and, 2, 61–63
  productivity and, 151–152

Kahn, R. F., 101
Kennedy, John F., 150, 183
Keynes, John Maynard, 8–9, 29, 78–79, 97,
    114, 160, 178, 195, 215–216, 229, 273,

274, 276, 277, 278, 279, 280, 281, 282, 283, 286
inflation and, 171, 176
on interest rates, 154, 167, 192
on labor, 73–74, 147
liquidity preference and, 17, 44
on mercantilism, 192
on savings and investment, 103–105
Keynes, John Neville, 68, 276
Knight, Frank H., 78, 263, 283, 290
Kondratieff, Nikolai D., 171
Korea, Republic of (South), 211, 214, 219

L, 51, 52, 111
labor, 73–86, 89, 126
capital vs., 130
COLAs and, 187–188
cost of, 66, 180–183, 202–203, 207–208, 245
division of, 3, 5, 62, 197–198, 203, 256
employee ownership and, 138–139, 262
exploitation of, 101, 207–208
power of, 192, 210–211, 212
socially necessary, 74
as standard of value, 73–75, 126
technological advances and, 130–131
Third World, 207–211
U.S. comparative advantage and, 201–202
U.S. expansion of, 163
wages and, 75, 76, 80–84, 86, 153, 179, 180–181, 207–208
Labor Theory of Right, 126–127, 262
land, 122, 126, 153–154, 222
Laplace, Pierre Simon de, 32, 275
Larson, Eric D., 277
Latin America:
inflation in, 171–172, 175–176
see also specific countries
Law of Comparative Advantage, 198–199, 215
law of diminishing returns, 176
"Laws of Returns under Competitive Conditions, The" (Sraffa), 256–257, 289
Lectures on Political Economy (Wicksell), 289
Legal Foundations of Capitalism (Commons), 124, 280, 281
Lehrer, Tom, 35
lender of last resort, 226
lending, 50
by banks, 53–54, 55, 58, 90, 158, 159, 165–166, 186, 188, 205–207
to Third World, 158, 205–207
see also interest, interest rates
Lenin, V. I., 209, 282
Leontief, Wassily, 201–202, 207, 208, 270–271, 285, 290
Leontief's Paradox, 271
Lerner, Abba, 240
"Lerner on the Economics of Control" (Friedman), 287

less-developed countries (LDCs), see Third World; specific countries
Leven, Maurice, 286
leveraged buyouts, 158, 226–227
Leviathan, The (Hobbes), 287
Levins, Richard, 236, 287
liberals, 141, 150, 214
libertarians, 232, 233
Liddy, G. Gordon, 279
Limitist, The (Raymond), 290
limitist law, 263–264
liquid finance, 124–126, 221–223, 281–282
liquidity preference, 17–18, 44–45, 59, 106, 112, 113
liquidity trap, 282
Locke, John, 85, 277
logic, 13, 23
Lombardi, Richard, 158, 281
love, 69–72, 84
loyalty to enterprise, 129
Lundberg, Ferdinand, 195
Luther, Martin, 190
Luxemburg, Rosa, 209
Lydia, money in, 39, 43, 59

M1, 51, 110, 111, 162–163, 184
M2, 51, 111, 163, 184, 259
M3, 51, 111
MacDougal, G. D. A., 269, 290
Machlup, Fritz, 244–245, 288
macroeconomics, 104, 105, 111
foreign trade and, 220
incompatibility of microeconomics and, 142–151
Macroeconomics (Tobin), 275
Magna Carta, 7
maldistribution, 111–113, 221–223, 227, 228, 286
Malthus, Thomas, 92, 234–235
management:
business, 77, 78, 80, 82, 115, 125–126, 129, 143, 147, 261
household, 2–3, 37
of mutual and money funds, 129
Sloan system of, 204–205
worker participation in, 138
Manual of Political Economy (Pareto), 289
Mao Zedong, 77, 89
Marcuse, Herbert, 17
margin, defined, 243
marginal analysis, 176, 231, 243–245
"Marginal Analysis and Empirical Research" (Machlup), 288
marginal efficiency of capital, 280
marginal utility, 238–243
market basket, 45–46
market equilibrium, 253
market price, 63–64, 66
markets, 64–66
commodities, 108, 110
control of, 204, 210
free, 6–7, 66, 70, 84, 185–186
instability of, 26–27

markets *(cont.)*
  not cleared, 52, 66
  stock, *see* stock, stock market
Marshall, Alfred, 29–30, 154, 274, 281
Marx, Karl, 4, 17, 45, 58, 74–79, 88, 91,
    130, 146, 171, 175, 209, 212, 273, 274,
    275, 276, 277, 284, 286
Marx-Engels Reader, The (Tucker, ed.),
    273, 274, 277
mass production, 221, 223
mathematics, 12, 19–30, 232–233
  equilibrium and, 246–247
  errors in, 24
  reciprocity in, 30
  stability of, 26–27, 30
  statistics and, 20–23, 26
Maxwell, James Clerk, 25, 26
Mayer, Thomas (of World Bank) 282
Mayer, Thomas (of University of California,
    Davis), 276, 279
Means, Gardiner C., 77, 277
measurement, 39–45
  comparison with a standard and, 40–41
  of money supply, 51–52
  physical vs. monetary, 43–45
  of production, 93
  reciprocity and, 41, 45
  science and, 42–43
  of time, 41–42
mechanism, mechanics, 4, 25, 229
Medicare, 193
"me generation," 13–14, 227
Menger, Carl, 238, 241, 287
mercantilism, 18, 21, 22, 52, 91, 191–193,
    197
  transition to capitalism from, 51, 70
merchant adventurers, 101–102, 198
mergers, 58, 129, 174
meter, length of, 40, 41
metric system, 40–43
Metzler, Lloyd A., 290
Mexico, 171–172, 202
microeconomics, 104, 105
  foreign trade and, 219–220
  incompatibility of macroeconomics and,
    142–151
Middle Ages, 2, 7, 61, 63, 91
  ethical doctrine in, 5
  production in, 101, 102
*Midworld of Symbols and Functioning
    Objects, The* (Miller), 288
Milgate, Murray, 276, 289
military spending, 160
Mill, James, 265
Mill, John Stuart, 77, 78, 90, 265, 271, 277,
    290
Miller, John William, 4, 288
Mills, C. Wright, 81
Minnesota Rate Case, 124
Minsky, Hyman P., 283, 286
Mirowski, Philip, 247, 288
Mitchell, Wesley Clair, 9, 25–26, 274

*Modern Corporation and Private Property,
    The* (Berle and Means), 277
monetarism, 57, 58, 188, 259–260
Monetary Equilibrium (Myrdal), 280
monetary policy, *see* Federal Reserve Board;
    interest, interest rates
money, 28, 38–60, 137, 240
  ambiguity of, 44
  commerce created by, 48
  as convenience, 39, 44
  counting of, 49–50
  credit and, 47–50
  as debt, 50, 70
  demand for, 54, 162
  faith in, 59–60
  Federal Reserve definitions of, 51
  functions of, 153
  invention of, 39, 43
  limits of, 58
  as liquid capital, 102, 103
  loss vs. consumption of, 48
  as measuring unit, 43–45, 48
  as non-commodity, 51–52
  purchasing power of, 45, 166, 187
  quantity theory of, 289
  as rare and durable commodity, 47, 70
  in speculation, 107–114, 117
  spending of, 10–11
  as store of buying power, 48
  as store of value, 44, 48, 85–86, 172
  velocity of, 109, 259
  wealth vs., 49
  withholding of, 18, 53, 112
Money, Banking and the Economy (Mayer,
    Duesenberry, and Aliber), 279
Money and the Real World (Davidson),
    275, 283
money market, 110, 154, 156, 162
money market funds, 128–129, 156, 157
money supply, 259–260
  Federal Reserve and, 51–57, 110, 111,
    115–116, 117, 155, 168, 184, 260
  inflation and, 52–53, 155, 183–184
  interest rates and, 162–163, 165
  measurement of, 51–52
  stock market and, 109–110
"Money Supply" (Brunner), 276
monopolies, 64, 197, 231, 232, 256
mortgages, 163, 164, 186, 188, 193
motivation, 18–19, 240
Moulton, Harold C., 286
multinational corporations, 198, 199,
    204–205, 207–211
Mumford, Lewis, 138
mutual funds, 128–129, 156
Myrdal, Gunnar, 280

NAACP Legal Defense Fund, 163
Nader, Ralph, 138
nation:
  distinguishing marks of, 196
  as household, 2–3, 7, 37
  wealth of, 1, 5–6, 90–91, 97, 191

National Income and Product Accounts, 98
natural price, 63–64, 66, 246
natural resources, 87, 90, 126, 208, 209, 220
nature, 3, 4, 31, 33
    nurture vs., 81
    reliability of, 27
Nature and Logic of Capitalism, The
    (Heilbroner), 280
neoclassical economics, 58, 176, 246
neo-imperialism, 209–216
New Class, The (Djilas), 290
New Deal, 85, 156, 163–164, 179–180, 194, 195
New Leader, The, 278
Newman, Peter, 276, 289
Newman, Philip C., 274, 287
New Palgrave: Money, The (Eatwell, Milgate, and Newman, eds.), 276, 289
Newton, Sir Isaac, 20, 22, 27, 29, 35, 42
Newtonian physics, 6, 20, 22, 23, 25, 36, 45
New York Times, 116
Nichomachean Ethics (Aristotle), 275, 276
Nigeria, 211
nothingness, 34, 67
NOW accounts, 156
Nuñes de Castro, Alfonso, 200–201

objectivity, 237, 240–242, 255
    of science, 27–29
observers:
    autonomy of, 36
    impartiality of, 27
"Of Cheating, Which Is Committed in Buying and Selling" (St. Thomas), 276
"Of Money" (Hume), 275
Ohlin, Bertil, 270, 290
oikonomia (household management), 2–3
oil prices, 159, 173
Okun, Arthur, 69, 275
oligopolies, 64, 133, 232, 257
On Ethics and Economics (Sen), 274
opportunity cost, 182, 185, 187, 224, 285, 286
optics, 26, 27
option trading, 108
Organization of Petroleum Exporting Countries (OPEC), 159, 173, 205, 206, 210
Origin of Species, The (Darwin), 95, 277
Ortega y Gasset, José, 36, 275
Other People's Money (Brandeis), 281
Our Knowledge of the External World (Russell), 275
outputs, 147, 149, 250–251
    real, 55, 56
    total, 147, 150
overproduction, 89

pain, utility analysis and, 237–242
panics, financial, 110, 111
Paradox of Cost Reduction, 225
Pareto, Vilfredo, 245, 257, 258, 289
partial analysis, 14–15

past, 33–34, 37
    denial of, 32
    exchange-value and, 124–125
    historical view of, 32
Pauling, Linus, 28
Pechman, Joseph A., 278, 286
Peirce, Charles, 167
pension funds, 129, 187
Pepsi Cola, 244
perfect competition, 231–233
Pericles, 133
personality, 70, 237
Petty, Sir William, 20–22, 274
Phelps, Edmund S., 246, 288
Philippines, 214
Phillips, W. A., 282
Phillips curve, 176
Philosophical Essay on Probabilities, A (Laplace), 275
Philosophy of Loyalty, The (Royce), 280
Philosophy of Physics, The (Planck), 274, 275
photons, 26
Physicist's Conception of Nature, The (Heisenberg), 33
physics, 24, 26, 35, 36, 68
    Newtonian, 6, 20, 22, 23, 25, 36, 45
    perfect competition and, 232
    as value free, 27–29
Pickett, S. T. A., 288
Pigou, A. C., 281
Planck, Max, 28, 274
Plato, 2, 3, 101, 276
pleasure, utility analysis and, 237–242
Plessy v. Ferguson, 152
Pogo, 241
Poland, 116
Political Discourses (Hume), 275
Political Economy (Phelps), 288
political vs. economic problems, 3, 92
Politics (Aristotle), 277
pollution, 141, 146
Polyani, Karl, 223
Portugal, 198, 199, 265–267
Positive Economics (Friedman), 286
postmodernism, 36
poverty, 79, 86, 92, 95, 190, 207, 224
    GNP and, 151
    in Great Depression, 227–228
power:
    diffusion of, 133
    economic, 99–100, 133
    of labor, 192, 210–211, 212
"power elite," 81
present, 32, 33–34
price, prices, 29, 61–72
    competition and, 134–136
    as economic fact, 71
    equilibrium, 64, 246
    histories of, 67
    increase of, 18, 25, 52–53, 54, 56, 58, 172
    interest rates and, 54, 56, 185

price *(cont.)*
  just, 2, 61–63
  marginal analysis and, 244
  market and, 64–66
  money supply and, 52–53, 110
  natural, 63–64, 66, 246
  nominal and real, 73
  profits' effect on, 121
  reduction of, 56
  regress and, 66, 68, 71
  setting of, 53, 61–72, 149
  speculation and, 108, 110, 116, 117–118
  sticky, 167
  of stock, 108, 110
  transactions form of the quantity of
    money equation and, 259–260
  utility analysis and, 240, 242
price fixing, 63
price takers, 53, 64, 71
Principles of Economics (Marshall), 274,
  281
Principles of Economics (Menger), 287
Principles of Political Economy (Mill), 277,
  290
*Principles of Political Economy and
  Taxation, The* (Ricardo), 276, 284, 285
Prisoner's Dilemma, 235–236
Producer Price Index, 45
producers' goods, 97–104, 124, 279
production, 28, 50, 55, 56, 58, 155
  ancient vs. modern modes of, 101–102
  conservation and, 141–142
  consumption vs., 91–96
  costs of, 244
  growth of, 3, 58, 93
  marginal analysis and, 243–244
  mass, 221, 223
  means of, 122
  money for speculation and, 112, 113, 115,
    185
  priority of, 100–101
  profit maximization and, 10–13
  saving and, 100–101, 103
  Say's law and, 177–178
  as system of flows, 101, 102
  time frame of, 92–93
*Production of Commodities by Means of
  Commodities* (Sraffa), 284
productivity, 133, 140–152, 282
  as function of "hours worked," 146–147,
    149
  microeconomics-macroeconomics
    incompatibility and, 142–151
profit, 48, 50, 113, 119–122
  actual, 182
  defined, 119
  expected, 125
  normal, 120–121, 154, 182, 183, 186,
    225, 280, 284
  productivity and, 148–149
profit centers, of firms, 143–144
profit (or income) maximization, 10–13, 15,
    16, 77, 149, 150

microeconomics-macroeconomics
    incompatibility and, 143–145
profit motive, 18–19
profit sharing, 262
progress, workers and, 131
proletariat, 4
property, 119–139
  competition and, 133–136
  consumers' goods as, 123
  exchange-value and, 124–125, 223
  private, 85
  producers' goods as, 124
  as rights, 124–128, 132
  state, 122
prosperity, 107, 115, 151, 174
psychology, 8–19, 34–35
  behaviorist, 4, 9, 25
  consistency and, 36
  equilibrium and, 246
  greed and, 13–17
  profit and utility maximization and,
    10–13, 15, 16
  self-interest and, 9, 13–15, 17
  of speculation, 114, 118
Psychology (James), 276
publishing, 107, 236
  competition in, 134–135
  goods in, 89–90, 93
Purchasing Power of Money, The (Fisher),
  289

qualitative vs. quantitative methods, 25–26
"Quantitative Analysis in Economic Theory"
  (Mitchell), 274
"Quantity Theory of Money" (Friedman),
  289

"Radical Currency Reform: Germany, 1948"
  (Mayer and Thumann), 282
rationality, 16, 68, 69, 70, 132, 240, 261
Raumer, Hans von, 47, 275
Raymond, Fred I., 263–264, 290
Readings in International Economics (Caves
  and Johnson), 285
*Readings in the Theory of International
  Trade* (Ellis and Metzler), 290
Reagan administration, 169
"real bills" theory, 55–56, 283
real estate, 98–100, 104, 110
reality vs. appearance, 10, 166–167
recession, 2, 116, 130, 149, 168, 171, 185,
  190
Reconstruction of Economic Theory, The
  (Mirowski), 288
recovery, economic, 2, 151, 160, 163
"Reducing the Deficits: Send the Bill to
  Those Who Went to the Party"
  (Faux), 281
Regulation Q, 58, 156, 205, 264
"Relationship between the Rate of Change
  of Money-Wage Rates and
  Unemployment in the United

Kingdom, 1861–1957, The" (Phillips), 282
religion, 5, 10, 15, 91–92
Religion and the Rise of Capitalism (Tawney), 277
Renaissance, ix, 2, 5, 63
  merchants in, 101–102
rent, renting, 113, 119, 125, 153, 208
Report on Manufactures (Hamilton), 273
Republic, The (Plato), 62, 276
resource allocation, 2, 3, 87–88, 220
"Response to Burns, A" (Friedman), 275
responsibility, 16, 34, 69, 71, 113, 120
  of CEOs, 80
  of consumers, 96
  of owners of corporations, 123, 129, 131–132
Rhodes, Cecil, 209
Ricardo, David, 66, 73, 88, 92, 133, 182, 191, 215, 216, 276, 284, 285
  comparative advantage and, 198–199, 265, 267–271
right, rights, 84–85
  Labor Theory of, 126–127, 262
  property as, 124–128, 132
Rise and Fall of the Medici Bank, The (de Roover), 276
Risk, Uncertainty and Profit (Knight), 283
risk taking, 78–79, 80, 107, 127, 132
Rivlin, Alice M., 281
Road to Serfdom, The (Hayek), 280
Robinson, Joan, 125, 280
Ross, Marc H., 277
Rousseau, Jean Jacques, 4, 6
Royce, Josiah, 280
Russell, Bertrand, 49, 275

Sadowski, Zdzislaw, 116
sales, increasing of, 149, 157
sales tax, 105, 240
Samuelson, Paul, 268
satisfaction, 71, 79
  utility analysis and, 237–243
satisfaction (or utility) maximization, 10–13, 15, 16, 17, 252
saving, 97–105, 113, 225, 278, 286
  Keynes's views on, 103–105
  production and, 100–101, 103
Say, Jean-Baptiste, 176, 177, 242, 275, 283, 287
Say's law, 177–178
Schacht, Hjalmar, 209
Schuker, Stephen A., 282
Schumacher, E. F., 138
Schumpeter, Joseph A., 68, 78, 170–171, 182, 214, 276, 277, 281, 284, 289
Schwartz, John E., 285
science:
  economics as, 6, 22–29, 68
  exact, 26
  laws of, 33
  logical vs. mathematical, 23
  measurement and, 42–43

natural vs. social, 22–23, 26–29
  objectivity of, 27–29
  precision in, 42, 44
scientific method, 4, 27
Scope and Method of Political Philosophy, The (Neville Keynes), 276
Second Treatise of Government (Locke), 277
Secrets of the Temple (Greider), 271
Selected Papers on Economic Theory (Wicksell), 288
self-assertion, 33–34, 36–37
self-definition, 72, 79, 85, 96
self-interest, 9, 13–15, 17, 26, 33, 36, 271
  employee ownership and, 139
  enlightened, 9–10
  Smith's views on, 5–6
self-maintenance, 34, 36, 37
Sen, Amartya, 13, 274
Senior, Nassau, 281
services:
  as economic goods, 88–90
  see also goods and services
Shackle, G. L. S., 283
silver, 47, 51, 57, 191–192
Singapore, 203
Slaughter House Cases, 124
slavery, 88, 132, 221
smallness, beauty of, 132–133, 138
Smith, Adam, 1–3, 5–9, 70, 73, 91, 124, 191, 209, 273, 274, 276, 277, 280, 285, 287
  on division of labor, 3, 5, 62, 197–198, 203
  on free trade, 197–198
  invisible hand of, 5–6, 11, 63, 229, 239, 257
  natural price of, 63, 66, 246
  on profits, 121
  statistics rejected by, 21–22
Smoot-Hawley Tariff, 218–219
Snow, C. P., 34
Social Darwinism, 69, 235
Social Economics (Wieser), 290
social science, natural science compared with, 22–23, 26–29
Social Security, 193–195
  COLAs and, 187–188, 189, 193
  critics of, 193–194
Social Security tax, 105, 193–194, 225
society:
  consumption and, 95–96
  dimensions of, 31
  faith in, 59–60
  individual and, 95, 151
  normal profit and, 121
  technological advances and, 130–131
  work and, 84–85
Source Readings in Economic Thought (Newman, Gayer, and Spencer, eds.), 274, 287
space, 41, 233
space shuttle, GNP and, 140

Spain, 97–98, 99, 191
    stagnation and decline of, 200–201
speculation, 18, 44, 48, 55, 58, 86, 99,
    106–118, 123, 155, 158, 166, 222,
    226–227, 279, 285–286
    causes of, 114, 129
    control of, 118
    enterprise replaced by, 77–78, 116, 118,
        185
    gambling compared with, 107
    interest rates and, 113–117, 184–185, 186
    money lost in, 48, 110–114
    "real bills" theory and, 55–56
    in stock, 106–115
    useful, 117
Spencer, Milton H., 274
Sraffa, Piero, 256–257, 284, 289
stability, 26–27, 30, 116, 183, 188
Stabilizing an Unstable Economy (Minsky),
    283, 286
stagnation, 116, 200–201, 286
Stalin, Joseph, 209
Standard and Poor's index, 110
standard of living, 193
    decline of, 190, 200–201, 206
state, 58
    as employer of last resort, 85
statistics, 20–23, 26, 120
Stein, Herbert, 136–138
Stetson, Harlan, 24
Steuart, Sir James, 16, 274
Stevin, Simon, 22, 233
Stigler, George L., 280, 290
stock, stock market, 49, 104–115, 223, 279
    bull market, 110, 112–114, 224, 226
    corporate, 122–123, 128–132, 138,
        261–262
    crash of, 110–112, 114, 226
    speculation in, 106–115
storytelling, storytellers, 34–35, 36
Structure of Monetarism, The (Mayer), 276
subjectivity, 238, 240–242, 255
subsistence, 3, 7, 88, 92, 193, 207
Summa Theologica (St. Thomas), 275, 276
supply, 26, 56
    aggregate, 55
    of money, see money supply
    profit maximization and, 10–12
    of stock, 109, 110
supply and demand, law of:
    price and, 61, 65–66, 71
    reformulation of, 61–72
supply curve, 65, 71, 243
"supply side" tax cuts, 113, 160–161
Supreme Court, U.S., 124, 163
Sweden, 202
Switzerland, 176, 206
system, as basis of wealth, 90–91

Tariff History of the United States, The
    (Taussig), 219, 285
tariffs, 218–219
Taussig, Frank, 219, 285

Tawney, R. H., 77, 91, 195, 276
taxes, 105, 113–114, 118, 143, 206, 207,
    240, 241, 286
    cuts in, 113, 160–161
    Social Security, 105, 193–194, 225
technology, 78, 130–131, 208, 223
Teresa, Mother, 13, 14
textbooks:
    competition and, 134–135
    economic, 86, 134–135
textiles, 202–203
Thales, 232
Theory of Interest, The (Fisher), 281
Theory of Moral Sentiments, The (Smith), 8,
    273
Theory of Political Economy (Jevons), 274,
    287
Theory of the Leisure Class, The (Veblen),
    277
Theory of Value (Debreu), 247–254, 276,
    288, 289
Third World:
    debt of, 168, 172, 205–207
    international trade and, 201–203,
        205–217
Thirteenth Amendment, 124
Thomas Aquinas, Saint, 7, 62, 154, 275, 276
Thoreau, Henry, 12, 79
Thumann, Gunther, 282
Thurow, Lester, 99, 100, 278
time:
    allocation of, 12
    as business factor, 144, 178
    existence and, 33–34
    historical, 30, 32
    labor and, 75
    measurement of, 41–42
    see also future; past; present
Tinbergen, Jan, 29
Tobin, James, 275
Tocqueville, Alexis de, 7
"too much money," 55, 165, 172–173, 177,
    186
Townsend, Robert, 80
trade, 48
    ancient vs. modern, 101–102
    favorable balance of, 191–192
    international, 196–220; see also
        international trade
    measurement and, 43
    price and, 61–62, 67–70
    reciprocity and, 61–62
transactions form of the quantity of money
    equation, 259–260
Treasury, U.S., 116, 161
Treasury bills, 157
Treasury bonds, 162, 188
Treatise on Political Economy, A (Say), 283,
    287
trigonometry, 232–233
Trollope, Anthony, 70
Truman, Harry S., 183
trust, 137–138

truth, error and, 35–36
Tucker, Robert C., 273, 274, 277
Turgot, Anne Robert Jacques, 176
Twain, Mark, 141

uncertainty, 44–45, 50, 55, 56, 120, 151
    speculation and, 117, 118
uncertainty principle, 33
unemployment, 2, 168, 188, 190, 206, 218,
    219, 226, 227
    inflation control and, 2, 113, 116,
    174–176, 283
    productivity and, 145, 149
United States Steel Corporation, 281
Updike, John, 70
Up the Organization (Townsend), 80
use-value, 74, 124, 223
usury, 2, 5, 58
utilitarianism, 237–238
utility analysis, 237–243
utility (or satisfaction) maximization, 10–13,
    15, 16, 17, 252

value:
    in economics vs. science, 27–29
    exchange-, 74, 124–125, 223
    labor as standard of, 73–75, 126
    money as store of, 48, 85–86, 172
    price and, 71–72
    social, 86
    surplus, 75
    use-, 74, 124, 223
    utility analysis and, 240, 242
Value and Capital (Hicks), 288
variables, dependent vs. independent, 24, 71,
    162–163
Veblen, Thorstein, 11, 91, 94, 277
Velikovsky, Immanuel, 24
Venice, merchants of, 101–102
Vietnam War, 95, 227
"Volatility in the Equity Market" (Fedack),
    279
Volcker, Paul A., 116, 162, 275

wage-fund theory, 182–183, 283–284
wage-price spiral, 185, 187
wages:
    economic service defined by, 88–89
    equilibrium and, 254
    inflation and, 173, 175, 185–186, 187
    international trade changes and, 202,
    207–211, 213, 214–215
    labor and, 75, 76, 80–84, 86, 153, 179,
    180–181, 207–208

productivity and, 147, 148
profit and, 119–120, 121
speculation and, 58, 113
wage-scale theory of foreign competition,
    213, 214–215
Wallis, Allen, 290
Walras, Léon, 68, 238–241, 255, 257, 258,
    276, 287, 289
war, 37, 72, 95, 120, 151, 227
Warburton, Clark, 286
War of the Spanish Succession, 191
Watson, John B., 9
wealth, 6–7, 107, 219
    distribution of, 99
    money as store of, 44
    money vs., 49
    of nations, 1, 5–6, 90–91, 97, 191
    natural resources vs., 90
    system as basis of, 90–91
Wealth of Nations, The (Smith), 2, 5–6, 21,
    92, 273, 274, 276, 277, 280, 285, 287
Weimar Republic, hyperinflation of, 47,
    171–172, 175
Weintraub, E. Roy, 288
Weintraub, Sidney, 214
welfare, general, 7
"Whether It Is a Sin To Take Usury for
    Money Lent" (St. Thomas), 275
Wicksell, Knut, 245, 257–258, 288, 289
Wicksteed, Philip H., 288
Wieser, Friedrich von, 290
Wilde, Oscar, 71
will, 12, 34, 37, 67–69, 229, 244
    labor and, 76
    rights and, 128
Williams, Robert H., 277
Wilson, Charles E., 142
women, 11, 81, 82, 145, 163, 227
wool trade, 102
Wordsworth, William, 10
work, 77, 84–85, 88
work ethic, 91–92, 218
Works and Days (Hesiod), 79
World Bank, 211
Worldly Philosophers, The (Heilbroner),
    274
World of Goods, The (Douglas and
    Isherwood), 94–95, 277

yard, length of, 40
Young, Allyn A., 256, 289
Yugoslavia, 202, 211

Zeno's paradox, 32
zero-sum games, 107

ABOUT THE AUTHOR

George P. Brockway writes a monthly column for *The New Leader* under the rubric "The Dismal Science" and has contributed articles to *Challenge, Journal of Post Keynesian Economics,* the *New York Times,* and other periodicals. He has published a brief monograph titled *Political Deals That Saved Andrew Johnson* (he is an honorary fellow of the Society of American Historians) and is coauthor (with his late wife, Lucile H. Brockway, an anthropologist) of a travel book on Greece. He was for many years editor and CEO of W. W. Norton & Company and president of the board of governors of Yale University Press. He holds an honorary Litt.D. from Williams College, of which he is a graduate. He is the father of seven children and lives in Chappaqua, New York.